Praise for *Prayer* by Timothy Keller

"Books on prayer abound, but few, if any, are better than this one."
—*World*

"If you follow Keller into the arsenal, you will be powerfully equipped to overcome the world/flesh/Devil and see your prayers for kingdom advance answered by almighty God. And if you follow Keller to the banqueting table, you will increasingly feast on new and old treasures of awe and intimacy with your heavenly Father."
—*The Gospel Coalition*

"Hugely encouraging, thought-provoking, and insightful . . . It is one of the best books on prayer, period."
—*Reformation 21*

"Emotionally affecting and practical . . . If you're looking for guidance to found your prayers securely on biblical truth and also raise your prayers into experiential moments with God, pick up this book."
—*The Anchor Course*

"A valuable reference tool for the student of prayer."
—*The Christian Chronicle*

"Unique, fresh, and deeply rooted in history—this book is vintage Keller in his most carefully researched and most Reformed self. . . . When I finished this book, it instantly topped this year's book list. Reformed to the core, practical, comprehensive, God-centered, Christ-focused, and joy-saturated—the book is rich on many levels."
—*Desiring God*

"An important book for anyone desiring to pray more effectively and understand why intimacy with God matters."
—*Deseret News*

"Keller provides a contextually rich guide and companion to prayer."
—*Kirkus Reviews*

PENGUIN BOOKS

PRAYER

Timothy Keller was born and raised in Pennsylvania and educated at Bucknell University, Gordon-Conwell Theological Seminary, and Westminster Theological Seminary. He was first a pastor in Hopewell, Virginia. In 1989 he started Redeemer Presbyterian Church in New York City with his wife, Kathy, and their three sons. Today, Redeemer has more than five thousand regular Sunday attendees and has helped to start more than two hundred and fifty new churches around the world. He is also the author of *Encounters with Jesus, Walking with God through Pain and Suffering, Every Good Endeavor, The Meaning of Marriage, Generous Justice, Counterfeit Gods, The Prodigal God, Jesus the King*, and *The Reason for God*. Timothy Keller lives in New York City with his family.

By Timothy Keller

The Reason for God
Belief in an Age of Skepticism

The Prodigal God
Recovering the Heart of the Christian Faith

Counterfeit Gods
The Empty Promises of Money, Sex, and Power, and the Only Hope that
Matters

Generous Justice
How God's Grace Makes Us Just

Jesus the King
Understanding the Life and Death of the Son of God

The Meaning of Marriage (with Kathy Keller)
Facing the Complexities of Commitment with the Wisdom of God

Every Good Endeavor
Connecting Your Work to God's Work

Walking with God through Pain and Suffering

Encounters with Jesus
Unexpected Answers to Life's Biggest Questions

Prayer
Experiencing Awe and Intimacy with God

Preaching
Communicating Faith in an Age of Skepticism

The Songs of Jesus (with Kathy Keller)
A Year of Daily Devotions in the Psalms

REDEEMER

TIMOTHY KELLER

PRAYER

*Experiencing Awe and
Intimacy with God*

PENGUIN BOOKS

PENGUIN BOOKS
An imprint of Penguin Random House LLC
375 Hudson Street
New York, New York 10014
penguin.com

First published in the United States of America by Dutton,
an imprint of Penguin Random House LLC, 2014
Published in Penguin Books 2016

All Bible references are from the New International Version (NIV), unless otherwise noted.

THE LIBRARY OF CONGRESS HAS CATALOGED THE
HARDCOVER EDITION AS FOLLOWS:
Keller, Timothy J., 1950–
Prayer : experiencing awe and intimacy with God / Timothy Keller. — First [edition].
pages cm
At head of title: Redeemer
Includes bibliographical references.
ISBN 978-0-525-95414-9 (hc.)
ISBN 978-0-14-310858-0 (pbk.)
1. Prayer—Christianity. I. Title. II. Title: Redeemer.
BV210.3.K457 2014
248.3'2—dc23
2014025011

Printed in the United States of America
7   9   10   8   6

Set in ITC Galliard Std
Designed by Leonard Telesca

While the author has made every effort to provide accurate telephone numbers,
Internet addresses, and other contact information at the time of publication, neither the
publisher nor the author assumes any responsibility for errors or for changes that occur
after publication. Further, the publisher does not have any control over and does not
assume any responsibility for author or third-party websites or their content.

To Dick Kaufmann,
friend and man of prayer

CONTENTS

Contents

Introduction

Why Write a Book on Prayer?

Some years ago I realized that, as a pastor, I didn't have a first book to give someone who wanted to understand and practice Christian prayer. This doesn't mean there aren't great books on prayer. Many older works are immeasurably wiser and more penetrating than anything I could possibly produce. The best material on prayer has been written.

Yet many of these excellent books are written in an archaic idiom inaccessible to most contemporary readers. In addition they tend to be primarily theological or devotional or practical, but seldom do they combine the theological, experiential, and methodological all under one cover.[1] A book on the essentials of prayer should treat all three. Also, nearly all the classic books on prayer spend a fair amount of time warning readers about practices in their day that were spiritually unhelpful or even damaging. Such cautions must be updated for readers living in each generation.

Two Kinds of Prayer?

Recent writers on prayer tend to have one of two views on the subject. Most now emphasize prayer as a means to experience God's love and to know oneness with him. They promise a life of peace and of continual resting in God. Such authors often give radiant testimonies of feeling regularly surrounded by the divine presence. Other books, however, see the essence of prayer not as inward resting but as calling on God to bring in his kingdom. Prayer is viewed as a wrestling match, often—or perhaps ordinarily—without a clear sense of God's immediate presence. One book of this sort is *The Still Hour*, by Austin Phelps.[2] He begins with the premise that a sense of the absence of God is the norm for the Christian at prayer, and that the experience of God's presence is difficult for most people to find.

Another book with the same approach is Donald G. Bloesch's *The Struggle of Prayer*. He criticizes what he calls "Christian mysticism."[3] He resists the teaching that prayer's ultimate goal is personal communion with God. He thinks this makes prayer a selfish "end in itself."[4] In his view, the highest aim of prayer is not peaceful reflection but fervent supplication for the kingdom of God to come to fruition in the world and in our own lives. The ultimate aim of prayer is "obedience to God's will, not the contemplation of his being."[5] Prayer is not mainly for an inner state but for conformity to God's purposes.

What accounts for these two views—what we could call "communion-centered" and "kingdom-centered" prayer? One explanation is that they reflect people's actual experience. Some discover that their emotions are unresponsive toward God and that even paying attention in prayer for more than a few minutes is extremely difficult. Others regularly experience a feeling of God's presence. This accounts at least in part for the different views. However, theological differences also play a role. Bloesch argues that mystical prayer fits more with the Catholic view that God's grace is infused directly into us through baptism and the Mass rather than with the Protestant belief that we are saved through faith in God's word of gospel promise.[6]

Which view of prayer is the better one? Is peaceful adoration or assertive supplication the ultimate form of prayer? That question assumes that the answer is completely either-or, which is unlikely.

Communion and Kingdom

For help, we should turn first to the Psalms, the inspired prayer book of the Bible. There we see that both experiences of prayer are well represented. There are Psalms such as Psalm 27, 63, 84, 131, and the "long hallelujah" of Psalms 146–150 that depict adoring communion with God. In Psalm 27:4, David says that there is one primary thing he asks of the Lord in prayer—"to gaze on the beauty of the Lord." While David did in fact pray for other things, he means at the very least that nothing is better than to know the presence of God. Therefore he says: "O God . . . my soul thirsts for you. . . . I have seen you in the sanctuary and beheld your power and your glory. Because your love is better than life, I will praise you" (Ps 63:1–3). When he adores God in his presence, he says his "soul is satisfied as with the richest of foods" (Ps 63:5). This is indeed communion with God.

There are, however, even more Psalms of complaint, of cries for help, and of calls for God to exercise his power in the world. There are also stark expressions of the experience of God's absence. Here we indeed see prayer as a struggle. Psalms 10, 13, 39, 42–43, and 88 are just a very few examples. Psalm 10 begins asking why God "stands far off" and "hides" himself in times of trouble. Suddenly the author cries, "Arise, Lord! Lift up your hand, O God. Do not forget the helpless" (Ps 10:12). Yet then he seems to speak almost to himself as well as to the Lord. "But you, O God, *do* see trouble and grief. You consider it to take it to hand. . . . You are the helper of the fatherless"

(Ps 10:14). The prayer ends with the psalmist bowing to God's timing and wisdom in all matters yet still fiercely calling out for justice on the earth. This is the wrestling match of kingdom-centered prayer. The Psalter, then, affirms both the communion-seeking and kingdom-seeking kinds of prayer.

Besides looking at the actual prayers of the Bible, we should consider also the Scripture's theology of prayer—the reasons in God and in our created nature that human beings are able to pray. We are told that Jesus Christ stands as our mediator so that we, though undeserving in ourselves, can boldly approach God's throne and cry out for our needs to be met (Heb 4:14–16; 7:25). We are also told that God himself dwells within us through the Spirit (Rom 8:9–11) and helps us to pray (Rom 8:26–27) so that even now by faith we may gaze and contemplate the glory of Christ (2 Cor 3:17–18). Thus the Bible gives us theological support for both communion-centered and kingdom-centered prayer.

A little reflection will show us that these two kinds of prayer are neither opposites nor even discrete categories. Adoring God is shot through with supplication. To praise God is to pray "hallowed be thy name," to ask him to show the world his glory so that all would honor him *as* God. Yet just as adoration contains supplication, so seeking God's kingdom must include prayer to know God himself. The Westminster Shorter Catechism tells us that our purpose is to "glorify God and enjoy him forever." In this famous sentence we see reflected both kingdom-prayer and communion-prayer. Those two things—glorifying God and enjoying God—do not always coincide in this life, but in the end they must be the same thing. We may pray for the coming of God's kingdom, but if we don't enjoy God supremely with all our being, we are not truly honoring him as Lord.[7]

Finally, when we consult many of the greatest of the older writers

on prayer—such as A[ugustine] [...] and Joh[n] [...]
see th[...] [...] mp.[8] Indeed [...]
pro[...] [...] theologian [...] lthasar has s[o]ught to
[...] to the [...] [...] rayer tradition. He
[...] [...] nplative prayer . . .
[...] [...] [rather] a reverent
[...] [...] the [...] Word of God."[9]

[handwritten note: We must know the awe of praising his glory, the intimacy of finding his grace and the struggle of asking his help, all of which can lead to the spiritual reality of his pre[sence]]

Whe[...] [...] edge between
seeki[...] [...] dvance of his
kingd[...] [...] and if they are kept together,
then c[...] [...] ot be just wordless mystical awareness on the
one hand, and our petitions will not be a way of procuring God's favor
"for our many words" (Matt 6:7) on the other.

This book will show that prayer is both conversation *and* encounter
with God. These two concepts give us a definition of prayer and a set of
tools for deepening our prayer lives. The traditional forms of prayer—
adoration, confession, thanksgiving, and supplication—are concrete practices as well as profound experiences. We must know the awe of praising
his glory, the intimacy of finding his grace, and the struggle of asking his
help, all of which can lead us to know the spiritual reality of his presence.
Prayer, then, is both awe *and* intimacy, struggle *and* reality. These will not
happen every time we pray, but each should be a major component of our
prayer over the course of our lives.

J. I. Packer and Carolyn Nystrom's book on prayer has a subtitle
that sums all this up nicely. Prayer is "Finding Our Way through Duty
to Delight." That is the journey of prayer.

PART ONE

Desiring Prayer

ONE

The Necessity of Prayer

"We're Not Going to Make It"

In the second half of my adult life, I discovered prayer. I had to.

In the fall of 1999, I taught a Bible study course on the Psalms. It became clear to me that I was barely scratching the surface of what the Bible commanded and promised regarding prayer. Then came the dark weeks in New York after 9/11, when our whole city sank into a kind of corporate clinical depression, even as it rallied. For my family the shadow was intensified as my wife, Kathy, struggled with the effects of Crohn's disease. Finally, I was diagnosed with thyroid cancer.

At one point during all this, my wife urged me to do something with her we had never been able to muster the self-discipline to do regularly. She asked me to pray with her every night. *Every* night. She used an illustration that crystallized her feelings very well. As we remember it, she said something like this:

> Imagine you were diagnosed with such a lethal condition that the doctor told you that you would die within hours unless you took a particular medicine—a pill every night before going to sleep. Imagine that you were told that you

could never miss it or you would die. Would you forget? Would you not get around to it some nights? No—it would be so crucial that you wouldn't forget, you would never miss. Well, if we don't pray together to God, we're not going to make it because of all we are facing. I'm certainly not. We *have* to pray, we can't let it just slip our minds.

Maybe it was the power of the illustration, maybe it was just the right moment, maybe it was the Spirit of God. Or, most likely of all, it was the Spirit of God using the moment and the clarity of the metaphor. For both of us the penny dropped; we realized the seriousness of the issue, and we admitted that anything that was truly a nonnegotiable necessity was something we could do. That was more than twelve years ago, and Kathy and I can't remember missing a single evening of praying together, at least by phone, even when we've been apart in different hemispheres.

Kathy's jolting challenge, along with my own growing conviction that I just didn't *get* prayer, led me into a search. I wanted a far better personal prayer life. I began to read widely and experiment in prayer. As I looked around, I quickly came to see that I was not alone.

"Can't Anyone Teach Me to Pray?"

When Flannery O'Connor, the famous Southern writer, was twenty-one years old and studying writing in Iowa, she sought to deepen her prayer life. She had to.

In 1946 she began keeping a handwritten prayer journal. In it she describes her struggles to be a great writer. "I want very much to succeed in the world with what I want to do. . . . I am so discouraged about my work. . . . Mediocrity is a hard word to apply to oneself . . . yet it is impossible not to throw it at myself. . . . I have nothing to be proud of yet myself. I am stupid, quite as stupid as the people I ridicule." These kinds of declarations can be found in the journal of any aspiring artist, but O'Connor did something different with these feelings. She prayed them. Here she followed a very ancient path, as did the psalmists in the Old Testament, who did not merely identify, express, and vent their feelings but also processed them with brutal honesty in God's presence. O'Connor wrote of

> effort at artistry in this rather than thinking of You and feeling inspired with the love I wish I had. Dear God, I cannot love Thee the way I want to. You are the slim crescent of a moon that I see and my self is the earth's shadow that keeps me from seeing all the moon . . . what I am afraid of, dear God, is that my self shadow will grow so large that it blocks the whole moon, and that I will judge myself by the shadow that is nothing. I do not know You God because I am in the way.[10]

Here O'Connor recognizes what Augustine saw clearly in his own prayer journal, the *Confessions*—that living well depended on the reordering of our loves. To love our success more than God and our neighbor hardens the heart, making us less able to feel and to sense. That, ironically, makes us poorer artists. Therefore, because O'Connor *was* a writer of extraordinary gifts who could have become haughty and self-absorbed, her only hope was in the constant soul reorientation of prayer. "Oh God please make my mind clear. Please make it clean. . . . Please help me to get down under things and find where You are."[11]

She reflected on the discipline of writing out her prayers in the journal. She recognized the problem of the form. "I have decided this is not much as a direct medium of prayer. Prayer is not even as premeditated as this—it is of the moment and this is too slow for the moment."[12] Then there was the danger that what she was writing down wasn't really prayer but ventilation. "I . . . want this to be . . . something in praise of God. It is probably more liable to being therapeutical . . . with the element of self underlying its thoughts."[13]

Yet with the journal she believed, "I have started on a new phase of my spiritual life . . . the throwing off of certain adolescent habits and habits of mind. It does not take much to make us realize what fools we are, but the little it takes is long in coming. I see my ridiculous self by degrees."[14] O'Connor learned that prayer is not simply the solitary exploration of your own subjectivity. You are with Another, and he is unique. God is the only person from whom you can hide nothing. Before him you will unavoidably come to see yourself in a new, unique light. Prayer, therefore, leads to a self-knowledge that is impossible to achieve any other way.

Cutting through everything else in O'Connor's journal was a simple longing to learn truly how to pray. She knew intuitively that prayer was the key to everything else she needed to do and to be in life. She wasn't content with the perfunctory religious observances of her past. "I do not mean to deny the traditional prayers I have said all my life; but I have been saying them and not feeling them. My attention is always fugitive. This way I have it every instant. I can feel a warmth of love beating me when I think and write this to You. Please do not let the explanations of the psychologists about this make it turn suddenly cold."[15]

At the end of one entry, she simply called out, "Can't anyone teach me how to pray?"[16] Millions of people today are asking the same question. There is a sense of the necessity of prayer—we *have* to pray. But how?

A Confusing Landscape

Across Western society an interest has been growing in spirituality, meditation, and contemplation that began a generation ago, perhaps inaugurated by the highly publicized interest of the Beatles in Eastern forms of meditation and fueled by the decline of institutional religion. Fewer and fewer people know the routine of regular religious services, yet some kind of spiritual craving remains. Today no one blinks to read a passing reference in a *New York Times* article that Robert Hammond, one of the founders of the High Line urban park in the Western Chelsea neighborhood of Manhattan, is going to India for a three-month meditation retreat.[17] Scores of Westerners flood to ashrams and other spiritual retreat centers in Asia every year.[18] Rupert Murdoch recently tweeted that he was learning Transcendental Meditation. "Everyone recommends," he said. "Not that easy to get started, but said to improve everything!"[19]

Within the Christian church, there has been a similar explosion of interest in prayer. There is a strong movement toward ancient meditation and contemplative practices. We now have a small empire of institutions, organizations, networks, and practitioners that teaches and coaches in methods such as centering prayer, contemplative prayer, "listening" prayer, *lectio divina*, and many others of what are now called "spiritual disciplines."[20]

All this interest should not be characterized as a single, coherent "wave," however. Rather, it is a set of powerful crosscurrents causing dangerously choppy waters for many inquirers. There have been substantial criticisms lodged against much of the new emphasis on contemplative spirituality, within both the Catholic and Protestant churches.[21] As I looked around for resources to help me with my prayer life as well as others', I saw how confusing the landscape was.

"An Intelligent Mysticism"

The way forward for me came by going back to my own spiritual-theological roots. During my first pastorate in Virginia, and then again in New York City, I had the experience of preaching through St. Paul's letter to the Romans. In the middle of chapter 8, Paul writes:

> The Spirit you received does not make you slaves, so that you live in fear again; rather, the Spirit you received brought about your adoption to sonship. And by him we cry, "Abba, Father." The Spirit himself testifies with our spirit that we are God's children. (vv. 15–16)

The Spirit of God assures us of God's love. First, the Spirit enables us to approach and cry to the great God as our loving father. Then he comes alongside our spirit and adds a more direct testimony. I first came to grips with these verses by reading the sermons of D. Martyn Lloyd-Jones, a British preacher and author of the mid-twentieth century. He made the case that Paul was writing about a profound experience of God's reality.[22] Eventually I found that most modern biblical commentators generally agreed that these verses describe, as one New Testament scholar put it, "a religious experience that is ineffable" because the assurance of secure love in God is "mystical in the best sense of the word." Thomas Schreiner adds that we must not "underemphasize the emotional ground" of experience. "Some veer away from this idea because of its subjectivity, but the abuse of the subjective in some circles cannot exclude the 'mystical' and emotional dimensions of Christian experience."[23]

Lloyd-Jones's exposition also pointed me back to writers I had read in seminary, such as Martin Luther, John Calvin, the seventeenth-century British theologian John Owen, and the eighteenth-century American philosopher and theologian Jonathan Edwards. There I discovered no choice offered between truth *or* Spirit, between doctrine *or* experience. One of the most accomplished of the older theologians— John Owen—was especially helpful to me at this point. In a sermon on the gospel, Owen gave due diligence to laying the doctrinal foundation of Christian salvation. Then, however, he exhorted his hearers to "get an *experience* of the power of the gospel . . . in and upon your own hearts, or all your profession is an expiring thing."[24] This heart experience of the gospel's power can happen only through prayer— both publicly in the gathered Christian assembly and privately in meditation.

In my pursuit of a deeper prayer life, I chose a counterintuitive course. I deliberately avoided reading any new books on prayer at all. Instead, I went back to the historical texts of Christian theology that had formed me and began asking questions about prayer and the experience of God—questions I had not had in my mind very clearly when I studied these texts in graduate school decades before. I discovered many things I had completely missed. I found guidance on the inward life of prayer and spiritual experience that took me beyond the dangerous currents and eddies of the contemporary spirituality debates and movements. One I consulted was the Scottish theologian John Murray, who provided one of the most helpful insights of all:

It is necessary for us to recognize that there is *an intelligent mysticism* in the life of faith . . . of living union and communion with the exalted and ever-present Redeemer. . . . He communes with his people and his people commune with him in conscious reciprocal love. . . . The life of true faith cannot be that of cold metallic assent. It must have the passion and warmth of love and communion because communion with God is the crown and apex of true religion.[25]

Murray was not a writer given to lyrical passages. Yet when he speaks of "mysticism" and "communion" with the one who died and ever lives for us, he is assuming that Christians will have a palpable love relationship with him and do have a potential for a personal knowledge and experience of God that beggars the imagination. Which, of course, means prayer—but what prayer! In the midst of the paragraph, Murray quotes Peter's first epistle: "Though you have not seen him, you love him; and even though you do not see him now, you believe in him and are filled with an inexpressible and glorious joy." The older King James version calls it "joy unspeakable and full of glory." Some translate it "glorified joy beyond words."[26]

As I pondered that verse, I had to marvel that Peter, in writing to the church, could address all his readers like this. He didn't say, "Well, some of you with an advanced spirituality have begun to get periods of high joy in prayer. Hope the rest of you catch up." No, he assumed that an experience of sometimes overwhelming joy in prayer was normal. I was convicted.

One phrase of Murray's resonated particularly, that we were called to an *intelligent* mysticism. That means an encounter with God that involves not only the affections of the heart but also the convictions of the mind. We are not called to choose between a Christian life based on truth and doctrine *or* a life filled with spiritual power and experience. They go together. I was not being called to leave behind my theology and launch out to look for "something more," for experience. Rather, I was meant to ask the Holy Spirit to help me experience my theology.

Learning to Pray

As Flannery O'Connor asked so plaintively, how, then, do we actually learn how to pray?

In the summer after I was treated successfully for thyroid cancer, I made four practical changes to my life of private devotion. First, I took several months to go through the Psalms, summarizing each one. That enabled me to begin praying through the Psalms regularly, getting through all of them several times a year.[27] The second thing I did was always to put in a time of meditation as a transitional discipline between my Bible reading and my time of prayer. Third, I did all I could to pray morning and evening rather than only in the morning. Fourth, I began praying with greater expectation.

The changes took some time to bear fruit, but after sustaining these practices for about two years, I began to have some breakthroughs. Despite ups and downs since then, I have found new sweetness in Christ *and* new bitterness too, because I could now see my heart more clearly in the new light of vital prayer. In other words, there were more restful experiences of love as well as more wrestling to see God triumph over evil, both in my own heart and in the world. These two experiences of prayer we discussed in the introduction grew together like twin trees. I now believe that is how it should be. One stimulates the other. The result was a spiritual liveliness and strength that this

Christian minister, for all my preaching, had not had before. The rest of the book is a recounting of what I learned.

Prayer is nonetheless an exceedingly difficult subject to write about. That is not primarily because it is so indefinable but because, before it, we feel so small and helpless. Lloyd-Jones once said that he had never written on prayer because of a sense of personal inadequacy in this area.[28] I doubt, however, that any of the best authors on prayer in history felt more adequate than Lloyd-Jones did. The early-twentieth-century British writer P. T. Forsyth expressed my own feeling and aspiration better than I can:

> It is a difficult and even formidable thing to write on prayer, and one fears to touch the Ark. . . . But perhaps also the effort . . . may be graciously regarded by Him who ever liveth to make intercession as itself a prayer to know better how to pray.[29]

Prayer is the only entryway into genuine self-knowledge. It is also the main way we experience deep change—the reordering of our loves. Prayer is how God gives us so many of the unimaginable things he has for us. Indeed, prayer makes it safe for God to give us many of the things we most desire. It is the way we know God, the way we finally treat God *as* God. Prayer is simply the key to everything we need to do and be in life.

We must learn to pray. We have to.

TWO

The Greatness of Prayer

*For this reason, ever since I heard about your faith in the Lord
Jesus and your love for all God's people, I have not stopped
giving thanks for you, remembering you in my prayers. I keep
asking that the God of our Lord Jesus Christ, the glorious Father, may give you the Spirit of wisdom and revelation, so that
you may know him better. I pray that the eyes of your heart
may be enlightened in order that you may know the hope to
which he has called you, the riches of his glorious inheritance in
his holy people, and his incomparably great power for us who
believe.*

Ephesians 1:15–19

The Supremacy of Prayer

A quick comparison of this prayer from Ephesians 1 with those in
Philippians 1, Colossians 1, and later in Ephesians 3 reveals that
this is how Paul customarily prayed for those he loved. At the gram-
matical heart of Paul's long sentence is a striking insight into the greatness and importance of prayer. In verse 17 he writes: "I keep asking
that . . . you may know him better."

It is remarkable that in all of his writings Paul's prayers for his friends contain no appeals for changes in their circumstances. It is certain that they lived in the midst of many dangers and hardships. They faced persecution, death from disease, oppression by powerful forces, and separation from loved ones. Their existence was far less secure than ours is today. Yet in these prayers you see not one petition for a better emperor, for protection from marauding armies, or even for bread for the next meal. Paul does not pray for the goods we would usually have near the top of our lists of requests.

Does that mean it would have been wrong to pray for such things? Not at all. As Paul knew, Jesus himself invites us to ask for our "daily bread" and that God would "deliver us from evil." In 1 Timothy 2, Paul directs his readers to pray for peace, for good government, and for the needs of the world. In his own prayers, then, Paul is not giving us a universal model for prayer in the same way Jesus did. Rather, in them he reveals what he asked most frequently for his friends—what he believed was the most important thing God could give them.

What is that? It is—to *know him better.* Paul explains this with color and detail. It means having the "eyes of their hearts . . . enlightened" (Ephesians 1:18). Biblically, the heart is the control center of the entire self. It is the repository of one's core commitments, deepest loves, and most foundational hopes that control our feeling, thinking, and behavior. To have the "eyes of the heart enlightened" with a particular truth means to have it penetrate and grip us so deeply that it changes the whole person. In other words, we may know that God is holy, but when our hearts' eyes are enlightened to that truth, then we not only understand it cognitively, but emotionally we find God's holiness wondrous and beautiful, and volitionally we avoid attitudes and behavior that would displease or dishonor him. In Ephesians 3:18, Paul says he wants the Spirit to give them "power . . . to grasp" all the past, present, and future benefits they received when they believed in Christ. Of course, all Christians know about these benefits in their minds, but the prayer is for something beyond that—it is to have a more vivid sense of the reality of God's presence and of shared life with him.

Paul sees this fuller knowledge of God as a more critical thing to receive than a change of circumstances. Without this powerful sense of God's reality, good circumstances can lead to overconfidence and spiritual indifference. Who needs God, our hearts would conclude, when matters seem to be so in hand? Then again, without this enlightened heart, bad circumstances can lead to discouragement and despair, because the love of God would be an abstraction rather than the infinitely consoling presence it should be. Therefore, knowing God better is what we must have above all if we are to face life in any circumstances.

Paul's main concern, then, *is for their public and private prayer life.* He believes that the highest good is communion or fellowship with God. A rich, vibrant, consoling, hard-won prayer life is the one good that makes it possible to receive all other kinds of goods rightly and beneficially. He does not see prayer as merely a way to get things from God but as a way to get more of God himself. Prayer is a striving to "take hold of God" (Is 64:7) the way in ancient times people took hold of the cloak of a great man as they appealed to him, or the way in modern times we embrace someone to show love.

By praying in this way, Paul was assuming the priority of the inner life with God.[30] Most contemporary people base their inner life on their outward circumstances. Their inner peace is based on other people's valuation of them, and on their social status, prosperity, and performance. Christians do this as much as anyone. Paul is teaching that, for believers, it should be the other way around. Otherwise we will be whiplashed by how things are going in the world. If Christians do not base their lives on God's steadfast love, then they will have "to accept as success what others warrant to be so, and to take their happiness, even their own selves, at the quotation of the day. They tremble, with reason, before their fate."[31]

The Integrity of Prayer

If we give priority to the outer life, our inner life will be dark and scary. We will not know what to do with solitude. We will be deeply uncomfortable with self-examination, and we will have an increasingly short attention span for any kind of reflection. Even more seriously, our lives will lack integrity. Outwardly, we will need to project confidence, spiritual and emotional health and wholeness, while inwardly we may be filled with self-doubts, anxieties, self-pity, and old grudges. Yet we won't know how to go into the inner rooms of the heart, see clearly what is there, and deal with it. In short, unless we put a priority on the inner life, we turn ourselves into hypocrites. The seventeenth-century English theologian John Owen wrote a warning to popular and successful ministers:

> A minister may fill his pews, his communion roll, the mouths of the public, but what that minister is on his knees in secret before God Almighty, *that he is and no more.*[32]

To discover the real you, look at what you spend time thinking about when no one is looking, when nothing is forcing you to think about anything in particular. At such moments, do your thoughts go toward God? You may want to be seen as a humble, unassuming person, but do you take the initiative to confess your sins before God?

You wish to be perceived as a positive, cheerful person, but do you habitually thank God for everything you have and praise him for who he is? You may speak a great deal about what a "blessing" your faith is and how you "just really love the Lord," but if you are prayerless—is that really true? If you aren't joyful, humble, and faithful in private before God, then what you want to appear to be on the outside won't match what you truly are.

Just prior to giving his disciples the Lord's Prayer, Jesus offered some preliminary ideas, including this one: "When you pray, do not be like the hypocrites, for they love to pray standing in the synagogues and on the street corners to be seen by others. . . . But when you pray, go into your room, close the door and pray to your Father, who is unseen . . . in secret" (Matt 6:5–6). The infallible test of spiritual integrity, Jesus says, is your private prayer life. Many people will pray when they are required by cultural or social expectations, or perhaps by the anxiety caused by troubling circumstances. Those with a genuinely lived relationship with God as Father, however, will inwardly *want* to pray and therefore will pray even though nothing on the outside is pressing them to do so. They pursue it even during times of spiritual dryness, when there is no social or experiential payoff.

Giving priority to the inner life doesn't mean an individualistic life. Knowing the God of the Bible better can't be achieved all by yourself. It entails the community of the church, participation in corporate worship as well as private devotion, and instruction in the Bible as well as silent meditation. At the heart of all the various ways of knowing God is both public and private prayer.

A pastor and friend of mine, Jack Miller, once said he could tell a great deal about a person's relationship with God by listening to him or her pray. "You can tell if a man or woman is really on speaking terms with God," he said. My first response was to make a mental note never to pray aloud near Jack again. I've had years to test out Jack's thesis. It is quite possible to become florid, theologically sound, and earnest in your public prayers without cultivating a rich, private prayer life. You can't manufacture the unmistakable note of reality that only comes from speaking not toward God but with him. The depths of private prayer and public prayer grow together.

The Hardness of Prayer

I can think of nothing great that is also easy. Prayer must be, then, one of the hardest things in the world. To admit that prayer is very hard, however, can be encouraging. If you struggle greatly in this, you are not alone.

The Still Hour, a classic book on prayer by nineteenth-century American theologian Austin Phelps, starts with the chapter "Absence of God, in Prayer" and the verse from Job 23:3—"Oh that I knew where I might find him!" Phelps's book begins with the premise that "a consciousness of the *absence of God* is one of the standing incidents of religious life. Even when the forms of devotion are observed conscientiously, the sense of the presence of God, as an invisible Friend, whose society is a joy, is by no means unintermittent."[33]

Phelps goes on to explain the numerous reasons why there is such dryness in prayer and how to endure through that sense of God's unreality. The first thing we learn in attempting to pray is our spiritual emptiness—and this lesson is crucial. We are so used to being empty that we do not recognize the emptiness as such until we start to try to pray. We don't feel it until we begin to read what the Bible and others have said about the greatness and promise of prayer. Then we finally begin to feel lonely and hungry. It's an important first step to fellowship with God, but it is a disorienting one.

When your prayer life finally begins to flourish, the effects can be remarkable. You may be filled with self-pity, and be justifying resentment and anger. Then you sit down to pray and the reorientation that comes before God's face reveals the pettiness of your feelings in an instant. All your self-justifying excuses fall to the ground in pieces. Or you may be filled with anxiety, and during prayer you come to wonder what you were so worried about. You laugh at yourself and thank God for who he is and what he's done. It can be that dramatic. It is the bracing clarity of a new perspective. Eventually, this can be the normal experience, but that is never how the prayer life starts. In the beginning the feeling of poverty and absence usually dominates, but the best guides for this phase urge us not to turn back but rather to endure and pray in a disciplined way, until, as Packer and Nystrom say, we get through duty to delight.

We must beware of misunderstanding such phrases, however. Seasons of dryness can return for a variety of causes. We don't spend a discrete amount of time in dryness until we break through permanently into joy and feeling. Instead, the vivid reorientation of mind, and the overall sense of God on the heart, comes more frequently and sometimes in startling ways—interspersed with times of struggle and even absence. Nevertheless, the pursuit of God in prayer eventually bears fruit, because God seeks for us to worship him (John 4:23) and because prayer is so infinitely rich and wondrous.

The Centrality of Prayer

The Bible is all about God, and that is why the practice of prayer is so pervasive throughout its pages. The greatness of prayer is nothing but an extension of the greatness and glory of God in our lives. The Scripture is one long testimony to this truth.

In Genesis we see every one of the patriarchs—Abraham, Isaac, and Jacob—praying with familiarity and directness. Abraham's doggedly insistent prayer for God's mercy on the pagan cities of Sodom and Gomorrah is remarkable (Gen 18:23ff). In Exodus, prayer was the way Moses secured the liberation of Israel from Egypt. The gift of prayer makes Israel great: "What other nation is so great as to have their gods near them the way the Lord our God is near us whenever we pray to him?" (Deut 4:7).[34]

To fail to pray, then, is not to merely break some religious rule—it is a failure to treat God as God. It is a sin against his glory. "Far be it from me," said the prophet Samuel to his people, "that I should sin against the *Lord* by failing to pray for *you*" (1 Sam 12:23 [italics mine]).[35] King David composed much of the Psalter, God's inspired prayer book, filled with appeals to "you who answer prayer" (Ps 65:2). His son Solomon built the temple in Jerusalem and then dedicated it with a magnificent prayer.[36] Solomon's main petition for the temple was that from it God would hear his people's prayers—indeed, Solomon's highest prayer was for the gift *of* prayer itself.[37] Beyond that, he hoped those from other nations would "hear of your great name . . . and pray toward this temple" (1 Kings 8:42). Again we see prayer is simply a recognition of the greatness of God.

The Old Testament book of Job is largely the record of Job's suffering and pain—worked through with prayer. In the end, God is angry with Job's callous friends and tells them he will refrain from their punishment only if Job prays for them (Job 42:8). Prayer permeated the ministry of all the Old Testament prophets.[38] It may have been the ordinary means by which the Word of God itself came to them.[39] The Jews' preservation and return from exile in Babylon was essentially carried out through prayer. Their exile began with a call to pray for the pagan city and their neighbors (Jer 29:7). Daniel, nearly executed by the Babylonian authorities over his insistence on prayer three times a day, prays a prayer of repentance for his people, asks for their return, and is heard.[40] Later, Nehemiah rebuilds the wall around Jerusalem with a series of great prayers interspersed with wise leadership.[41]

Jesus Christ taught his disciples to pray, healed people with prayers, denounced the corruption of the temple worship (which, he said, should be a "house of prayer"), and insisted that some demons could be cast out only through prayer. He prayed often and regularly with fervent cries and tears (Heb 5:7), and sometimes all night. The Holy Spirit came upon him and anointed him as he was praying (Luke 3:21–22), and he was transfigured with the divine glory as he prayed (Luke 9:29). When he faced his greatest crisis, he did so with prayer. We hear him praying for his disciples and the church on the night before he died (John 17:1–26) and then petitioning God in agony in the Garden of Gethsemane. Finally, he died praying.[42]

Immediately after their Lord's death, the disciples prepare for the future by being "constantly in prayer" together (Acts 1:14). All church gatherings are "devoted . . . to prayer" (Acts 2:42; 11:5; 12:5, 12). The power of the Spirit descends on the early Christians in response to powerful prayer, and leaders are selected and appointed only with prayer. All Christians are expected to have a regular, faithful, devoted, fervent prayer life. In the book of Acts, prayer is one of the main signs that the Spirit has come into the heart through faith in Christ. The Spirit gives us the confidence and desire to pray to God and enables us to pray even when we don't know what to say. Christians are taught that prayer should pervade their whole day and whole life—they should "pray without ceasing" (1 Thess 5:17).[43]

Prayer is so great that wherever you look in the Bible, it is there. Why? Everywhere God is, prayer is. Since God is everywhere and infinitely great, prayer must be all-pervasive in our lives.

The Richness of Prayer

One of the greatest descriptions of prayer outside of the Bible was written by the poet George Herbert (1593–1633) in his "Prayer (I)." The poem is remarkable for tackling the immense subject of prayer in just one hundred words and without a single verb or prose construction. Instead, Herbert gives us some two dozen word pictures.

In the next chapters, we will work at defining prayer, but there is a danger in doing that. A definition seeks to reduce things to the essence. George Herbert wants instead to move us in the opposite direction. He wants to explore the richness of prayer with all its infinities and immensities. He does so by overwhelming both our analytical and our imaginative faculties.

> PRAYER the Churches banquet, Angels age,
>   Gods breath in man returning to his birth,
>   The soul in paraphrase, heart in pilgrimage,
> The Christian plummet sounding heav'n and earth;
>
> Engine against th' Almightie, sinner's towre,
>   Reversed thunder, Christ-side-piercing spear,
>   The six daies world-transposing in an houre,
> A kinde of tune, which all things heare and fear;

Softnesse, and peace, and joy, and love, and blisse,
  Exalted Manna, gladnesse of the best,
  Heaven in ordinarie, man well drest,
The milkie way, the bird of Paradise,

  Church-bels beyond the stars heard, the souls bloud,
  The land of spices, something understood.

Prayer is "Gods breath in man returning to his birth." Many who are otherwise skeptical or nonreligious are shocked to find themselves praying despite not even formally believing in God. Herbert gives us his explanation for that phenomenon. The Hebrew word for "Spirit" and "breath" is the same, and so, Herbert says, there is something in us from God that knows we are not alone in the universe, and that we were not meant to go it alone. Prayer is a natural human instinct.

Prayer can be "softnesse, and peace, and joy, and love, and blisse"— the deep rest of soul that we need. It is "the souls bloud," *the* source of strength and vitality. Through prayer in Jesus' name and trust in his salvation we come as a "man well drest," spiritually fit for the presence of the king. That is why we can sit down with him at "the Churches banquet." Feasts were never mere feedings but a sign and means of acceptance and fellowship with the Host. Prayer is a nourishing friendship.

Prayer also is "a kinde of tune." Prayer tunes your heart to God. Singing engages the whole being—the heart through the music as well as the mind through the words. Prayer is also a tune others can hear besides you. When your heart has been tuned to God, your joy has an effect on those around you. You are not proud, cold, anxious, or bored—you are self-forgetful, warm, profoundly at peace, and filled with interest. Others will notice. All "heare and fear." Prayer changes those around us.

Prayer can be a "land of spices," a place of sensory overload, of exotic scents and tastes—and a "milkie way," a place of marvels and wonders. When that happens, prayer is truly of "Angels age," an experience of timeless eternity. Yet no one in history has found that "land of spices" quickly or easily. Prayer is also the "heart in pilgrimage," and in Herbert's time a pilgrim was someone who was engaged on a long, difficult, and exhausting trek. To be *in* pilgrimage is to have not yet arrived. There is a longing in prayer that is never fulfilled in this life, and sometimes the deep satisfactions we are looking for in prayer feel few and far between. Prayer is a journey.

Even in spiritually lean times, prayer can serve as a kind of heavenly Manna" and quiet "gladnesse" that keeps us going, just as the manna in the wilderness kept Israel moving toward its hope. Manna was simple food, especially savory, but hardly a banquet. Yet it sustained them wonderfully, a kind of travelers' waybread that brought an inner endurance. Prayer helps us endure.

One reason for the arduousness is because true prayer is "the soul in paraphrase." God does not merely require our petitions but our *selves*, and no one who begins the hard, lifelong trek of prayer knows yet who they are. Nothing but prayer will ever reveal you to yourself, because only before God can you see and become your true self. To paraphrase something is to get the gist of it and make it accessible. Prayer is learning who you are before God and giving him your essence. Prayer means knowing yourself as well as God.

Prayer is not all quiet, peace, and fellowship. It is also an "engine against th' Almightie," a startling phrase that clearly refers to the siege engines filled with archers that were used in Herbert's day to storm a city. The Bible contains laments and petitions and pleadings, for prayer is rebellion against the evil status quo of the world—and they are not in vain, for they are as "church-bels beyond the stars heard" and indeed are "reversed thunder." Thunder is an expression of the awesome power of God, but prayer somehow harnesses that power so that our petitions are not heard in heaven as whispers but as crack, boom, and roar. Prayer changes things.

Yet Herbert also states that prayer is a "sinner's towre." An arrogant spirit cannot rightly use the power of prayer's siege engines. "Sinner's towre" means that prayerful dependence on the grace of Jesus is our only refuge from our own sin. We cannot go into God's presence unless we are dependent on Christ's forgiveness and his righteousness before God, not on our own. Indeed, prayer is the "Christ-side-piercing spear." When we pray for forgiveness on the basis of the sacrifice of Jesus on our behalf, grace and mercy come flowing down even as the spear in his side brought water and blood gushing out. Prayer is a refuge.

Though prayer is a kind of artillery that changes the circumstances of the world, it is as much or even more about changing our own understanding and attitude toward those circumstances. Prayer is "a kinde of tune" that transposes even "the six daies world." The six days is not the Sabbath day of formal worship but the workweek of ordinary life. Yet the one "houre" of prayer completely transposes it all, as the transposition of a piece of music changes its key, tone, and timbre. Through prayer, which brings heaven into the ordinary, we see the world differently, even in the most menial and trivial daily tasks. Prayer changes us.

As plumb lines measured the depths of waters beneath boats, prayer is a "plummet sounding heav'n and earth." That means it can plunge us by the power of the Spirit into the "deep things of God" (1 Cor 2:10). This includes the indescribable journey that prayer can take us through the breadth, length, height, and depth of Christ's saving love for us (Eph 3:18). Prayer unites us with God himself.

How does Herbert end this dazzling succession of word pictures? He concludes, surprisingly, that prayer is "something understood." Many scholars have debated the apparent anticlimax of this great poem. It seems to be an "abandonment of metaphor . . . [yet] its final crowning."[44] After all the lofty images, Herbert comes down to earth. Through prayer "something"—not everything—is understood, and prayer's conquests are indeed often modest. Paul says believers in this world see things only "in part," just as the reflections in ancient mirrors were filled with distortions (1 Cor 13:12). Prayer, however, gradually clears our vision. When the psalmist was spiraling down into deadly despair, he went in prayer to "the sanctuary of God; then I understood" (Ps 73:17).

Prayer is awe, intimacy, struggle—yet the way to reality. There is nothing more important, or harder, or richer, or more life-altering. There is absolutely nothing so great as prayer.

PART TWO

Understanding Prayer

THREE

What Is Prayer?

What is prayer? Are the innumerable forms of prayer in the world all at heart the same? And if not, how do we define and discern real prayer?

A Global Phenomenon

In the great monotheistic religions of Islam, Judaism, and Christianity, prayer is at the very heart of what it means to believe. Muslims are called to pray five times a day, while Jews have traditionally prayed three times a day. Each branch of the Christian church is saturated with various traditions of common prayer, private prayer, and pastoral prayer.

Prayer is not, of course, limited to monotheistic religions. Buddhists use prayer wheels, which fling prayers for compassion into the atmosphere, in order to knit the spiritual and natural, to relieve suffering, and release kindness.[45] While Hindus may pray for help or peace in the world to any of several gods, the ultimate goal is union with the

Supreme Being, Brahman, and escape from the cycles of reincarnation.[46] People in other cultures, such as the Beaver Indians of southwestern Canada and the Papago Indians of the U.S. Southwest, pray through singing. Their poetry and music serve as prayers that unite the spiritual and physical realms.[47] Prayer is one of the most common phenomena of human life.

Even deliberately nonreligious people pray at times. Studies have shown that in secularized countries, prayer continues to be practiced not only by those who have no religious preference but even by many of those who do not believe in God.[48] One 2004 study found that nearly 30 percent of atheists admitted they prayed "sometimes,"[49] and another found that 17 percent of nonbelievers in God pray regularly.[50] The frequency of prayer increases with age, even among those who do not return to church or identify with any institutional faith.[51] Italian scholar Giuseppe Giordan summarized: "In virtually all studies of the sociology of religious behavior it is clearly apparent that a very high percentage of people declare they pray every day—and many say even many times a day."[52]

Does this mean that everyone prays? No, it does not. Many atheists are rightly offended by the saying "There are no atheists in foxholes." There are many people who do not pray even in times of extreme danger. Still, though prayer is not literally a universal phenomenon, it is a global one, inhabiting all cultures and involving the overwhelming majority of people at some point in their lives.[53] Efforts to find cultures, even very remote and isolated ones, without some form of religion and prayer have failed. There has always been some form of attempt to "communicate between human and divine realms."[54] There seems to be a human instinct for prayer. Swiss theologian Karl Barth calls it our "incurable God-sickness."[55]

To say prayer is nearly universal is not, however, to say all prayer is the same. Prayer presents a dizzying variety to the eye of the observer. Just look at the religious trances of Native American shamanists; the chanting in Benedictine monasteries; devotees doing yoga in Manhattan offices; the hour-long pastoral prayers of the seventeenth-century Puritan ministers; speaking in tongues in Pentecostal churches; Muslims engaging in *sujud*, with forehead, hands, and knees on the ground toward Mecca; Hasidim swaying and bowing in prayer; and the Anglican priest reading from the Book of Common Prayer.[56] This leads to the question: In what ways are all these kinds of prayer the same and in what ways are they different?

Types of Prayer

Some of the first modern theorists of prayer were Edward B. Tylor (1832–1917); James Frazer (1854–1941), author of *The Golden Bough*; and Sigmund Freud (1856–1939). Each of them used a Darwinian model that theorized prayer as a way for human beings to adapt to their environment, to get control of the forces of nature. According to this theory, prayer began when the collective human mind was "similar to the mentality of the child and the neurotic, the chief trait of which is infantile magical thinking."[57]

As time went on, prayer evolved to more refined, meditative forms. It did not try so much to seek communication with a personal God but rather looked inward and sought changes of consciousness and inner peace. In this view, the contemplative exercises of Greek philosophers were an improvement over sacrifices and petitions to Zeus to bring rain for the harvest. Yet in the end, these theorists believed, the future of human prayer was bleak. Since prayer was born amid prescientific efforts to use religion and magic to control the world, now that science has emerged, prayer no longer helps us adapt to our environment. In these conditions it "will wither away."[58]

Another important thinker to be considered is early-twentieth-century psychologist Carl Jung, whose understanding of religious experience also viewed prayer more as a turning inward rather than a reaching outward.[59] Jung believed, as did Eastern thinkers, that human individuals were all part of a cosmic life force.[60] We move into health and wholeness as we realize our oneness with all reality and the interconnected world.[61] Jung pointed out the similarities between this process and the Zen Buddhist experience of satori.[62] Jung's followers discouraged the idea that we should seek contact with a personal God outside of ourselves.[63] Better, in their view, was the transformation of consciousness, pure awareness, and the sense of oneness with all reality that spiritual contemplation brings.[64]

Mystical versus "Prophetic" Prayer

It is worth noting that in both the Freudian and the Jungian assessment of religion, contemplation is seen as a higher, more sophisticated kind of prayer than the petition to a personal divine being. A very different assessment, however, was proposed by the German scholar Friedrich Heiler. Heiler spoke of inwardly focused "mystical" and outwardly focused "prophetic" prayer, and unlike earlier theorists, he saw the latter as superior.

While Heiler believed the most purely mystical prayer was found in Eastern religions, he critiqued some forms of mystical Christian prayer as well.[65] Mysticism, according to Heiler, plays down the difference between God and the person praying, the aim being that "human personality is dissolved, disappears and is absorbed in the infinite unity of the Godhead."[66] Mystical religion, therefore, sees silent, tranquil, wordless contemplation as the highest form of prayer. When we achieve it, we no longer talk to God—we are part of God. This Heiler contrasted to the "passionate crying and groaning . . . [the] complaint and pleading"—the wrestling, verbal prayer of prophetic religion.[67] By this term he meant the kind of prayers we see in the Bible in the writings of the prophets, psalmists, and, later, the apostles and Jesus himself.

In Heiler's view, the two kinds of prayer differ principally in their conception of God.[68] Mystical prayer, he believed, emphasizes God as more immanent than transcendent. He is within us and within all things. The main way, then, to connect to God is to go down into yourself and sense your continuity with the Divine. For example, Orthodox theologian Anthony Bloom, in his famous book *Beginning to Pray*, says, "The Gospel tells us that the kingdom of God is within us first of all. . . . If we cannot meet God within, in the very depth of ourselves, our chances of meeting Him outside ourselves are very remote. . . . So it is inward we must turn."[69] Prophetic prayer by contrast emphasizes that God is outside us, transcendent above us, holy, glorious, and "Other."[70]

Another great difference between the two, Heiler thought, was in their understanding of grace. The mystical, he believed, could become "a thing . . . meritorious," a means by which people tried to save their own souls.[71] Mystical prayer often entails a long process of "purgation"—a "weary climbing by degrees to the heights of vision and union with God"[72]—through which the worshipper achieves a state of pure love and becomes fit and worthy of God's presence.[73]

In the prophets and psalmists, however, Heiler perceived that prayer was not a way of purifying oneself for God but of relying on "the 'prevenience and givenness' of the grace of God. Prayer is not our discovery or achievement but is rather *God's* work in man."[74] The aim of prophetic prayer is not absorption into God but nearness to God—the nearness of child to parent or friend to friend. Mystical prayer climaxes in tranquility without words, while prophetic prayer finds its final expression in words of praise and an outburst of powerful emotions. While mystical prayer tends toward the loss of the boundary between the self and God, prophetic prayer leads to a much greater sense of the difference between the self and the majestic God—an awareness of sinfulness. Yet it also revels in the grace that nonetheless opens the way to intimacy with God. Mystics believe prayer consists of successive stages, moving from petition upward through confession and finally on into adoring, wordless contemplation.[75] Prophetic prayer, however, refuses to see one of these forms of prayer as higher than the others. It mixes meditation, petition and thanksgiving, confession, and adoration all at once. Indeed, in prophetic prayer the forms stimulate and deepen and lead into one another.[76]

The Mystical Prophetic

Whose view of prayer is right? Those who champion the mystical inward turn or those who reject it as too "Eastern" and not fully biblical?[77] One response is to reject both views. Philip and Carol Zaleski's *Prayer: A History* criticizes both the older "evolutionary" theories as well as Heiler's. Each approach, they say, is too negative about some forms of prayer and therefore "excludes a significant percentage of the world's repertoire of prayer."[78] How, they ask, can anyone rule out most of human prayer as simply invalid? While acknowledging some differences, they refuse to see any one kind of prayer as better than any other.[79]

The Zaleskis' analysis is informative, but it ultimately fails to do justice to the profound differences between the forms of human prayer. For example, their gallant effort to liken the ecstatic trances of the Hindu Sri Ramakrishna with Pentecostal tongues-speaking[80] fails to persuade. The *bhava samadhi* (ecstatic consciousness) of Ramakrishna and speaking in tongues share the external likeness of emotional joy, but they are seeking contradictory things. One Hindu monk describing *samadhi* says that when he attained it, "there was no god to speak of, except myself." He goes on to say that "orthodox Jews, Christians, and Muslims really cannot seek this union and be pious at the same time, because losing one's identity and becoming the cosmic ground is a deadly heresy in these teachings."[81] Since the goals and the gods are so divergent in the minds of those who are praying, it is very misleading to insist that all forms of prayer are basically the same.

I believe that Heiler is far wiser than the Zaleskis in his distinctions and correct in his basic thrust. He believed prayer that assumed God's personality was better than prayer that lost the sense of communication between persons.[82] He saw prayer primarily as a verbal conversation rather than a mystical, wordless encounter. Yet some of Heiler's distinctions are overdrawn. He contrasts the calmness and serenity sought by mystical prayer with the loud cries and wrestling of prophetic prayer. However, some of the Psalms *do* speak about a calm contemplation of God's beauty (Ps 27:4) or of his glory and love (Ps 63:1–3). In Psalm 131:2, David speaks of deep spiritual contentment in God: "I have calmed and quieted myself, I am like a weaned child with its mother; like a weaned child I am content." Someone like Jonathan Edwards—very much more in the Protestant "prophetic" than the Catholic mystical tradition of prayer—can nonetheless speak of being "emptied and annihilated" in prayer. In his "Personal Narrative," a kind of diary of Edwards's spiritual experiences, he wrote:

Once . . . *anno* 1737 . . . [in] divine contemplation and
prayer, I had a view that for me was extraordinary, of the
glory of the Son of God, as Mediator between God and
man, and his wonderful, great, full, pure and sweet grace
and love, and meek and gentle condescension. . . . The person of Christ appeared ineffably excellent with an excellency
great enough to swallow up all thought and conception . . .
which continued as near as I can judge, about an hour;
which kept me the greater part of the time in a flood of
tears, and weeping aloud. I felt an ardency of soul to be,
what I know not otherwise how to express, emptied and
annihilated; to lie in the dust, and to be full of Christ alone;
to love him with a holy and pure love; to trust in him; to live
upon him; to serve and follow him; and to be perfectly sanctified and made pure, with a divine and heavenly purity.[83]

Anyone at all acquainted with Edwards's theology knows that he is
not speaking of becoming merged with the Godhead nor of a pantheistic dissolution of the boundaries between the self and the universe.
Heiler is right to point out that the mystics were often seeking a kind
of self-salvation through meditation, and that is as far as can be from
Edwards's understanding of redemption through faith alone and grace
alone. Nevertheless, his experience of fellowship with God sounds
similar to many of the experiences of deep love and delight in the accounts of the mystical writers.

Why, then, can Edwards talk about prayer to a personal, transcendent God with such mystical overtones? Because, while the biblical
God is not Same-as-Me, he is also not utterly, inaccessibly Far-
from-Me. Christian believers have "Christ in you, the hope of glory"
(Col 1:27) through the Holy Spirit. Also, God has given us his Word,

the Scriptures, and because God is divine, the Bible is not just a repository of information but a dynamic spiritual power. Edwards wrote:

> I had then, and at other times, the greatest delight in the holy scriptures, of any book whatsoever. Oftentimes in reading it, every word seemed to touch my heart. I felt a harmony between something in my heart, and those sweet and powerful words. I seemed often to see so much light exhibited by every sentence, and such a refreshing food communicated, that I could not get along in reading; often dwelling long on one sentence, to see the wonders contained in it; and yet almost every sentence seemed to be full of wonders.[84]

This is deeply mystical *and* richly prophetic—at once. Edwards is not going down into himself to touch the impersonal ground of being. He is meditating on the words of God in the Scriptures, and the resulting experience is not one of just wordless tranquility. This is not the "pure awareness" that gets beyond predication and rational thought. In fact, Edwards is overwhelmed with the power of the words and the reality to which the words point. I believe Heiler is right in this regard—that prayer is ultimately a verbal response of faith to a transcendent God's Word and his grace, not an inward descent to discover we are one with all things and God. Heiler's "prophetic" prayer is closer to the biblical understanding of prayer than that of the other thinkers we have surveyed. Yet while his warnings against mysticism are crucial, we need to recognize that prayer also can lead regularly to personal encounter with God, which can be indeed a wondrous, mysterious, awe-filled experience.[85]

An Instinct, a Gift

We have seen that prayer is a global phenomenon and yet there are genuine, irreducible differences among kinds of prayer. This brings us back to the question: What is the essence of prayer? How can we define it so that we are able to make sense of its pervasiveness in human life and yet grow in faithful practice toward real prayer?

From the biblical point of view, the near-universal phenomenon of prayer is not surprising. All human beings are made in the "image of God" (Gen 1:26–27). Bearing God's image means that we are designed to reflect and relate to God. This is why the sixteenth-century Reformer John Calvin wrote of the *divinitatis sensum*, the sense of deity that all human beings have. "There is within the human mind, and indeed by natural instinct, an awareness of divinity," and therefore "the seed of religion is planted in all."[86] Other theologians have also understood this *divinitatis sensum* as the reason prayer is so pervasive across the human race. Romans 1:19–20 says we can look at the world and conclude that some great power created and sustains it. An experience of weakness and precariousness can then trigger this primal knowledge into prayerful cries for help.

English theologian John Owen also believed that the natural impulse to pray is present in all people, that it is "original in the law of nature" and a "natural, necessary, fundamental acknowledgement of that Divine Being." He added that many non-Christian religions and cultures put Christians to shame in the diligence of their prayers.[87] Jonathan Edwards added that "God is sometimes pleased to answer the prayers of unbelievers," not because of any obligation but strictly out of his "pity" and "sovereign mercy," citing the biblical examples of God hearing the cries of the Ninevites in Jonah 3 and even of the wicked king Ahab (1 Kings 21:27–28).[88]

With all this in view, we can define prayer as a *personal, communicative response to the knowledge of God*. All human beings have some knowledge of God available to them. At some level, they have an indelible sense that they need something or someone who is on a higher plane and infinitely greater than they are. Prayer is seeking to respond and connect to that being and reality, even if it is no more than calling out into the air for help.

That is, I believe, the common denominator of all human prayer. However, because our definition understands prayer as a response to the knowledge of God, it means that prayer is profoundly altered by the amount and accuracy of that knowledge. While everyone may have a *sensus divinitatis*, Calvin observed that we all refashion that sense of deity to fit our own interests and desires unless through the Spirit and the Scripture our view of God is corrected and clarified.[89]

Prayer, then, is a response to the knowledge of God, but it works itself out at two levels. At one level, prayer is a human instinct to reach out for help based on a very general and unfocused sense of God. It is an effort to communicate, but it cannot be a real conversation because the knowledge of God is too vague. At another level, prayer can be a spiritual gift. Christians believe that through the Scripture and the power of the Holy Spirit, our understanding of God can become unclouded. The moment we are born again by the Spirit through faith in Christ (John 1:12–13; 3:5), that Spirit shows us that we are not simply God's subjects but also his children, and we can converse with him as our Father (Gal 4:5–6).[90]

The knowledge of God for instinctive prayer comes intuitively and generally through nature (Rom 1:20). What Christians know about God comes with verbal specificity through the words of the Scripture and its main message—the gospel. In the Bible, God's living Word, we can hear God speaking to us and we respond in prayer, though we should not call this simply a "response." Through the Word and Spirit, prayer becomes *answering God*—a full conversation.[91]

A Conversation, an Encounter

Here, then, we have a definition of prayer that both affirms the pervasiveness of human prayer and helps us make an important distinction. All prayer is responding to God. In all cases God is the initiator—"hearing" always precedes asking. God comes to us first or we would never reach out to him.[92] Yet all prayers are not alike or equally effective in relating to God. The clearer our understanding of who God is, the better our prayers. Instinctive prayer is like an emergency flare in reaction to a general sense of God's reality. Prayer as a spiritual gift is a genuine, personal conversation in reply to God's specific, verbal revelation.

Yet prayer can be even more than that. Many or perhaps most of our conversations are relatively superficial. Persons can exchange information without much self-disclosure. Some conversations, however, go deep and we sense that both of us are revealing not just information but our very selves. The conversation then becomes a personal encounter, a true connection.

C. S. Lewis's novel *That Hideous Strength* relates the conversion of one of the characters, Jane Studdock, after a crucial conversation. She had thought of "religion" as being like a cloud of incense "steaming up from especially gifted souls towards a receptive Heaven," which would then respond in various rewards and blessings. Suddenly she got a very different picture in her mind, not of our efforts upward but of "God . . . of strong, skillful hands thrust down to make and mend." Then, on the basis of this new information, she felt herself come "into the presence of a Person. Something expectant, patient, inexorable, met her with no veil or protection between." God met her. As a result, everything changed. "The mould under the bushes, the moss on the path, and the little brick border were not visibly changed. But they were changed. A boundary had been crossed."[93]

Almost immediately, voices arose in her mind. The first was a frontal assault. "'Take care. Draw back. Keep your head. Don't commit yourself,' they said." The second was far more subtle, urging her to turn the feeling into a life-enriching experience that would help her enjoy her current life better. "'You have had a religious experience. This is very interesting. Not everyone does. How much better you will now understand the Seventeenth-century poets!'" Lewis the narrator adds in conclusion, "But her defenses had been captured and these counter-attacks were unsuccessful." [94]

Lewis entitled this chapter "Real Life Is Meeting."[95] Indeed it is, and this is particularly true of life in Christ. Jane's life was changed when she met God. The Bible speaks of our relationship with God as knowing and being known (Gal 4:9; 1 Cor 13:12). The goal is not just the sharing of ideas but also of ourselves. Communication can lead to two-way personal revelation that produces what can only be called a dynamic experience. J. I. Packer, in his famous work *Knowing God*, writes:

> Knowing God is a matter of personal dealing. . . . Knowing God is more than knowing about him; it is a matter of dealing with him as he opens up to you, and being dealt with by him. . . . Friends . . . open their hearts to each other by what they say and do. . . . We must not lose sight of the fact that knowing God is an emotional relationship, as well as an intellectual and volitional one, and could not indeed be a deep relationship between persons if it were not so.[96]

What is prayer, then, in the fullest sense? Prayer is continuing a conversation that God has started through his Word and his grace, which eventually becomes a full encounter with him.

Listening and Answering

Throughout most of the great Old Testament book that bears his name, Job cries out to God in agonized prayer. For all his complaints, Job never walks away from God or denies his existence—he processes all his pain and suffering through prayer. Yet he cannot accept the life God is calling him to live. Then the skies cloud over and God speaks to Job "out of the whirlwind" (Job 38:1). The Lord recounts in vivid detail his creation and sustenance of the universe and of the natural world. Job is astonished and humbled by this deeper vision of God (Job 40:3–5) and has a breakthrough. He finally prays a mighty prayer of repentance and adoration (Job 42:1–6).

The question of the book of Job is posed in its very beginning. Is it possible that a man or woman can come to love God for himself alone so that there is a fundamental contentment in life regardless of circumstances (Job 1:9)?[97] By the end of the book we see the answer. Yes, this is possible, but only through prayer.

What had happened? The more clearly Job saw who God was, the fuller his prayers became—moving from mere complaint to confession, appeal, and praise. In the end he broke through and was able to face anything in life. This new refinement and level of character came through the interaction of listening to God's revealed Word and answering in prayer. The more true his knowledge of God, the more fruitful his prayers became, and the more sweeping the change in his life.

The power of our prayers, then, lies not primarily in our effort and striving, or in any technique, but rather in our knowledge of God. You may respond, "But God spoke audible words to Job out of a storm. I wish God spoke to me like that." The answer is—we have something better, an incalculably clearer expression of God's character. "In the past God spoke to our ancestors through the prophets at many times and in various ways, but in these last days he has spoken to us by his Son . . . the radiance of God's glory and the exact representation of his being" (Heb 1:1–3).

Jesus Christ is *the* Word of God (John 1:1–14) because no more comprehensive, personal, and beautiful communication of God is possible. We cannot look directly at the sun with our eyes. The glory of it would immediately overwhelm and destroy our sight. We have to look at it through a filter, and then we can see the great flames and colors of it. When we look at Jesus Christ as he is shown to us in the Scriptures, we are looking at the glory of God through the filter of a human nature. That is one of the many reasons, as we shall see, that Christians pray "In Jesus' name." Through Christ, prayer becomes what Scottish Reformer John Knox called "an earnest and familiar talking with God," and John Calvin called an "intimate conversation" of believers with God, or elsewhere "a communion of men with God"—a two-way communicative interaction.[98] "For through [Christ] we . . . have access to the Father by one Spirit" (Eph 2:18).

FOUR

Conversing with God

We have learned that prayer is both an instinct and a spiritual gift. As an instinct, prayer is a response to our innate but fragmentary knowledge of God. It is like a note in a bottle to "whatever gods there be." As a gift of the Spirit, however, prayer becomes the continuation of a conversation God has started. If that conversation proceeds, as in the best conversations, praying becomes meeting with God—heaven in the ordinary.

Since prayer is our reply to God, we must now explore how it is that he first speaks to us, and then how we can learn to answer him.

Meeting a Personal God

If God were impersonal, as the Eastern religions teach, then love—something that can happen only between two or more persons—would be an illusion. We can go further and say that even if God were only unipersonal, then love could not have appeared until after God began to create other beings. That would mean God was more fundamentally power than he was love. Love would not be as important as power.

The Christian doctrine of the Trinity, however, teaches that there is one God in three persons who have known and loved one another from before the dawn of time.[99] If God is triune, then words and language are seen in a new light. In John 14–17 Jesus refers to his life within the Godhead before he came to earth, speaking of "the glory I had with [the Father] before the world began" (John 17:5) and of "the words" he has received from the Father (John 17:8). Within the Trinity from all eternity, there has been communication by words—the Father speaks to the Son, the Son speaks to the Father, and the Father and the Son speak to the Spirit.[100] In John 17, we get a glimpse of this speaking in Jesus' prayer to his Father. It is divine discourse.[101]

Many philosophers have said that God is a pure spirit and so it is inappropriate to talk about God speaking.[102] Yet Jesus said, "Heaven and earth will pass away, but my words will never pass away" (Matt 24:35). Philosopher Nicholas Wolterstorff and others deny the idea that God cannot and does not speak. Wolterstorff applies J. L. Austin's speech-act theory, which points out that words are also actions. They not only say things, they accomplish things. If God exists and has power to act, then there is no reason he could not speak, because words are also actions. Also, since the Godhead contains a community of persons, and because language is intrinsic to personal relationship, there is every reason to expect that God communicates through words.

Therefore, Christian prayer is not plunging into the abyss of unknowing and a state of wordless hyperconsciousness. That condition is created not by words per se but by sounds. "The techniques that prepare for [the mantra meditation state of *samadhi*] feature repetitive sounds, sights, or actions. Analytical thought is mesmerized to favor intuitive awareness, a relaxed state in which one's consciousness of individual identity is suspended."[103] Rather, Christian prayer is fellowship with the personal God who befriends us through speech. The biblical pattern entails meditating on the words of Scripture until we respond to God with our entire being, saying, "Give me an undivided heart, that . . . I may praise you, Lord my God, with all my heart" (Ps 86:11–12).

Meeting God through His Word

Speech-act theory makes a convincing case that our words not only convey information, they get things done. However, God's words have a power infinitely beyond our own. Timothy Ward's book *Words of Life* argues that God's words are identical with his actions.[104] He quotes Genesis 1:3, "'Let there be light,' and there was light." Ward observes that the passage does not say that first God spoke and then he proceeded to do what he said he would do. No, his word itself brought the light about. When God names someone, his very word also constitutes the person. When he renames Abram to be Abraham— "father of a multitude"—that word makes the aged man and his wife biologically and spiritually capable of being the progenitors of a whole race (Gen 17:5). Psalm 29 is an entire hymn of praise of the power of God's voice. "The voice of the Lord breaks the cedars—the Lord breaks in pieces the cedars of Lebanon. The voice of the Lord shakes the desert—the Lord shakes the Desert of Kadesh" (Ps 29:5, 8). We see again that what God's voice does, God does. God's speaking and acting are equated. Isaiah 55:10–11 puts this theological principle most powerfully:

As the rain and the snow
come down from heaven,
and do not return to it
without watering the earth
and making it bud and flourish,
so that it yields seed for the sower and bread for the eater,
so is my word that goes out from my mouth:
It will not return to me empty,
but will accomplish what I desire
and achieve the purpose for which I sent it.

We humans may say, "Let there be light in this room," but then we have to flick a switch or light a candle. Our words need deeds to back them up and can fail to achieve their purposes. God's words, however, cannot fail their purposes because, for God, speaking and acting are the same thing. The God of the Bible is a God who "by his very nature, acts through speaking."[105]

When the Bible talks of God's Word, then, it is talking of "God's active presence in the world."[106] To say that God's word goes out to do something is the same as to say God has gone out to do something. To break one of God's commands or words is to break one's relationship with him. "Thus (we may say) God has *invested* himself with his words, or we could say that God has so *identified* himself with his words that whatever someone does to God's words . . . they do to God himself. . . . God's . . . *verbal actions are a kind of extension of himself.*"[107]

The implications of this basic teaching of the Bible about itself are immense. One of them directly relates to the subject of prayer. "More mystically minded people sometimes suppose that words by their very nature are an obstruction to the goal of a deep communion with God, but that is just not so." If God's words are his personal, active presence, then to put your trust in God's words *is* to put your trust in God. "Communication from God is therefore communion with God, when met with a response of trust from us." Of course, there can be, in prayer, times of simple stillness in his presence, but even at the human level, "a man and a woman sitting in a restaurant gazing silently into each other's eyes . . . are engaging in a much more genuine relationship if they are doing so with twenty years of conversation-filled marriage behind them, than if they are on their first date and have not yet spoken to each other."[108]

How are we to receive God's words? They come to us in the Scripture. The Bible says that God will put his words in the mouths of the prophets (Deut 18:15–20; Jer 1:9–10). Once a prophet receives God's words, they can be written down and can effectively be read as God's speech when the prophet is not present or even after he is dead and gone (Jer 36:1–32). The Bible, then, is God's Word written, and it remains God's Word when we read it today.

The conclusion is clear. God acts through his words, the Word is "alive and active" (Heb 4:12), and therefore the way to have God dynamically active in our lives is through the Bible. To understand the Scripture is not simply to get information about God. If attended to with trust and faith, the Bible is the way to actually hear God speaking and also to meet God himself.

Prayer through Immersion in God's Word

We know who we are praying to only if we first learn it in the Bible. And we know how we should be praying only by getting our vocabu-

lary from the Bible. None of this should be a surprise, since we
basic dynamic played out in the development of every new human
being.

Eugene Peterson reminds us that "because we learned language so
early in our lives we have no memory of the process" and would therefore imagine that it was we who took the initiative to learn how to
speak. However, that is not the case. "Language is spoken into us; we
learn language only as we are spoken to. We are plunged at birth into
a sea of language. . . . Then slowly syllable by syllable we acquire the
capacity to answer: mama, papa, bottle, blanket, yes, no. Not one of
these words was a first word. . . . All speech is answering speech. We
were all spoken to before we spoke."[109] In the years since Peterson
wrote, studies have shown that children's ability to understand and
communicate is profoundly affected by the number of words and the
breadth of vocabulary to which they are exposed as infants and tod-
dlers. We speak only to the degree we are spoken to.

It is therefore essential to the practice of prayer to recognize what
Peterson calls the "overwhelming *previousness* of God's speech to our
prayers."[110] This theological principle has practical consequences. It
means that our prayers should arise out of immersion in the Scripture.
We should "plunge ourselves into the sea" of God's language, the Bible. We should listen, study, think, reflect, and ponder the Scriptures
until there is an answering response in our hearts and minds. It may
be one of shame or of joy or of confusion or of appeal—but that response to God's speech is then truly *prayer* and should be given to
God.

If the goal of prayer is a real, personal connection with God, then
it is only by immersion in the language of the Bible that we will learn
to pray, perhaps just as slowly as a child learns to speak. This does not
mean, of course, that we must literally read the Bible before each indi-

vidual prayer. A sponge needs to be saturated in water only periodically in order to do its work. We can cry out to God all during the day as long as we regularly spend time with his Word. Peterson looks at the prayers of the writers and figures of the Bible and concludes that they were

> not prayed by people trying to understand themselves. They are not the record of people searching for the meaning of life. They were prayed by people who understood that . . . God, not their feelings, was the center. . . . Human experiences might provoke the prayers, but they do not condition them. . . . It is not simply a belief in God that conditions these prayers . . . but a *doctrine* of God.[111]

In the Bible we discover a real and complex God. If you have a personal relationship with any real person, you will regularly be confused and infuriated by him or her. So, too, you will be regularly confounded by the God you meet in the Scriptures—as well as amazed and comforted. Your prayer must be firmly connected to and grounded in your reading of the Word. This wedding of the Bible and prayer anchors your life down in the real God.

Verbal Prayer as Response to God's Person

In his chapter "Prayer and Mysticism," theologian Donald Bloesch writes about the writings of medieval mystics Meister Eckhart and John Tauler. He observes that "in the deepest sense, the mystical experience is beyond the rational, beyond words and ideas."[112] As Catholic author Thomas Merton writes, "The mystical knowledge of

God . . . is above concepts. It is a knowledge that registers itself in the soul passively *without an idea*."[113] The mystic wants to attend strictly to God, not to words and ideas about God. Rationality is seen as a limitation, a barrier between the heart and God.

Yet Paul calls Christians to keep their rationality as they pray. "I will pray with my spirit, but I will also pray with my understanding; I will sing with my spirit, but I will also sing with my understanding" (1 Cor 14:15). We are, after all, praying in words to the Father through the Son, who is *the* Word (John 1:1). Martin Luther was adamant that we must never get "beyond" God's words in the Bible or we can't know whom we are conversing with. "We must first hear the Word, and then afterwards the Holy Ghost works in our hearts; he works in the hearts of whom he will, and how he will, but never without the Word."[114]

A contemporary writer who makes similar arguments is John Jefferson Davis in his helpful work *Meditation and Communion with God*.[115] Davis concludes that, though they are not without their merits, the methods of "Centering Prayer" and "the Jesus Prayer" are not entirely appropriate for those who understand prayer as a response to God's verbal revelation in the Bible and as a gift given to those secure in God's grace. Centering Prayer is based, like the fourteenth-century work *The Cloud of Unknowing*, on the idea of God as pure spirit within us and beyond all thoughts, concepts, and images.[116] The goal is "apophatic prayer"—to get beyond discursive thoughts and to experience pure attentiveness to God the Spirit through the quiet, reflective, and repetitive use of a single word such as *God* or *love*.[117] Davis rightly criticizes this by insisting that the use of language is not incidental but is instead essential to God's eternal being as a unity of three persons, and that believers are to be sanctified in the form of the truthful words given to Jesus by the Father (John 17:8, 17) and conveyed to us by the Spirit (1 Cor 2:13).[118] He also points out that the movement of

Christian prayer in the Bible is not so much inward (though there must be self-examination and repentance) but upward, to realize our true status in Christ and to align our hearts with that. "Since, then, you have been raised with Christ, set your hearts on things above. . . . Set your minds on things above, not on earthly things" (Col 3:1–2). We are not to stop thinking and using language but to direct our words and ideas heavenward.[119]

Davis is somewhat less critical of "the Jesus Prayer" ("Lord Jesus Christ, Son of God, have mercy on me, a sinner") but still advises against relying on it too much. This is an ancient prayer used in the Eastern Orthodox Church, to be said repeatedly for long periods of time or to be repeated under the breath and in the heart all day long. Davis points out that even though this is a sentence of words, many use the repetition to block out all thoughts, and so it may be used for the same suppression of conversation, interchange, language, and thought that marks Centering Prayer and other forms of Eastern meditation. Repeated sounds along with rhythmic breathing can produce psychosomatic effects similar to the prayers of the Islamic Sufi *dhikr*.[120] Also, Davis notes that the Jesus Prayer does not include prayer to the Father through Christ, though this is the essence of prayer according to Jesus himself (Matt 6:9ff). The Father is not mentioned and we come only as "sinners," not as children secure in his love, so the prayer makes no reference to our status as already forgiven and accepted.[121] The Jesus Prayer could easily be used as a kind of magic or mantra, a way to procure God's attention through its "many words" (Matt 6:7). Davis therefore proposes developing ways of doing meditation and prayer that are grounded in a more robust understanding of the personality of the speaking God and of our security as justified and adopted children.

As usual, a balance must be found, and J. I. Packer finds it. He takes on "the distinct belief, stemming from Asian religions and from Gnostic and Neoplatonic aberrations among Christians, that God is to be realized and contemplated as an impersonal presence rather than a personal friend." He goes on to say that a "non-cognitive closeness to God in which the mind is emptied of all personal thoughts about him, and indeed of all thoughts whatsoever," is Eastern "mysticism in [W]estern dress."[122]

However, Packer reminds us that "there is [indeed] a place for silence before God . . . after we have spoken to him, while joy at God's love invades the soul." It is appropriate some time to admire and adore God silently because "when two people love each other there are times when they smilingly look at each other in silence, not needing to speak, simply enjoying their close rapport."[123] Yet even people who are deeply in love will instinctively search for words and exclamations of wonder to convey and express what they feel. Therefore, he concludes, "wordless prayer is not the pinnacle . . . but the periodic punctuation of verbal prayer."[124]

Varied Prayer as Response to God's Glory

In prayer we are to use words, but what kind? All kinds. The Psalms reveal a great range in the modes of prayer. They include exclamations of wonder, virulent complaints, reasoned arguments, pronouncements and verdicts, appeals and requests, summonses and calls, and verdicts of self-condemnation. They represent not only radically different types of discourse but of attitudes and emotions as well. Left to ourselves, to our cultures and natural temperaments, there are many kinds of language that we would never use. The Psalms contain heights and exuberant outbursts that melancholic types would never produce on their own. There are depths of heart insight that extroverted people might never discover. There are complaints and blunt questions to God of which introverted and compliant people are less capable.

We would never produce the full range of biblical prayer if we were initiating prayer according to our own inner needs and psychology. It can only be produced if we are responding in prayer according to who God is as revealed in the Scripture. The biblical God is majestic and tender, holy and forgiving, loving and inscrutable. That is why prayer can never be primarily abject confessions or triumphant praise or plaintive appeals—it cannot be mainly any one type of expression. Some prayers in the Bible are like an intimate conversation with a friend, others like an appeal to a great monarch, and others approximate a wrestling match. Why? In every case the nature of the prayer is determined by the character of God, who is at once our friend, father, lover, shepherd, and king. We must not decide how to pray based on what types of prayer are the most effective for producing the experiences and feelings we want. We pray in response to God himself. God's Word to us contains this range of discourse—and only if we respond to his Word will our own prayer life be as rich and varied.

The Tragedy of Untethered Prayer

Eugene Peterson says that your starting point for prayer must be immersion in God's Word. A different approach is seen in Anne Lamott's book on prayer entitled *Help, Thanks, Wow: The Three Essential Prayers*. She declares up front that your view of God is not really important for prayer:

> Let's say [prayer is to] what the Greeks called the Really
> Real, what lies within us, beyond the scrim of our values,

positions, convictions, and wounds. Or let's say it is a cry
from within to Life or Love, with capital L's. Nothing could
matter less than what we call this force. . . . Let's not get
bogged down on whom or what we pray to. Let's just say
prayer is communication from our hearts to the great mystery, or Goodness . . . to the animating energy of love we
are sometimes bold enough to believe in: to something unimaginably big, and not us. We could call this force Not
Me . . . or for convenience we could just say "God." [125]

It may be that she is simply trying to invite people unsure of belief
in God to begin reaching out to him. If understood in this way, Lamott's book is a disarming invitation to the doubter to pray, but that can
only at best serve as a provisional first step. Telling someone to pray
and not worry about who God is or what we believe about him cannot
serve as a sustaining operating principle of prayer, because you cannot
grow in a relationship with a person unless you learn who he or she is.
Lamott memorably names three of the traditional categories of
prayer: Help (supplication), Thanks (thanksgiving), and Wow (adoration). It is striking, though, that the book leaves out one of the most
crucial classical categories of prayer, namely confession and repentance.[126] If we contrast Lamott's short book with similar-length treatises on prayer by Augustine and Luther, and with the Lord's Prayer
itself, the lack of emphasis on confession is a glaring omission.[127] My
guess is this is because she uses a starting point that is not the knowledge of God in the Bible. We should not get "bogged down" in who
God is. We should just pray. The problem is that if God is not the
starting point, then our own perceived emotional needs become the
drivers and sole focus of our prayer.[128] That will inevitably narrow
prayer down from its full biblical spectrum.

Edmund P. Clowney wrote, "The Bible does not present an art of prayer; it presents the God of prayer."[129] We should not decide how to pray based on the experiences and feelings we want. Instead, we should do everything possible to behold our God as he is, and prayer will follow. The more clearly we grasp who God is, the more our prayer is shaped and determined accordingly.

Without immersion in God's words, our prayers may not be merely limited and shallow but also untethered from reality. We may be responding not to the real God but to what we wish God and life to be like. Indeed, if left to themselves our hearts *will* tend to create a God who doesn't exist. People from Western cultures want a God who is loving and forgiving but not holy and transcendent. Studies of the spiritual lives of young adults in Western countries reveal that their prayers, therefore, are generally devoid of both repentance and of the joy of being forgiven.[130] Without prayer that answers the God of the Bible, we will only be talking to ourselves. Peterson has put this very bluntly:

> Left to ourselves, we will pray to some god who speaks what we like hearing, or to the part of God we manage to understand. But what is critical is that we speak to the God who speaks to us, and to everything that he speaks to us. . . . There is a difference between praying to an unknown God whom we hope to discover in our praying, and praying to a known God, revealed through Israel and Jesus Christ, who speaks our language. In the first, we indulge our appetite for religious fulfillment; in the second we practice obedient faith. The first is a lot more fun, the second is a lot more important. What is essential in prayer is not that we learn to express ourselves, but that we learn to answer God.[131]

If we leave the Bible out, we may plumb our impressions and feelings and imagine God saying various things to us, but how can we be sure we are not self-deceived? The eighteenth-century Anglican clergyman George Whitefield was one of the spearheads of the Great Awakening, a period of massive renewal of interest in Christianity across Western societies and a time of significant church growth. Whitefield was a riveting orator and is considered one of the greatest preachers in church history. In late 1743 his first child, a son, was born to he and his wife, Elizabeth. Whitefield had a strong impression that God was telling him the child would grow up to also be a "preacher of the everlasting Gospel." In view of this divine assurance, he gave his son the name John, after John the Baptist, whose mother was also named Elizabeth. When John Whitefield was born, George baptized his son before a large crowd and preached a sermon on the great works that God would do through his son. He knew that cynics were sneering at his prophecies, but he ignored them.

Then, at just four months old, his son died suddenly of a seizure. The Whitefields were of course grief-stricken, but George was particularly convicted about how wrong he had been to count his inward impulses and intuitions as being essentially equal to God's Word. He realized he had led his congregation into the same disillusioning mistake. Whitefield had interpreted his own feelings—his understandable and powerful fatherly pride and joy in his son, and his hopes for him—as God speaking to his heart. Not long afterward, he wrote a wrenching prayer for himself, that God would "render this mistaken parent more cautious, more sober-minded, more experienced in Satan's devices, and consequently more useful in his future labors to the church of God."[132]

The lesson here is not that God never guides our thoughts or prompts us to choose wise courses of action, but that we cannot be sure he is speaking to us unless we read it in the Scripture.

Finding the Heart to Pray

When David the king was at the height of his power, he decided to build a temple for God. God sent him a message through the prophet Nathan that he should not build the temple, but then he made David a promise: "The Lord himself will establish a house for you. . . . I will raise up your offspring to succeed you. . . . He is the one who will build a house for my Name, and I will establish the throne of his kingdom forever" (2 Sam 7:11–13). David wanted to build God a house, but God said, "No, I will build *you* a house." It's a play on words, and a powerful one. David wanted to build God a place that displayed his glory. God said, in effect, that he had a counterproposal. He would establish David's royal family line and it would ultimately reveal God's glory in a more permanent, far-reaching, and universal way.

In response to this gracious promise, David says: "Lord Almighty, God of Israel, you have revealed this to your servant, saying, 'I will build a house for you.' So your servant has found courage to pray this prayer to you" (2 Sam 7:27). This reveals the inner dynamic of how prayer works. In the New International Version translation of verse 27, David's words are rendered that he had received the "courage to pray." The Hebrew text, however, literally says that God's Word enabled David to "find the heart [Hebrew *leb*] to pray this prayer to you." The Word of God created within David the desire, drive, and strength to pray. The principle: God speaks to us in his Word, and we respond in prayer, entering into the divine conversation, into communion with God.

David's prayer in 2 Samuel 7 is a mighty one, but Christians have every advantage over even the greatest Old Testament saints. Surely, David must have wondered how his throne could be established "forever." Is that just ancient imperial hyperbole, like "O may the king live forever"? No. The prophet Isaiah tells us of one who will "reign on David's throne . . . forever" and "of the increase of his government and peace there will be no end" (Is 9:7). How could there be an individual human being who reigns forever? Isaiah's answer is that the child who is to be born will be the "Mighty God" (Is 9:6). He will be "born"—therefore human—but divine. One of David's descendants will take up a kingdom and never relinquish it, because of the divine power of his indestructible life (Heb 7:16). Jesus, the ultimate Son of David, will do this.

There is more. We who believe in him will ourselves become God's "house"—a temple of living stones indwelt by the Holy Spirit (1 Pet 2:4–5; Eph 2:20–22). The same divine glory that would have been fatal to Moses on contact (Ex 33:20) now comes into the hearts of those pardoned by Christ (John 1:14; 2 Pet 1:4). No wonder Christ could say, to the astonishment of his hearers, that while John the Baptist was the greatest prophet before Christ, the least of Jesus' disciples was greater than he (Matt 11:11). God's Word of power "dwells richly" in all believers, giving them hearts to praise, sing, and pray to God with a joy and reality that neither David nor John the Baptist could know (Col 3:16).

David found the heart to pray when he received God's Word of promise—that he would establish his throne and build him a house. Christians, however, have an infinitely greater Word of promise. God will not merely build us a house, he will make us *his* house. He will fill us with his presence, beauty, and glory. Every time Christians merely remember who they are in Christ, that great word comes home to us and we will find, over and over again, a heart to pray.

FIVE

Encountering God

Prayer is conversation with God. However, conversations can remain mere exchanges of information that do not lead to true personal encounter and relationship. We do not want just to know *about* God, but to *know* God, to seek his face and presence. Timothy Ward has shown that the words of God given to the prophets and the apostles, written down in the Bible, comprise the main way we encounter God. "To encounter the words of the Scripture is to encounter God in action."[133] We must not, therefore, pit theological truth against existential encounter. Rather, we must experience the truth. How does that happen? In this chapter we will examine what the Bible says about experiencing God. To do that we must explore who the God is that we pray to and then how the Scripture says we can encounter him.

Whom We Encounter: A Tri-Personal God

The primary theological fact about prayer is this: We address a triune God, and our prayers can be heard only through the distinct work of every person in the Godhead.

In the New Testament the triune nature of God becomes explicit,[134] but few places are as compressed and direct as Matthew 28:19, where Jesus sends his disciples into the world to baptize "in the name of the Father and of the Son and of the Holy Spirit." It does not say "in the names" but rather states that the Father, Son, and Holy Spirit all have a single name. For us the term *name* may be just a label or a brand that can be discarded or changed at will, but in biblical times, it denoted the very nature and being of a person.[135] This means the Father, Son, and Holy Spirit all share one divine nature, that they are one being. There is only one God—not three. Though Paul continually speaks of Christ's divinity, saying that *all* the fullness of the deity dwells in him (Col 2:9), yet he also says there is "no God but one" (1 Cor 8:4)—God has one nature, name, and being.

Yet the Father, the Son, and the Holy Spirit are all equally God. Biblical scholar R. T. France says, "For 'the Son' to take his place as the middle member between the Father and the Holy Spirit, in a threefold object of the disciples' allegiance . . . [and] the rightful object of worship . . . is extraordinary."[136] Therefore, there are three persons within the unity of God's being, who are equally divine, who know and love one another, and who from all eternity have together worked for our salvation.[137]

The implications of the Triunity of God for prayer are many. It means, to begin with, that God has always had within himself a perfect friendship. The Father, the Son, and the Holy Spirit are adoring one another, giving glorifying love to one another, and delighting in one another. We know of no joy higher than being loved and loving in return, but a triune God would know that love and joy in unimaginable, infinite dimensions. God is, therefore, infinitely, profoundly *happy*, filled with perfect joy—not some abstract tranquility but the fierce happiness of dynamic loving relationships. Knowing this God is not to get beyond emotions or thoughts but to be filled with glorious love and joy.

If God did not need to create other beings in order to know love and happiness, then why did he do so? Jonathan Edwards argues, in *A Dissertation Concerning the End for Which God Created the World*, that the only reason God would have had for creating us was not to *get* the cosmic love and joy of relationship (because he already had that) but to *share* it.[138] Edwards shows how it is completely consistent for a triune God—who is "other-oriented" in his very core, who seeks glory only to give it to others—to communicate happiness and delight in his own divine perfections and beauty to others.

As Augustine wrote in his great work *On the Trinity*, our ability to love other persons is just an image of the internal Trinitarian love that we were created to reflect.[139] We can see why a triune God would call us to converse with him, to know and relate to him. It is because he wants to share the joy he has. Prayer is our way of entering into the happiness of God himself.

Whom We Encounter: Our Heavenly Father

While God was called Father only occasionally in the Old Testament, it is when the Trinity becomes explicit in the New Testament that the character of God's fatherhood also becomes prominent and clear. The Father sends the Son to save us from our sins so that we can become God's adopted sons and daughters (Eph 1:3–10). When we are born again through faith in Christ, we receive the right to be his children and call on him as father (John 1:12–13). The Spirit then puts the actual life of God in us—the "family resemblance," God's own nature. "God sent his Son, born of a woman, born under the law, to redeem those under the law, that we might receive adoption to sonship. Because you are his sons, God sent the Spirit of his Son into our hearts, the Spirit who calls out, '*Abba*, Father'" (Gal 4:4–6).

Many people ask, Aren't all people God's children? The Bible occasionally speaks of all human beings as God's "offspring" since he created all persons (Acts 17:28). The word used in Acts 17 is the Greek word *genos*, meaning "descendants," and it is true that God is father of all in the sense that Henry Ford is father of the Model T. However, the word *father* also denotes a relationship of love and care. Have you ever heard a conversation (or been in one) where a young person says to an older man, "You were never a real *father* to me!" Perhaps the man responds, "But you are my own flesh and blood." The younger party will then retort: "It takes more than that to be a father! You were never there for me."

Just because someone is my biological progenitor doesn't mean he has a real father relationship to me. The Bible takes the same perspective. It reserves the richness of the term "children of God" for those who have been adopted into God's family by grace through faith. To be adopted is a legal event, but of course it means more than that. To be adopted into a new family means a revolution in how you live your life day to day. In Christ, therefore, believers are not only legally but personally established in God's fatherly love.[140] In a remarkable passage, Jesus prays to the Father for his followers "[that] the world will know that you sent me and have loved them *even as* you have loved me" (John 17:23). To be adopted means that now God loves us as if we had done all Jesus had done. This means Christ, as one theologian said, "has not merely paid the penalty" for our sins but "also he has positively merited for us eternal life . . . merited for [us] the reward by his perfect obedience to God's law," so we can run to our Father without fear.[141] We have the most intimate and unbreakable relationship possible with the God of the universe.

To be a child of God means *access*. We know God is attentively listening to us and watching us. Think about what it takes to get in to see the president of the United States. Only people who merit his time and attention would be allowed in. They must have credentials, accomplishments, and perhaps a power base of their own. If you are one of his children, however, it is different. In the same way, the God of the universe is "mindful" of you (Ps 8:4).

Prayer is the way to sense and appropriate this access and fatherly love, and to experience the calm and strength in one's life that results from such assurance of being cared for.

How We Encounter: The Spirit of Adoption

In Ephesians 2:18, Paul said that our access to God as Father comes through and "by one Spirit." Jonathan Edwards says that "prayer is . . . only the voice of faith."[142] Anyone with real faith will desire to pray because, through the Spirit, prayer is faith become audible. Paul gives us more detail on this work of the Spirit in prayer as he writes:

> For those who are led by the Spirit of God are the children of God. The Spirit you received does not make you slaves, so that you live in fear again; rather, the Spirit you received brought about your adoption to sonship. And by him we cry, "*Abba*, Father." The Spirit himself testifies with our spirit that we are God's children. (Rom 8:14–16)

Paul tells us that, rather than fear, the Spirit of God fills Christians with confidence in God's loving attention, analogous to the trust of a little child toward a parent. The Spirit leads us to "*cry*"—a Greek word, *krazdo*, that means a loud, fervent cry, which is often used in the Old Testament to denote fervent prayer, as in "*Abba*, Father." As biblical scholar C. E. B. Cranfield writes, this is "in origin an exclamatory form used by small children," easy to pronounce, somewhat like the term *Papa*.[143] He observes that this was considered too "homely and affectionate" to be an appropriate address to God in Judaism, and that Jesus' own adoption of it in his own prayer life (e.g., Mark 14:36) "expressed his consciousness of a unique relationship to God, and His authorizing his disciples to address God in this way is to be understood as His giving them a share in his relationship to God."[144]

This is no "emergency flare" or desperate, anxious gamble. The Spirit gives believers an existential, inward certainty that their relationship with God does not now depend on their performance as it does in the relationship between an employee and a supervisor. It depends on parental love. The Holy Spirit takes a theological proposition and turns it into an inner confidence and joy. You know that God responds to your cry with the intense love and care of a parent responding to the cry of pain of his or her child—because you are in Jesus, the true Son. You can go to God with the confidence of receiving that kind of attention and love. Put another way, the Holy Spirit gives us a confident faith that turns naturally into prayer.

This confidence was the heart of Martin Luther's powerful theology and practice of prayer. Well-known for praying at least two hours a day and emerging with great boldness, Luther told any Christian to begin to pray by saying the following to the Lord:

> Although . . . you could rightly and properly be a severe
> judge over us sinners . . . now through your mercy implant
> in our hearts a comforting trust in your fatherly love, and
> let us experience the sweet and pleasant savor of a childlike

certainty that we may joyfully call you Father, knowing and loving you and calling on you in every trouble.[145]

According to Paul, however, "Abba" prayer is not the only kind of prayer we are given by the Spirit. Paul doesn't speak merely of the Spirit of adoption but also of the Spirit as "intercessor":

> Likewise the Spirit helps us in our weakness; for we do not know how to pray as we ought, but the Spirit himself intercedes for us with sighs too deep for words. And he who searches the hearts of men knows what is the mind of the Spirit, because the Spirit intercedes for the saints according to the will of God. We know that in everything God works for good with those who love him, who are called according to his purpose. (Rom 8:26–28)

There has been debate over the meaning of "the Spirit's groans."[146] Some believe this is the Spirit helping us when we are desperate and groaning, but it is unlikely that this is describing only times of depression. Rather, the "weakness" referred to in verse 26 is the weakness described in the preceding verses, which refer not just to times of despondency but to our entire human situation of frustrated longings as we await the future glory (vv. 18–25, especially v. 23). We know that God is working out all things for our good according to his will (v. 28), but seldom can we discern what that good actually is. In other words, most of the time, we don't know exactly what outcome we should pray for.[147] The Spirit, however, makes our groaning *his* groaning, putting his prayers to the Father inside our prayers. He does so by placing within us a deep, inexpressible longing to do God's will and see his glory. This aspiration—this "groaning" desire to please him—comes through in our petitions to God. In every specific request, then, the Father hears us praying for what is both truly best for us and pleasing to him, "and the intercession of the Spirit is answered as God works all things for our good."[148] The Spirit enables us to long for the future glory of God and his will, even though we don't know the specific thing we should pray for here and now.[149]

Prayer is the way to experience a powerful confidence that God is handling our lives well, that our bad things will turn out for good, our good things cannot be taken from us, and the best things are yet to come.

How We Encounter: The Mediator

We come to the Father not only in the Spirit but through the Son. We can only be confident that God is our father if we come to him through the mediation of Christ, in Jesus' name.

A teacher of mine, Edmund P. Clowney, once told me that he went to one of his own teachers, John Murray, to discuss a private matter. Murray offered to pray for him, and when he did, the power of the prayer was stunning. Murray's address combined intimate familiarity with a sense of God's absolute majesty. The presence of God was instantly palpable. It was clear that Murray knew both the nearness of God as well as his transcendence.

Murray was being Ed's "mediator," though only in a secondary sense. He was bringing him into God's presence and speaking for him. Murray's trust in God's grace and confidence in his approach enabled Ed to rest in God's sovereign love, and that was the thing he most needed at that moment. Of course Murray the theologian knew that the two men were going together into the presence of God only through the mediation of Christ. In his commentary on Romans, Murray treats the verse—"Christ Jesus . . . is at the right hand of God and is also interceding for us" (Rom 8:34)—arguing that Jesus' "intercession" for us at the right hand of God, securing the Father's help for our needs because of his atoning work, must not be regarded as "mythical any more than may we regard as mythical the resurrection." He goes on:

> Nothing serves to verify the intimacy and constancy of the Redeemer's preoccupation with the security of his people, nothing assures us of his unchanging love more than the tenderness which his heavenly intercession bespeaks and particularly as it comes to expression in intercession for us.[150]

Ed said to me, "I was so helped by this godly man's intercession before God for me. Then I realized—if I find this comforting, how much more comforted should I be by the knowledge of Christ's intercession for me?"

As encouraging as this experience was for Ed, it was also deeply convicting. Just hearing Murray pray to God revealed to him that his own prayers were wooden, formal, mechanical. He knew little of familiar conversation with God in his presence. He realized that he was not taking seriously the meaning of the mediation of Jesus for his prayer life.

Jesus is the mediator between us and God (1 Tim 2:5; cf. Heb 8:6; 12:24). All ancient lands and cultures had temples, because human beings once knew innately that there was a gap, a yawning chasm, between us and the divine. God is great and we are small—God is perfect and we are flawed. Temples were places where an effort was made to bridge that gap. Sacrifices and offerings were made and rituals observed by professional "mediators" (priests) who sought to bring the remote divinity near. All such efforts were understood to be partial and fragmentary. No religion claimed that the gap could be closed. Aristotle, for example, said that while it might be possible to venerate and appease the gods, actual intimate friendship with a god was impossible. The philosopher reasoned that friendship requires that both parties share much in common as equals. They must be alike. But since God is infinitely greater than human beings, "the possibility of friendship ceases."[151]

Now, however, we have the ultimate mediator and priest to end all priests (Heb 4:14–15). He eliminates the gap so that we can know God as friend (cf. Ex 33:11). It is because the Son of God was "made like them, fully human in every way, in order that he might become a merciful and faithful high priest" (Heb 2:17). And because "we do not have a high priest who is unable to sympathize with our weakness, but . . . has been tempted in every way, just as we are—yet without sin," we are able to "approach God's throne of grace with confidence" (Heb 4:15–16). Here, then, is a claim that Aristotle—indeed, all the other philosophers and religious teachers of the world—would find outrageous. How could God be our intimate friend? How could we approach him with complete confidence? It is because God became like us, equally mortal and subject to suffering and death. He did it so we could be forgiven and justified by faith apart from our efforts and merits. That is why we can draw near.

Because in Jesus God became human, he is not only the God on the other side of the chasm, he is the bridge over the gap. Thus he is the mediator of a new relationship with God that cannot fail because it is based on his faithfulness, not ours (Heb 9:14–16).

> Therefore, brothers and sisters, since we have confidence to enter the Most Holy Place by the blood of Jesus, by a new

and living way opened for us through the curtain, that is, his body, and since we have a great priest over the house of God, let us draw near to God with a sincere heart and with the full assurance that faith brings. (Heb 10:19–22)

Prayer in Jesus' Name

This leads us to an important related directive of the New Testament regarding Christian prayer—Jesus taught his disciples that they must always pray in his name (John 14:13–14; 15:16; 16:23–24). "Prayers in his name are prayers . . . in recognition that the only approach to God . . . the only *way* to God is Jesus himself."[152]

This is essentially about qualification and access. I remember how as a student in graduate school, I anxiously approached a well-known speaker after a lecture. He seemed distracted as he greeted other students with perfunctory pleasantries. I, however, was able to mention that I knew a friend of his. When I said the name, he immediately snapped to attention and spoke to me with warmth and interest. I got this kind of access to him not in my own name but in the name of our mutual friend. That is a very dim hint of how we have access to God the Father. Because we know Jesus, because we are "in Christ," God focuses his almighty love and attention on us when we pray.

Paul's version of this guidance from Jesus is found in his deeply Trinitarian formula for prayer found in Ephesians 2:18: "Through him [Christ] we both have access to the Father by one Spirit." The word *access* was commonly used when an ancient king granted someone an audience. No one could simply walk into the presence of a powerful monarch. The consequences could be imprisonment or even death (cf. Esther 4:9–16). That, however, describes the power differential only between an ancient oriental king and a commoner. The gulf between a holy God and sinful human beings is infinitely greater (1 Sam 6:20; Ps 130:3; Na 1:6). No human being can look upon God and live (Ex 33:20). Paul's claim that we now have access to God's very presence "through him" is therefore quite astounding. We always have an audience because of what Jesus Christ has done. His death on the cross reconciled us to God (Eph 2:16) and made him our Father.

Knowing God for Who He Is

Galatians 4:6–7 says that the Spirit leads us to call out passionately to God as our loving Father. Paul refers to this experience as "knowing God" (4:8). That's the ground motive of Spirit-directed, Christ-mediated prayer—to simply know him better and enjoy his presence.

Consider how different this is from the normal way we use prayer. In our natural state we pray to God to get things. We may believe in God, but our deepest hopes and happiness reside in things as in how successful we are or in our social relationships. We therefore pray mainly when our career or finances are in trouble, or when some relationship or social status is in jeopardy. When life is going smoothly, and our truest heart treasures seem safe, it does not occur to us to pray. Also, ordinarily our prayers are not varied—they consist usually of petitions, occasionally some confession (if we have just done something wrong). Seldom or never do we spend sustained time adoring and praising God. In short, we have no positive, inner desire to pray. We do it only when circumstances force us. Why? We know God is there, but we tend to see him as a means through which we get things to make us happy. For most of us, he has not *become* our happiness. We therefore pray to procure things, not to know him better.

All this changes when we discover that we have been mired all our lives in forms of self-salvation, and we turn to Christ. When we grasp his astonishing, costly sacrifice for us, transfer our trust and hopes from other things to Christ, and ask for God's acceptance and grace for Christ's sake, we begin to realize with the Spirit's help the magnitude of our benefits and blessings in Christ. Then we begin to want almost desperately to know and love God for himself. His love and regard make popularity and worldly status look pale and thin. Being delighted in him and delighting him become inherently fulfilling and beautiful.

> *To see the law by Christ fulfilled*
> *And hear his pard'ning voice*
> *Transforms a slave into a child*
> *And duty into choice.*
>
> —William Cowper, *Olney Hymns*

In the early chapters of his exposition of the Christian faith, *The Institutes of Christian Religion*, John Calvin argues that you may know a lot about God, but you don't truly *know* God until the knowledge of what he has done for you in Jesus Christ has changed the fundamental structure of your heart. "For the Word of God is not received by faith if it flits about in the top of the brain, but when it takes root in the depth of the heart . . . the heart's distrust is greater than the mind's blindness. It is harder for the heart to be furnished with assurance [of God's love] than for the mind to be endowed with thought."[153] When the gospel does take root in the heart, the sign of it is that Christians are led to "establish their complete happiness in him." Unless people experience this, "they will never give themselves truly and sincerely to him."[154] You don't have true saving knowledge of God until you *long* to know and serve him. Such a soul "restrains itself from sinning, not out of dread of punishment alone; but because it loves and reveres God as Father. . . . *Even if there were no hell, it would still shudder at offending him.*"[155]

That is a vivid way of saying that a Christian who understands the gospel in the power of the Holy Spirit seeks God not primarily to gain reward or avoid punishment (since both are guaranteed in Christ anyway). Christians seek God for themselves. Without the gospel, we may come and ask for things. Without the gospel, we may conceive of a holy God who is intimidating and who can be approached with petitions only if we are very good. Or we may conceive of a God whose "love" just means he regards everyone positively. To approach the first kind of "God" is fearsome; to approach the second kind of God is no big deal. Thus without the gospel, there is no possibility of passion and delight to praise and approach the true God.

The Zaleskis argue that all human prayer is an effort to exercise power through a form of sacrifice by which God or the gods are moved to answer. However, biblical prayer is offered on the basis of God's free saving grace and his steadfast, endless fatherly love. If God is your heavenly father, neither magic nor sacrifice is needed.[156]

The Cost of Prayer

How is such access and freedom possible? The only time in all the gospels that Jesus Christ prays to God and doesn't call him Father is on the cross, when he says, "My God, my God, why have you forgotten me? Why have you forsaken me?" Jesus lost his relationship with the Father so that we could have a relationship with God as father. Jesus was forgotten so that we could be remembered forever—from everlasting to everlasting. Jesus Christ bore all the eternal punishment that our sins deserve. That is the cost of prayer. Jesus paid the price so God could be our father.

Perhaps, you protest, your own father or mother did you wrong. That must not be a barrier to prayer, for only in Christ will you get the love that you need to make up for your unhappy family history. It does no good to say, "Why weren't they the parents they should have been?" There are no parents who are what they should be. Psalm 27:10 says: "Though my father and mother forsake me, the Lord will bear me up."[157] This new relationship with God is what you need if you have a bad family background. This is what you need if you feel like a failure, if you feel lonely, or if you are sinking further into despair. Because of the infinite price paid by your brother, Jesus, God your father will hold you up.

Conversation with God leads to an encounter with God. Prayer is not only the way we learn what Jesus has done for us but also is the way we "daily receive God's benefits."[158] Prayer turns theology into experience. Through it we sense his presence and receive his joy, his love, his peace and confidence, and thereby we are changed in attitude, behavior, and character.

PART THREE

Learning Prayer

SIX

Letters on Prayer

We have learned that prayer is the continuation of a conversation that God has started. He started it when he implanted knowledge of himself in every human being, when he spoke through the prophets and in his written Word, and especially when he called us to himself through the Holy Spirit sent into our hearts. We have also explored what could be called a theology of prayer. The character of prayer is determined by the character of the God we are reaching toward. The God to whom Christians pray is a triune God. We can pray because God is our loving Father, because Christ is our mediator giving us access to the throne of the universe, and because the Spirit himself indwells us.

From here on in, we will try to answer the practical questions. How do we actually build on this foundation? In God and the gospel we have the spiritual resources to pray, but how do we actually do it?

We turn first to three of the greatest teachers in the history of the Christian church—St. Augustine, Martin Luther, and John Calvin. Each of them wrote extensively on prayer in many places, but each of them also produced one timeless classic—three "master classes"—on the subject. Augustine and Luther each wrote a personal letter to an individual on how to pray, while Calvin included a magisterial treatment of prayer in his summary of doctrine, the *Institutes*.[159] In this and the following chapters, we will listen to and learn from them.

Augustine on Prayer

Anicia Faltonia Proba (died AD 432) was a Roman noblewoman who was a Christian believer. She had the distinction of knowing Augustine, who was the greatest theologian of the first millennium of Christian history, as well as John Chrysostom, who was its greatest preacher. We have two letters of Augustine to Proba, and the first (Letter 130) is the only writing wholly devoted to the subject of prayer that he ever produced. Proba wrote Augustine because she was afraid she wasn't praying as she should. Augustine responded with a brief, practical essay.[160]

Augustine's first principle is that before you know what to pray for and how to pray for it, you must become a particular kind of person. "You must account yourself 'desolate' in this world, however great the prosperity of your lot may be." The scales must have fallen from your eyes and you must see clearly that no matter how great your earthly circumstances become, they can never bring you the lasting peace, happiness, and consolation that are found in Christ. Unless you have that clearly in view, your prayers may go wrong.

Here again is one of the main themes of Augustine's theology, applied to prayer. We must see that our heart's loves are "disordered," out of order. Things we ought to love third or fourth are first in our hearts. God, whom we should love supremely, is someone we may acknowledge but whose favor and presence is not existentially as important to us as prosperity, success, status, love, and pleasure. Unless at the very least we recognize this heart disorder and realize how much it distorts our lives, our prayers will be part of the problem, not an agent of our healing. For example, if we look to our financial prosperity as our main source of safety and confidence in life, then when our wealth is in grave jeopardy, we will cry out to God for help, but our prayers will be little more than "worrying in God's direction." When our prayers are finished we will be more upset and anxious than before. Prayer will not be strengthening. It won't heal our hearts by reorienting our vision and helping us put things in perspective and bringing us to rest in God as our true security.

Augustine goes on. If you have settled this—if you have grasped the character of your heart and admitted your desolation apart from Christ—then, he says, you can begin to pray. And what should you pray for? With a bit of a smile (I think), he answers that you should pray for what everyone else prays for: "Pray for a happy life." What, however, will bring you a happy life? If you have embraced Augustine's first principle of prayer, you have realized that comforts and rewards and pleasures in themselves give only fleeting excitement and that, if you rest your heart in them, they will bring you less enduring happiness. He turns to Psalm 27:4 and points to the psalmist's great prayer: "One thing have I desired of the Lord, one thing will I seek after: that I may dwell in the house of the Lord to behold the beauty of the Lord."

This is the fundamental prayer for happiness from a mind that the Spirit has cleared of illusions. Augustine writes: "We love God, therefore, *for what He is in Himself,* and [we love] ourselves and our neighbors for His sake." That doesn't mean, he quickly adds, that we shouldn't pray for anything else but to know, love, and please God.

Not at all. The Lord's Prayer shows us that we need many things. However, if we have made God our greatest love, and if knowing and pleasing him is our highest pleasure, it transforms both what and how we pray for a happy life.

Augustine then cites Proverbs 30:7–9 as an example: "Give me neither poverty nor riches: Feed me with food appropriate for me lest I be full and deny you . . . or lest I be poor, and steal and take the name of my God in vain." This is an excellent test. Consider the petition "O Lord—give me a job so I won't be poor." That is an appropriate thing to ask God for. Indeed, it is essentially the same thing as to pray, "Give us this day our daily bread." Yet the Proverbs 30 prayer reveals the only proper motivation beneath the request. If you just jump into prayer without recognizing the disordered nature of the heart's loves, your prayer's intention will be, "Make me as wealthy as possible." The Proverbs 30 prayer is different. It is to ask, "Lord, meet my material needs, and give me wealth, yes, but only as much as I can handle without it harming my ability to put you first in life. Because ultimately I don't need status and comfort—I need you as my Lord."

Imagine an eight-year-old boy playing with a toy truck and then it breaks. He is disconsolate and cries out to his parents to fix it. Yet as he's crying, his father says to him, "A distant relative you've never met has just died and left you one hundred million dollars." What will the child's reaction be? He will just cry louder until his truck is fixed. He does not have enough cognitive capacity to realize his true condition and be consoled. In the same way, Christians lack the spiritual capacity to realize all we have in Jesus. This is the reason Paul prays that God would give Christians the spiritual ability to grasp the height, depth, breadth, and length of Christ's salvation (Eph 3:16–19; Eph 1:17–18). In general, our lack of joy is as Shakespeare wrote: "The fault, dear Brutus, is not in our stars, but in ourselves" (*Julius Caesar*, Act 1,

Scene 2). We are like the eight-year-old boy who rests his happiness in his "stars"—his circumstances—rather than recognizing what we have in Christ. This is why in the Lord's Prayer we don't get to the petition for our daily bread and needs until we have spent time remembering the greatness of God and reigniting our love for him. Only then can we pray rightly for happiness and for our needs.

Augustine's third directive is both comprehensive and practical, and we have already alluded to it. Once you have learned to pray in full awareness of the disorderedness of your heart and where true joys are found, he says, you can be guided in the specifics of how to pray by studying the Lord's Prayer. Look at all the kinds of prayer in it—adoration, petition, thanksgiving, confession. Look at the order and form of the petitions. Think long and hard about this great model of prayer and be sure your own appeals fit it. For example, Augustine writes:

> He who says in prayer . . . "Give me as much wealth as you have given to this or that man" or "Increase my honors; make me eminent in power and fame in the world," and who asks merely from a desire for these things, and not in order through them to benefit men agreeably to God's will, I do not think he will find any part of the Lord's Prayer in connection with which he could fit in these requests. Therefore let us be ashamed to ask these things.[161]

Augustine's fourth principle is about prayer in the dark times. He admits that even after following the first three rules, "we [still] know not what to pray for as we ought in regard to tribulations." Even the most godly Christians can't be sure what to ask for when we are enmeshed in difficulties and suffering. "Tribulations . . . may do us good . . .

and yet because they are hard and painful . . . we pray . . . that they may be removed from us." Should we pray, then, for a change in circumstances or just for strength to endure them? Augustine points to Jesus' own prayer in Gethsemane, which was perfectly balanced between honest desire—"let this cup pass from me"—and submission to God—"nevertheless, not my will but thine be done." He points also to Romans 8:26, which promises that the Spirit will guide our hearts and prayers when we are groaning and confused—and God will hear them even in their imperfect state. So, Augustine concludes, pour out your heart's desire, but remember the wisdom and goodness of God as you do so.

Anicia Proba was a widow by her early thirties and was present when Rome was sacked in 410. She had to flee for her life to Africa with her granddaughter Demetrias, where they met Augustine. Her former life had been upended, and from what we know about her from the historical record, she never again enjoyed the secure life she had previously known. Augustine, however, argues not only that we can grow in prayer in spite of these difficulties but because of them. He concludes the letter by asking his friend, "Now what makes this work [of prayer] specially suitable to widows but their bereaved and desolate condition?" Should a widow not, he asked, "commit her widowhood, so to speak, to her God as her shield in continual and most fervent prayer?" What a remarkable statement. Her sufferings were her "shield"—they defended her from the illusions of self-sufficiency and blindness that harden the heart, and they opened the way for the rich, passionate prayer life that could bring peace in any circumstance. He calls her to embrace her situation and learn to pray. There is every reason to believe she accepted his invitation.[162]

Martin Luther's "A Simple Way to Pray"

Martin Luther's most famous writing on prayer was also in the form of a letter to a friend. Luther was an extraordinary man of prayer himself. Veit Dietrich, one of Luther's friends, wrote: "There is not a day on which he does not devote at least three hours, the very ones most suitable for [work], to prayer. Once I was fortunate to overhear his prayer. Good God, what faith in his words! He speaks with the great reverence of one who speaks to his God, and with the trust and hope of one who speaks with his father and friend."[163]

Peter Beskendorf was the barber who shaved Luther and cut his hair. One day Peter asked Luther to give him a simple way to pray. Peter was a devout though flawed man. While intoxicated at a family meal, he stabbed his own son-in-law to death. Partly through Luther's intervention Peter was exiled rather than executed, but he endured difficult final years. However, he took with him one of the great texts on the subject of prayer in all of Christian history. Luther gave Peter a rich but practical set of guidelines for prayer.

To begin with, Luther counsels the cultivation of prayer as a *habit* through regular discipline. He proposes praying twice daily. "It is a good thing to let prayer be the first business of the morning and the last at night. Guard yourselves against those false, deluding ideas which tell you, 'Wait a little while. I will pray in an hour; first I must attend to this or that.'"[164] Luther is no romantic. He concludes, "We are as strictly and solemnly commanded to pray as in the others . . . not to kill, not to steal, etc."[165] We must pray whether we feel like it or not.

Next, Luther proposes ways to focus our thoughts and to warm and engage our affections for prayer. This is a balancing truth to that of prayer as a duty. Yes, we should pray regardless of feelings, and yet we should do everything we can to engage and warm our hearts, because prayer is a lifting of the heart to God (Lam 3:41).[166] It is wrong, he writes, that believers should be "cool and joyless in prayer," and therefore Luther proposes a preparation for prayer. He advises what he calls "recitation to yourself" of some part of the Scripture such as "the Ten Commandments [or] the words of Christ, etc."[167] This recitation is a form of meditation (or "contemplation," as Luther calls it) of the Scripture, but it is not mere Bible study. It is taking words of the Scripture and pondering them in such a way that your thoughts and feelings converge on God. By this practice, he says, "I want your heart to be stirred and guided . . . rightly warmed and inclined toward prayer." This meditation on the Word is then a kind of bridge as you move from a more formal study of the Bible to prayer.[168]

The Skill of Meditation

After advising meditation, Luther describes how to do it. He uses the metaphor of a garland. "I divide each [biblical] command into four parts, thereby fashioning a garland of four strands. That is I think of each commandment as first, instruction, which is really what it is intended to be, and consider what the Lord God demands of me so earnestly. Second, I turn it into a thanksgiving; third, a confession; and fourth, a prayer."[169] This turns every biblical text into "a school text, a song book, a penitential book, and prayer book." How does this work?

First, we are to discern the "instruction" of a text. That means we must distill its essential content, what the passage wants us to believe or do. This is the work of interpreting the biblical passage. Luther calls it the "school text" part of meditation. Obviously, this could be the work of a few seconds if you have already studied text in the past and have come to understand the teaching of the verse. Then you can simply summarize it and use that summary for the rest of the meditation. However, if you don't understand the text, you can't really meditate on it. For example, if you are meditating on the Ten Commandments, and you come to the second commandment and you are not sure what "taking God's name in vain" means, you will have to study that and settle it in your mind before you can summarize it and meditate on it.

Once we have drawn out the "instruction"—put the teaching of the text in a nutshell—then we ask how this teaching particularly leads us to praise and thank God, how it leads us to repent and confess sin, and how it prompts us to appeal to God in petition and supplication. For example, if we ponder the very beginning of the Lord's Prayer—"*Our* Father"—it could work like this: As instruction, it shows us that we cannot know God only on our own but must do so in community with others. Jesus did not teach us to pray "*my* father" but "*our* father." We may go on to praise God for all the friends who have helped us in our spiritual journey and for being a God who creates community and bonds of love. We may go on to confess that we do not pray much with others and do not allow our friends to hold us accountable on the consistency of our Christian walk. Finally, we may begin to pray for more close friends with whom we can share our walk of faith. These, of course, are only three out of many possible implications, applications, and reflections of the text.

Luther is teaching us how to generate a small but rich spectrum of insights that can be immediately lifted to God as prayer. Those who have practiced this particular discipline of meditation know that as it proceeds it creates its own energy. It ingeniously forces you off the theoretical plane to consider what that biblical truth you are pondering should actually *do* to you and in you—how it should lead you to praise God, to repent and change your heart, and also what it should lead you to do in the world. Sometimes the insights that are gained are very striking and moving, and you find yourself spontaneously moving to prayer. Over time this meditative habit of mind will often exert itself during the day, naturally turning your heart toward God. You may find many things you hear, see, and read spontaneously leading you to repent, and to praise and petition God. It helps you to habitually put God into every picture, seasoning your feelings and thoughts, lifting you up when disappointed, and humbling you when successful.

Luther gives brief yet full examples of how he meditates on each of the Ten Commandments. Here is an example of a meditation on the first commandment:

> "I am the Lord your God, etc. You shall have no other gods before me," etc. Here I earnestly consider that . . . my heart must not build upon anything else or trust in any other thing, be it wealth, prestige, wisdom, might, piety, or anything else. Second, I give thanks for his infinite compassion by which he has come to me in such a fatherly way and, unasked, unbidden, and unmerited, has offered to be my God, to care for me, and to be my comfort, guardian, help, and strength in every time of need. . . . Third, I confess . . . for having fearfully provoked his wrath by countless acts of idolatry. I repent of these and ask for his grace. Fourth, I pray . . . preserve my heart so that I shall never again become forgetful and ungrateful, that I may never seek after other gods or other consolation on earth or in any creature, but cling truly and solely to thee, my only God.[170]

Notice how Luther works out the truth of the text as it affects his relationship to God, to himself, and to the world. The meditations he records are blends of discursive thinking and personal address. They are not exactly Bible study, yet not exactly prayer. They are thinking in the presence of God—meditation. They are ways of inclining and preparing the heart for prayer by fully using the mind and taking the Scripture with utmost seriousness—all at the same time.

Spiritual "Riffing" on the Lord's Prayer

After meditation, do we launch into prayer? We could do that, yes, but Luther shares one more exercise that he does before praying free-form about the things on his heart. Luther suggests that after meditating on the Scripture, you should pray through each petition of the Lord's Prayer, paraphrasing and personalizing each one using your own needs and concerns.

He gives a personal example of how he would pray each petition. The prayers he conveys are something like musical riffs—improvisations on a theme. *"Give us . . . our daily bread,"* he says, and then immediately adds, "I commend to thee my house and property, wife and child. Grant that I can manage them well, supporting and educating them."[171] He is adamant that readers of his essay *not* recite the actual words Luther himself pens, lest it be "nothing but idle chatter and prattle, read word for word out of a book." That would defeat the purpose of the exercise. Indeed, Luther says that he himself would not be paraphrasing the Lord's Prayer the same way the following day. "I do not bind myself to such words or syllables, but say my prayers in one fashion today, in another tomorrow, depending on my mood and feeling."[172] He insists that the persons praying should personalize each section, putting their own needs and aspirations into their own words.

The value of this exercise is manifold. It addresses one of the great practical difficulties of prayer—distracting thoughts. We turn from

planning for an event to beginning to pray and find we are still thinking about the event. Ordinary prayer, which is either completely ex-
tempore or based on a list of prayer needs, often cannot draw the
mind's attention fully away from what occupied it previously. The exercise of elaborating on the Lord's Prayer commands the full mental
faculty, and this helps greatly with the problem of giving God full attention.

Also, praying the Great Prayer forces us to use all the full language
and basic forms of prayer. If left to ourselves we are likely to pray only
about the items that most trouble us at the moment. The petitions
"hallowed be thy name" and "thy kingdom come" lead us to pray for
the progress of the gospel in our community and society and relationships. "Thy will be done" presses us to accept some things that God
has allowed that are troubling us. "Forgive us our debts" brings us to
list our most recent sins and failings, while "as we forgive our debtors"
forces us to ask ourselves about our resentments and grudges. Praying
the Lord's Prayer forces us to look for things to thank and praise God
for in our dark times, and it presses us to repent and seek forgiveness
during times of prosperity and success. It disciplines us to bring every
part of our lives to God.

Finally, praying the Lord's Prayer, unlike meditation on a passage
of Scripture, is actual prayer. It is address to God—with the authority
of Jesus' own words. It brings boldness and comfort and, of course,
warms up the heart to slide right into the most passionate prayer for
our most urgent concerns.

This exercise is not burdensomely time-consuming. It often takes
only about two to three minutes, though as we will see in a moment,
this prayer could "catch fire" and last quite a long time.[173]

To summarize this point—Luther says we should start with meditation on a text we have previously studied, then after praising and

confessing in accordance with our meditation, we should paraphrase the Lord's Prayer to God. Finally, we should just pray from the heart. This full exercise, he adds, should be done twice a day.

The Preaching of the Holy Spirit

Luther gives one more piece of advice. It is not another "step" or practice to go along with the others but rather something to be kept in mind while going through all prayer and meditation. He calls praying believers to essentially keep a lookout for the Holy Spirit. If, as we are meditating or praying, "an abundance of good thoughts comes to us, we ought to disregard the other petitions, make room for such thoughts, listen in silence, and under no circumstances obstruct them. The Holy Spirit himself preaches here, and one word of his sermon is better than a thousand of our prayers. Many times I have learned more from one prayer than I might have learned from much reading and speculation."[174] This principle is important enough to be repeated. Again he writes, "If in the midst of such thoughts the Holy Spirit begins to preach in your heart with rich, enlightening thoughts, honor him by letting go of this written scheme. . . . Remember what he says and note it well and you will behold wondrous things in the law of God" (Ps 119:18).[175]

The balance here is noteworthy and rarely found in other works on prayer. Luther expects that we will hear God speak through his Word. Luther will not make the same mistake as George Whitefield, assuming that his inner impressions are revelations from God. God's communication to us is in the Scripture. That does not mean, however, that meditation is merely an exercise of the mind. He expects that the Spirit, as we reflect on the biblical truth before God, will sometimes fill our heart with rich thoughts and ideas that feel poignant and new to us, even when we are thinking about a text or truth that we have heard hundreds of times before. Luther is talking about the eyes of our hearts being enlightened (Eph 1:18) so that things we know with the mind become more fully rooted in our beings' core.

Of course, Luther believed that all prayer to our Father is enabled by the Spirit of adoption through the mediation of Jesus, the True Son. No prayer, then, happens without the work of the Spirit. Nevertheless, Luther came to see that the Spirit may particularly illumine our minds and assures our hearts with God's reality, as Paul hints in texts such as Romans 5:5 and 8:15–16.

To paraphrase Luther's little treatise—he tells us to build on our study of the Scripture through meditation, answering the Word in prayer to the Lord. As we do that, we should be aware that the Holy Spirit may begin "preaching" to us. When that happens, we must drop our routines and pay close attention.

SEVEN

Rules for Prayer

Our third "master class" on prayer is found in John Calvin's *Institutes of the Christian Religion*. Perhaps the most distinct part of Calvin's treatment is what he calls "the rules for prayer."

The Joyful Fear

Calvin's first rule for prayer is the principle of reverence or the "fear of God." Calvin calls Christians first of all to have a due sense of the seriousness and magnitude of what prayer is. It is a personal audience and conversation with the Almighty God of the universe. There is nothing worse than to be "devoid of awe."[176] We must instead come to prayer "so moved by God's majesty" that we are "freed from earthly cares and affections." Here, Calvin is touching on one of the most misunderstood yet important concepts in the Bible—the "fear of God." The fear of God obviously means to be afraid, but afraid of what—and why?

It is natural to think that the fear of God means to be afraid he is going to punish us. 1 John 4:18, however, tells us that "perfect love drives out fear" and adds that the kind of fear it drives out has "to do with punishment." Romans 8:1 teaches that there is no condemnation for those who are in Christ Jesus. From this we conclude that a Christian's fear of God can't mean we are constantly afraid of being spiritually lost if we don't live just right. Other texts, like the surprising Psalm 130:4, says that the experience of forgiveness actually *increases* the fear of God.

What, then, should a Christian be afraid of regarding God? Think of it like this. Imagine that you suddenly are introduced to some person you have always admired enormously—perhaps someone you have hero-worshipped. You reach out to shake her hand and suddenly it hits you. You can't believe you are actually meeting her. You discover to your embarrassment that you are trembling and sweating, and when you try to speak, you are out of breath. What is going on? You are not afraid of being hurt, or punished. Rather, you are genuinely afraid of doing something stupid or saying something that is inappropriate to the person and the occasion. Your joyful admiration has a fearful aspect to it. You are in awe, and therefore you don't want to mess up.

That is something we experience even in the presence of an admirable human being. How much more is this a proper response to God. In Kenneth Grahame's classic *The Wind in the Willows*, there is a chapter, "The Piper at the Gates of Dawn," in which the characters Mole and Rat meet the animals' deity, the god Pan, and hear him playing his pipes. They are stunned:

> "Rat," he found breath to whisper, shaking. "Are you afraid?"
>
> "Afraid?" murmured the Rat, his eyes shining with unutterable love. "Afraid! Of *Him*? O, never, never! And yet—and yet—O, Mole, I am afraid!" [177]

That captures the concept of the "fear of God" as well as anything I know. We could say that fear of punishment is a self-absorbed kind of fear. It happens to people wrapped up in themselves. Those who believe the gospel—who believe that they are the recipients of undeserved but unshakable grace—grow in a paradoxically loving yet joyful fear. Because of unutterable love and joy in God, we tremble with the privilege of being in his presence and with an intense longing to honor him when we are there. We are deeply afraid of grieving him. To put it another way—you would be quite afraid if someone put a beautiful, priceless, ancient Ming dynasty vase in your hands. You wouldn't be trembling with fear about the vase hurting you but about your hurting *it*. Of course, we can't really harm God, but a Christian should be intensely concerned not to grieve or dishonor the one who is so glorious and who did so much for us.

Calvin says that this sense of awe is a crucial part of prayer. Prayer both requires it and produces it. The very fact that we have access to God's attention and presence should concentrate the thoughts and elevate the heart.

Spiritual Insufficiency

Calvin's second rule for prayer is "the sense of need that excludes all unreality."[178] Calvin is here referring to what could be called "spiritual humility." It includes both a strong sense of our dependence on God, in general, and a readiness to recognize and repent our own faults in particular. Calvin warned against the common medieval (and modern) view that prayer was a way of putting on your best spiritual clothes, as it were, to impress God with your devoutness. He completely rejects the idea that God could be "appeased by devotions" or that he would hear prayers for "the sake of mere performance."[179] In fact, those who would pray fruitfully must come with an attitude that is exactly the opposite. We must be ruthlessly honest about our flaws and weaknesses. We do all we can to avoid the "unreality" of putting on our best face. We should come to God knowing our only hope is in his grace and forgiveness and being honest about our doubts, fears, and emptiness. We should come to God with the "disposition of a beggar."

Like the call for the "fear of God," this rule also can sound harsh to modern ears, but it need not. Calvin is simply telling us to drop all pretense, to flee from all phoniness. One author, Francis Spufford, using very contemporary idiom, calls for the same thing in this way. When discussing our sinfulness, he says:

> What we're talking about here is not just our tendency to lurch and stumble and screw up by accident, our passive role as agents of entropy. It's our active inclination to break stuff, "stuff" here including . . . promises, relationships we care about and our own well-being and other people's. . . . [You are] a being whose wants make no sense, don't harmonize: whose desires deep down are discordantly arranged, so that you truly want to possess and you truly want not to at the very same time. You're equipped, you realize, more for farce (or even tragedy) than happy endings. . . . You're human, and that's where we live; that's our normal experience.[180]

Until we fully acknowledge the chaos within us that the Bible calls sin, we live in what Calvin calls "unreality." Counselors will tell you that the only character flaws that can really destroy you are the ones you won't admit. Crucial to true prayer, then, is confession and repentance.

Again, prayer both requires and produces this humility. Prayer brings you into God's presence, where our shortcomings are exposed. Then the new awareness of insufficiency drives us to seek God even more intensely for forgiveness and help. Calvin writes: "Those who seek him with all their heart will find him (Jer 29:13–14). . . . Lawful prayer, therefore, demands repentance."[181] If you are smug, blaming others for your problems rather than taking responsibility for what you have done wrong, you will not be seeking God with all your heart. Prayer both requires and empowers the abandonment of self-justification, blame shifting, self-pity, and spiritual pride.

To the degree you can shed the "unreality" of self-sufficiency, to that degree your prayer life will become richer and deeper.

Restful Trust yet Confident Hope

Calvin's third and fourth rules for prayer should be paired and considered together. His third rule is that we should have a *submissive trust* of God. "Anyone who stands before God to pray . . . [must] abandon all thoughts of his own glory."[182] We are to trust in him even when things are not going as we wish them to go. This was Jesus' "law" for prayer too, because all who pray must say, "Thy will be done." One of the purposes of prayer is to bring our hearts to trust in his wisdom, not in our own. It is to say, "Here's what I need—but you know best." It is to leave all our needs and desires in his hands in a way that is possible only through prayer. That transaction brings a comfort and rest that nothing else can bring.

And yet. The fourth rule is just as crucial and must be kept beside the third. We are to pray with *confidence and hope*. Calvin writes, "[Though] cast down and overcome by true humility, we should be nonetheless encouraged to pray by a sure hope that our prayer will be answered."[183] He immediately acknowledges that "these are indeed things apparently contradictory." Then he goes on to argue why the contradiction is only apparent, not real.

If God's will is always right, and submission to it is so important, why pray for *any*thing with fervor and confidence? Calvin lists the reasons. God invites us to do so and promises to answer prayers—because he is good and our loving heavenly Father.[184] Also, God often waits to give a blessing until you have prayed for it. Why? Good things that we do not ask for will usually be interpreted by our hearts as the fruit of our own wisdom and diligence. Gifts from God that are not acknowledged as such are deadly to the soul, because they thicken the illusion of self-sufficiency that leads to overconfidence and sets us up for failure.

Finally, Calvin argues that these two balancing truths are not only *not* contradictory but are complementary. On the one hand, we know that we "have not because we ask not" (James 4:2). There are many goods that God will not give us unless we honor him and make our hearts safe to receive them through prayer. But on the other hand—what thoughtful persons, knowing the limits of their own wisdom, would dare to pray if they thought God would invariably give them their wishes? Endless stories of genies, lamps, and wishes illustrate the almost clichéd truth that our desires are, as we have seen, "discordantly arranged" and often fatally unwise. However, there is nothing to fear. God will not give us anything contrary to his will, and that will always include what is best for us in the long run (Rom 8:28). We can, therefore, pray confidently *because* he won't give us everything we want. "He so tempers the outcome of events according to his incomprehensible plan that the prayers of the saints, which are a mixture of faith and error, are not nullified."[185]

If we hold Calvin's third and fourth rules together, it creates enormous incentive to pray. "Ask and you shall receive" (Matt 7:7–8)—Ask with confidence and hope. Don't be afraid that you will ask for the wrong thing. Of course you will! God "tempers the outcome" with his incomprehensible wisdom. Cry, ask, and appeal—you will get many answers. Finally, where you do not get an answer, or where the answer is not what you want, use prayer to enable you to rest in his will.

The Rule against Rules

After Calvin expounded his four rules for prayer, he added an extended "coda" so significant that most readers understand it as a fifth rule.

The fifth rule is actually a major qualification of the very word *rule*. He says: "What I have set forth on the four rules of right praying is not so rigorously required that God will reject those prayers in which he finds neither perfect faith nor repentance, together with a warmth of zeal and petitions rightly conceived." Although this sounds like backpedaling, it isn't. "No one has ever carried out [prayer] with the uprightness that was due. . . . Without this mercy there would be no freedom to pray."[186] Calvin's fifth rule is the rule of grace. He urges us to *not* conclude that following any set of rules could make our prayers worthy to be heard. Nothing we formulate or do can qualify us for access to God. Only grace can do that—based not on our performance but on the saving work of Christ.

What, then, is the function of "rules"? Why does it matter how we pray if it's all by grace? The answer is that prayer should be shaped by and in accord with that grace. The joyful fear, the helplessness yet confidence, are all ways of approaching God that are possible only if our access is not earned but is received as a gift. Only when we see we cannot keep the rules, and need God's mercy, can we become people who begin to keep the rules. The rules do not earn or merit God's attention but rather align our prayers with who God is—the God of free grace—and thereby unite us to him more and more.

Here is an illustration that might help us think about this. When you flick the light switch, the bulbs illuminate. Does the light switch provide the power for the bulbs? No—that comes from the electricity. The switch has no power in itself, but rather it connects the bulbs to the power. In the same way, our prayers have no virtue to procure us access to the Father. Christ has done that. Prayers that are in accord with a gracious God, however, can connect us to him. If we pray without humility—if we pray filled with demanding impatience—it cuts us off from him. If instead we pray without any confidence or hope of being heard, that also blocks any sense of his presence. Both of these mistakes are failures to pray in Jesus' name, to come to God on the basis of undeserved mercy. Calvin says this in a passage that has set the course for Christian understanding of prayer for centuries:

> For as soon as God's dread majesty comes to mind, we cannot but tremble and be driven far away by the recognition of our own unworthiness, until Christ comes forward as intermediary, to change the throne of dreadful glory into the throne of grace. . . . "Hitherto," he says, "you have asked nothing in my name; ask and you will receive" [John 16:24] . . . as Paul says, "All God's promises find their yea and amen in him" [2 Cor 1:20]. That is, they are confirmed and fulfilled.[187]

Praying in Jesus' name, then, is not a magic formula. We must not think it means that only if we literally enunciate the words "in Jesus' name" will our prayers be answered. As we have seen, God can hear and answer the prayers of anyone, even those who do not pray with faith in Jesus. God often hears and answers the cries of the oppressed poor even when they are praying to a false god, Calvin argues, pointing to passages in the Bible that teach this. This is simply because he is a merciful God.[188] So "in Jesus' name" is not a magical incantation.

To pray in Jesus' name means to come to God in prayer consciously trusting in Christ for our salvation and acceptance and not relying on our own credibility or record. It is, essentially, to reground our relationship with God in the saving work of Jesus over and over again. It also means to recognize your status as a child of God, regardless of your inner state. God our Father is committed to his children's good, as any good father would be.

Jesus' Claims on the Father

Why are we always heard for Jesus' sake? Australian theologian Graeme Goldsworthy traces out how, ever since Adam was expelled from the family, God has promised to make us his children again. God called the nation of Israel "my firstborn son" (Ex 4:22–23) and called his son out of Egypt through the Exodus (Hos 11:1). He named the anointed kings of Israel—David and Solomon—to be his sons. Nevertheless, the history of Israel and of Israel's kings was one of a failure to trust and obey God and truly be his sons. At Jesus' baptism, however, God speaks from heaven: "You are my Son, whom I love; with you I am well pleased" (Luke 3:22). As Goldsworthy says, "One can almost hear heaven sigh with relief," for here, finally and at last, is a true Son, one who can and will perfectly trust, obey, and please his Father.[189]

Therefore, to him—and to him alone among all the human beings of the earth—does the privilege of prayer and access belong. He is the only one who can say with confidence to God, "I knew that you always hear me" (John 11:41–42). When we believe in Jesus Christ we are united to him. We are "in him," as Paul says repeatedly. This means that what is true of Jesus is true of us. Because he has the perfect and secure access of an obedient child to the Father, so now do we. "If the Father always hears the Son, then he always hears those who, in Christ, are his sons."[190] When we pray in Jesus' name, therefore, we do so with supreme confidence and yet humble dependence on unmerited grace.

The American preacher R. A. Torrey tells about a man he met when Torrey was preaching in Melbourne, Australia. One day as he was on the platform getting ready to speak, he was given an anonymous note. It was an appeal to address the problem of unanswered prayer in his sermon. The note read:

> Dear Dr. Torrey: I am in great perplexity. I have been praying for a long time for something that I am confident is according to God's will, but I do not get it. I have been a member of the Presbyterian Church for thirty years, and I have tried to be a consistent one all the time. I have been Superintendent in the Sunday school for twenty-five years, and an elder in the church for twenty years; and yet God does not answer my prayer and I cannot understand it. Can you explain it to me?

Torrey recognized the subtext of the argument and took a plunge. He walked to the podium, read the note, and used it to make a crucial point. He said that the problem was not hard to see. "This man thinks that because he has been a consistent church member for thirty years, a faithful Sunday school superintendent for twenty-five years, and an elder in the church for twenty years, that God is under obligation to answer his prayer. He is really praying in his own name." Doubtlessly, the man would have been dutifully intoning "in Jesus' name" at the end of each prayer, but only as part of his project to procure God's favor through perfect compliance with all the rules. "We must," Torrey continued, ". . . give up any thought that we have any claims upon God. . . . But Jesus Christ has great claims on God, and we should go to God in our prayers not on the ground of any goodness in ourselves, but on the ground of Jesus Christ's claims." After the close of the meeting, the writer of the note approached Torrey and revealed himself. "You have hit the nail on the head," he said.[191]

EIGHT

The Prayer of Prayers

None of our three master teachers of prayer, Augustine, Luther, and Calvin, developed their instruction primarily based on their own experiences. In each case, what they believed and practiced regarding prayer grew mainly out of their understanding of the ultimate master class in prayer—the Lord's Prayer in Matthew 6:9–13, in the heart of Jesus' Sermon on the Mount. The greatest part of Calvin's chapter 20 on prayer in the *Institutes* is given to a line-by-line study of Jesus' own model for prayer, as is much of Luther's classic letter. Each of these three great theologians expounded the Lord's Prayer at length in more than one place, not only in biblical commentaries and exegetical works, but also in pastoral and theological writings.[192]

In this chapter we will look at the Lord's Prayer through the insights of our three master teachers, thereby drawing out the fullness of their wisdom—and the depths of Jesus' prayer itself—on this subject.

The Danger of Familiarity

The Lord's Prayer may be the single set of words spoken more often than any other in the history of the world. Jesus Christ gave it to us as the key to unlock all the riches of prayer. Yet it is an untapped resource, partially because it is so very familiar.

Imagine you are, for the first time, visiting someone who has a home or an apartment near train tracks. You are sitting there in conversation, when suddenly the train comes roaring by, just a few feet from where you are sitting, and you jump to your feet in alarm. "What's that?" you cry. Your friend, the resident of the house, responds, "What was what?" You answer, "That sound! I thought something was coming through the wall." "Oh, that," she says. "That's just the train. You know, I guess I've gotten so used to it that I don't even notice it anymore." With wide eyes you say, "I don't see how that is possible." But it is.

It is the same with the Lord's Prayer. The whole world is starving for spiritual experience, and Jesus gives us the means to it in a few words. Jesus is saying, as it were, "Wouldn't you like to be able to come face-to-face with the Father and king of the universe every day, to pour out your heart to him, and to sense him listening to and loving you?" We say, of course, *yes.*

Jesus responds, "It's all in the Lord's Prayer," and we say, "In the *what?*" It's so familiar we can no longer hear it. Yet everything we need is within it. How do we overcome the deadly peril of familiarity? One of the best ways is to listen to these three great mentors, who plumbed the depths of the prayer through years of reflection and practice. What did they believe the Lord's Prayer to be saying?

"Our Father Who Art in Heaven"

This is called the address, not actually one of the petitions. Calvin explains that to call God "Father" *is* to pray in Jesus' name. "Who would break forth into such rashness as to claim for himself the honor of a son of God unless we had been adopted as children of grace in Christ?"[193] Luther also believed the address was a call to not plunge right into talking to God but to first recollect our situation and realize our standing in Christ before we proceed into prayer. We are to say to God, "You have taught us to regard you and call upon you as one Father of us all . . . although . . . you could rightly and properly be a severe judge over us." Therefore, we should start by asking God to "implant in our hearts a comforting trust in your fatherly love."[194] Calvin agrees that "by the great sweetness of this name [Father] he frees us from all distrust."[195]

"Hallowed Be Thy Name"

This first petition is somewhat opaque to contemporary English speakers. One reason is that the word *hallowed* is seldom used today, and another is that the idea of holiness (the basic meaning of the older English word *hallowed*) is alien in our secularized society. The third is a seeming problem of logic, expressed by Luther. "What are we praying for when we ask that His name become holy? Is it not holy already?" He immediately answers that of course it is holy, but that "in our use of it his name is not kept holy."[196] Luther points to the fact that all baptized Christians have God's name put upon them. As name bearers they represent a good and holy God, and so we are praying that God keep us from dishonoring the name by which we are called, that he would empower us to become ourselves good and holy. This petition, however, has a second meaning for Luther, who joins Augustine when he says it is a prayer that God "be glorified among all nations as you are glorified among us."[197] It is a request that faith in God would spread throughout the world, that Christians would honor God with the Christ-likeness or holiness of their lives, and that more and more people would honor God and call on his name.

Calvin agrees but adds a thought that goes deep into the heart. "What is more unworthy than for God's glory to be obscured partly by our ungratefulness?" In other words, ingratitude and an indifferent attitude toward God fails to honor his name. To "hallow" God's name is not merely to live righteous lives but to have a heart of grateful joy toward God—and even more, a wondrous sense of his beauty. We do not revere his name unless he "captivate[s] us with wonderment for him."[198]

"Thy Kingdom Come"

Augustine says God is reigning now, but just as a light is absent to those refusing to open their eyes, so it is possible to refuse God's rule.[199] This is the cause of all our human problems, since we were created to serve him, and when we serve other things in God's place, all spiritual, psychological, cultural, and even material problems ensue. Therefore, we need his kingdom to "come." Calvin believed there were two ways God's kingdom comes—through the Spirit, who "corrects our desires," and through the Word of God, which "shapes our thoughts."[200] This, then, is a "Lordship" petition: It is asking God to extend his royal power over every part of our lives—emotions, desires, thoughts, and commitments. It is reminiscent of Thomas Cranmer's "collect" for the fourteenth Sunday after Trinity, "that we may obtain that which thou dost promise, make us to love that which thou dost command." We are asking God to so fully rule us that we *want* to obey him with all our hearts and with joy.

Luther adds also an outward and a future dimension. The reign of God on earth is only partial now, but the fullness of the future kingdom is unimaginable. All suffering, injustice, poverty, and death will be ended. To pray "thy kingdom come" is to "yearn for that future life" of justice and peace, and to ask that "your future kingdom may be the end and consummation of the kingdom you have begun in us."[201]

"Thy Will Be Done"

Luther is the most vivid and forthright about the meaning of the third petition. He paraphrases like this: "Grant us grace to bear willingly all sorts of sickness, poverty, disgrace, suffering, and adversity and to recognize that in this your divine will is crucifying our will."[202] We may be reticent to make such a bold statement, but now we can discern the importance of the initial address. Unless we are profoundly certain God is our Father, we will never be able to say "thy will be done." Fathers are often inscrutable to little children. A four-year-old cannot understand many of his father's prohibitions—but he trusts him. Only if we trust God as Father can we ask for grace to bear our troubles with patience and grace.

Well, someone asks, how can we be sure God is trustworthy? The answer is that this is the one part of the Lord's Prayer Jesus himself prayed in the Garden of Gethsemane, under circumstances far more crushing than any of us will ever face. He submitted to his Father's will rather than following his own desires, and it saved us. That's why we can trust him. Jesus is not asking us to do anything for him that he hasn't already done for us, under conditions of difficulty beyond our comprehension.

Luther adds, following Augustine, that without this trust in God, we will try to take God's place and seek revenge on those who have harmed us.[203] We will be protected "from the horrible vices of character assassination, slander, backbiting . . . condemning others" only if we learn to commit ourselves to God.[204] If we can't say "thy will be done" from the bottom of our hearts, we will never know any peace. We will feel compelled to try to control people and control our environment and make things the way we believe they ought to be. Yet to control life like this is beyond our abilities, and we will just dash ourselves upon the rocks. This is why Calvin adds that to pray "thy will be done" is to submit not only our wills to God but even our feelings, so that we do not become despondent, bitter, and hardened by the things that befall us.[205]

We have considered the first three petitions of the Lord's Prayer. All our teachers observe the significance of their place in the order—that these petitions come first in prayer. The beginning of prayer is all about God. We are not to let our own needs and issues dominate prayer; rather, we are to give pride of place to praising and honoring him, to yearning to see his greatness and to see it acknowledged everywhere, and to aspiring to full love and obedience. George Herbert expressed it with beautiful economy:

> For my heart's desire
> Unto Thine is bent:
> I aspire
> To a full consent.[206]

Adoration and thanksgiving—God-centeredness—comes first, because it heals the heart of its self-centeredness, which curves us in on ourselves and distorts all our vision. Now that the prayer is nearly half over, and our vision is reframed and clarified by the greatness of God, we can turn to our own needs and those of the world.

"Give Us This Day Our Daily Bread"

Augustine reminds us that "daily bread" is a metaphor for necessities rather than luxuries. Since we have just spent the first three petitions of prayer recognizing God as our true food, wealth, and happiness, Jesus is charging us to now bring our "prayer list" of needs into line with this new frame of heart. As we have seen, Augustine believes the full petition should be Proverbs 30:8, "Give me neither poverty (lest I resent you) or riches (lest I forget you)."[207] Calvin follows Augustine's reasoning when he says that, in speaking of our daily bread, "we do not . . . bid farewell to God's glory . . . [but we] ask only what is expedient for him."[208] We come with our needs expectant of positive response, but we do so changed by our satisfaction in him and our trust of him. We do not come arrogantly and anxiously telling him what *has* to happen. Many things we would have otherwise agonized over, we can now ask for without desperation.

Luther sees a social dimension to this prayer as well. For all to get daily bread, there must be a thriving economy, good employment, and a just society. Therefore, to pray "give us—all the people of our land— daily bread" is to pray against "wanton exploitation" in business, trade, and labor, which "crushes the poor and deprives them of their daily bread." Ominously he warns those who do injustice about the power of this petition. "Let them beware of . . . the intercession of the church, and let them take care that this petition of the Lord's Prayer does not turn against them."[209] For Luther, then, to pray for our daily bread is to pray for a prosperous and just social order.

"Forgive Us Our Debts as We Forgive Our Debtors"

The fifth petition concerns our relationships, both with God and others. Luther, who for years struggled mightily and personally with the issues of guilt and pardon, gives a clarion call to seek God's forgiveness every day in prayer:

> If anyone insists on his own goodness and despises others . . . let him look into himself when this petition confronts him. He will find he is no better than others and that in the presence of God everyone must duck his head and come into the joy of forgiveness only through the low door of humility.[210]

Luther adds that this petition is not only a challenge to our pride but a test of spiritual reality. If we find confession and repentance intolerably traumatic or demeaning, it means "the heart is not right with God and cannot draw . . . confidence from his Gospel." If regular confession does not produce an *increased* confidence and joy in your life, then you do not understand the salvation by grace, the essence of the faith.

Jesus tightly links our relationship with God to our relationship with others. It works two ways. If we have not seen our sin and sought radical forgiveness from God, we will be unable to forgive and to seek the good of those who have wronged us. So unresolved bitterness is a sign that we are not right with God. It also means that if we are holding a grudge, we should see the hypocrisy of seeking forgiveness from God for sins of our own. Calvin puts it vividly:

> If we retain feelings of hatred in our hearts, if we plot revenge and ponder any occasion to cause harm, and even if we do not try to get back into our enemies' good graces, by every sort of good office deserve well of them, and commend ourselves to them, by this prayer we entreat God not to forgive our sins.[211]

"Lead Us Not into Temptation"

With this petition Augustine makes an important distinction. He says, "The prayer is not that we should not be tempted, but that we should not be brought [or led] *in*to temptation."[212] Temptation in the sense of being tried and tested is not only inevitable but desirable. The Bible talks of suffering and difficulty as a furnace in which many impurities of soul are "burned off" and we come to greater self-knowledge, humility, durability, faith, and love. However, to "*enter in*to temptation," as Jesus termed it (Matt 26:41), is to entertain and consider the prospect of giving in to sin. Calvin lists two categories of temptations from the "right" and from the "left." From the right comes "riches, power, and honors," which tempt us into the sin of thinking we do not need God. From the left comes "poverty, disgrace, contempt, and afflictions," which tempt us to despair, to lose all hope, and to become angrily estranged from God.[213] Both prosperity and adversity, then, are sore tests, and each one brings its own set of enticements away from trusting in God and toward centering your life on yourself and on "inordinate desires" for other things.[214]

"Deliver Us from Evil"

Calvin combined this phrase with "lead us not into temptation" and called it the sixth and last petition. Augustine and Luther, however, viewed "deliver us from evil" as a separate, seventh petition. It can also be translated "deliver us from the Evil One," that is, the devil. Luther writes that this petition is "directed against specific evils that emanate from the devil's kingdom . . . poverty, dishonor, death, in short . . . everything that threatens our bodily welfare."[215] Augustine indicates that while the sixth petition is for deliverance from the remaining evil inside us, this seventh petition is for protection from evil outside us, from malignant forces in the world, especially our enemies who wish to do us harm.[216]

"For Thine Is the Kingdom, the Power, and the Glory Forever"

Finally, there is what is called the ascription: "For thine is the kingdom, the power, and the glory, forever. Amen." Augustine does not mention it because it was not in most earlier manuscripts of the Bible or in the Latin Vulgate. Luther does not treat it. However, Calvin, while noting that "this is not extant in the Latin versions," believes that "it is so appropriate to this place that it ought not to be omitted." After descending into our needs, troubles, and limitations, we return to the truth of God's complete sufficiency. Here our hearts can end with "tranquil repose" in the remembrance that nothing can ever snatch away the kingdom, power, and glory from our heavenly, loving Father.[217]

"Give, Forgive, and Deliver—Us"

The concluding remarks on the Lord's Prayer by John Calvin are especially helpful. Like Luther in *A Simple Way to Pray*, Calvin insists that the Lord's Prayer does not bind us to its particular form of words but rather to its content and basic pattern. Indeed, even Luke does not set down Jesus' teaching on prayer in exactly the same words. The Lord's Prayer is a summary of all other prayers, providing essential guidance on emphasis and topics, on purpose and even spirit. Therefore in our prayers, "the words may be utterly different, yet the sense ought not to vary."[218] The Lord's Prayer must stamp itself on our prayers, shaping them all the way down. There could be no better way to ensure that than Luther's twice-daily exercise of paraphrasing and personalizing the Lord's Prayer as introduction to more free-form praise and petition.

An equally important insight is a reminder that the Lord's Prayer was given to us in plural form. *We* ask God to give *us* what we need, meaning that, as much as possible, "the prayers of Christians ought to be public . . . to the advancement of the believer's fellowship."[219] American theologian Michael S. Horton has pointed out that Calvin believed "public ministry shapes private devotion, not vice versa."[220] Calvin took great care to define public prayers and the liturgy because he wanted private prayers to be strongly shaped by the corporate worship of the Christian church.

Prayer is therefore not a strictly private thing. As much as we can, we should pray with others both formally in gathered worship and informally. Why? If the substance of prayer is to continue a conversation with God, and if the purpose of it is to know God better, then this can happen best in community.

C. S. Lewis argues that it takes a community of people to get to know an individual person. Reflecting on his own friendships, he observed that some aspects of one of his friend's personality were brought out only through interaction with a second friend. That meant if he lost the second friend, he lost the part of his first friend that was otherwise invisible. "By myself I am not large enough to call the whole man into activity; I want other lights than my own to show all his facets."[221] If it takes a community to know an ordinary human being, how much more necessary would it be to get to know Jesus alongside others? By praying with friends, you will be able to hear and see facets of Jesus that you have not yet perceived.

That is why, Lewis thinks, that the angels in Isaiah 6 are crying, "Holy, Holy, Holy" *to one another.* Each angel is communicating to all the rest the part of the glory it sees. Knowing the Lord is communal and cumulative, we must pray and praise together. That way "the more we share the Heavenly Bread between us, the more we shall all have."[222]

NINE

The Touchstones of Prayer

In this section of the book, we have been moving from theory toward practice by listening to the main insights on prayer given to us by some of the great teachers in the history of the church. Can we now amass and summarize all their individual rules and principles into a single set of points? The answer is no—and yes.

One problem we face in unifying their headings is that they are often saying the same thing from different perspectives. Calvin wrote more theologically, drawing out the implications of the doctrines of God, of sin, of Christ, and of the gospel for the pursuit of prayer. Luther's teaching on prayer is highly practical, because he was writing to a simple man who was asking for a concrete way to pray. Augustine came at prayer from the most existential perspective, focusing most on the motives of the heart. This means that the principles of each thinker intersect one another. Also, we must remember Calvin's own rule against ironclad rules. I fear that many contemporary books on prayer try to give readers a "key" or some kind of experience of "Aha! So that's the secret of prayer!" Such a thing simply does not exist.

The other extreme is to say only that prayer cannot be reduced to principles, and there's nothing to say about it other than to try hard and keep at it. But if prayer were completely ineffable, when the disciples asked Jesus, "Lord, teach us to pray" (Luke 11:1), Jesus would have responded, "I can't—it's just indefinable." He did not say that prayer is like the sound of one hand clapping. Rather, he gave his disciples a set of words, the Lord's Prayer.

Can we then distill what we have learned from our master teachers? I think we can. I'll call the result "touchstones." A touchstone is a small rock containing silica that was rubbed against a piece of gold or silver to test its degree of purity or genuineness. As we have seen, all prayer is somewhat impure. It is never done with fully proper motives of heart or with language worthy of its object. It is received and answered by God, therefore, only by grace. Yet there is every indication in the Bible that we should be striving to pray rightly. If our prayers are not done with dependence on Jesus (John 16:24–26) or with faith (James 1:6)—if they are done with selfish motives (James 4:3), or if we try to pray while willfully disobeying God in some area of life (Ps 66:18)—then our prayers may not be "powerful and effective" (James 5:16).

What follows is not a set of rules that merit or trigger God's response in some magical or mechanical way. Rather, they are twelve touchstones by which we can judge the relative strength or weakness of our prayers for honoring and connecting us to God. I have grouped them into four clusters of three each.

What Prayer Is

Work—Prayer Is a Duty and a Discipline

Prayer should be done regularly, persistently, resolutely, and tenaciously at least daily, whether we feel like it or not. "The worst sin is prayerlessness," wrote Peter T. Forsyth. "Overt sin . . . or the glaring inconsistencies which often surprise us in Christian people are the effect of this, or its punishment. . . . Not to want to pray, then, is the sin behind sin."[223] We should pray even if we are not getting anything out of it. Imagine that you are rooming with someone and he or she virtually doesn't speak to you. All she does is leave messages. When you mention it, she says, "Well, I don't get much out of talking to you. I find it boring and my mind flitting everywhere, so I just don't try." What will you conclude? Regardless of how scintillating a conversationalist you are, it's rude for her not to talk to you. She owes it to her suite mate to at least interact face-to-face. Of course *rudeness* is far too weak a word to use for a failure to directly address your Maker, Sustainer, and Redeemer, to whom you owe your every breath.

Prayer must be persevering. "I urge you," wrote Paul to the Christians at Rome, "to join me in my struggle by praying to God for me" (Rom 15:30). Prayer is striving. This means sticking with prayer through the ups and downs of feelings. "Do not say, 'I cannot pray. I am not in the spirit,'" writes Forsyth. "Pray till you are in the spirit."[224] It means that prayer also tends to have cumulative effect. Austin Phelps writes of watching people in the Royal Gallery at Dresden sitting for hours before a single masterpiece painting. "Weeks are spent every year in the study of that one work of Raphael. Lovers of art cannot enjoy it to the full, till they have made it their own by prolonged communion with its matchless form." He tells of a conversation with one of the painting's admirers, who said he had spent years looking at the painting and yet found it possible over and over to "discover some new beauty, and a new joy." How much more should we give this kind of patient attention to prayer? What painting, Phelps asks, could be anything like the great God himself, "which the soul needs to conceive *vividly*, in order to know the blessedness of prayer?"[225]

Prayer is always hard work, and often an agony. We sometimes have to wrestle even in order to pray. "When those hours of the day come in which we should be having our prayer-sessions with God, it often appears as though everything has entered into a conspiracy to prevent it." We often wrestle *in* prayer just to concentrate. "Your thoughts flit back and forth between God and the many pressing duties which await you."[226] While God can and will grant times of peace and tranquility, no Christian outgrows the need to struggle and persevere in prayer.

Responding to the Word—Prayer Is Conversing with God

In the Garden of Eden, God walked with us (Gen 3:8). To "walk with" someone in the Bible is to have a friendship, because people talk as they walk together. Prayer in Jesus' name and the power of the Spirit is the restoration of that single most precious thing we had with God in the beginning—free communication with him.

There are two ways of understanding prayer as a dialogue. The first is to understand prayer as responding to God's voice discerned subjectively within the heart. In this view we sit quietly and wait for intuitions, impressions, and feelings that we decide are not merely psychological but the voice of God within us. The other way is to understand God as primarily speaking to us through the Scripture. As we saw in Martin Luther, the Spirit convicts and illumines as we read it, and so we hear him through his Word. We have made the case earlier in this book that it is the latter understanding we should follow.

This has been one of the fundamental issues in the history of Christian piety and spirituality. One of its flash points was the seventeenth-century debate between the English Puritans and the early Quakers. For the Puritans, the Spirit's words *were* the Bible, as the Spirit speaks to us by and through the Word. Quakers and many others following in their footsteps have believed that while the Scripture was inspired, there was new, current, and inner revelation through the Spirit that was to be sought.[227] This would mean that the Scripture is not required for the conversation—we can go back and forth with God within our own hearts. We have explored the unreliability of this approach. J. I. Packer observes that once we understand prayer as conversation, we must regularly link thoughtful, scriptural meditation with prayer. Meditation is a bridge between biblical interpretation and study on the one hand and free prayer on the other. Packer's own practice is "reading Scripture, thinking through what my reading shows me of God, and turning that vision into praise before I go further [into prayer]." He adds that this is a vital means for "*knowing* God."[228]

Prayer Is a Balanced Interaction of Praise, Confession, Thanks, and Petition

The Lord's Prayer moves from adoration and praise ("Our heavenly Father, hallowed be thy name. Thy kingdom come. Thy will be done") to petitioning for our needs ("Give us this our daily bread . . . deliver us from evil"), to confessing our sins and asking for inner change ("forgive us our debts, as we forgive our debtors"), to thanksgiving for our blessings ("for thine is the kingdom, the power, and the glory") and even for our difficulties ("thy will be done"). The Lord's Prayer and the Psalter, the Bible's prayer book, show that all these "grammars," or dimensions of prayer, are crucial to use.

However, none of these forms of prayer should be preferred to any other. We should not think of some of them as lower stages preparing the way for other, higher stages. In fact, each of the forms is necessary for the others. They are interactive and stimulate one another. When we comprehend God's greatness, it leads us to a new grasp of our own sinfulness. Then a deeper recognition and a repentance for sin issues in thankful wonder at God's grace. "She who is forgiven much, loves much" (cf. Luke 7:47). The more we see God's power, the more we will want to depend on him for our needs. All these ways of praying to God should be present, interactive, and balanced when we pray.

What Prayer Requires

Grace—Prayer Must Be "In Jesus' Name," Based on the Gospel

We have addressed this crucial touchstone before. Our prayer must be in full, grateful awareness that our access to God as Father is a free gift won by the costly sacrifice of Jesus the True Son, and then enacted in us by the Holy Spirit, who helps us know inwardly that we are his children. To pray in Jesus' name is not meant to be a magic formula, as if the pronunciation of the words coerces God's power or mechanically taps into supernatural forces. Jesus' name is shorthand for his divine person and saving work. To come to the Father in Jesus' name, not our own, is to come fully cognizant that we are being heard because of the costly grace in which we stand. This is the one principle of prayer that makes it possible to be heard by God even though no one can follow all the other guidelines and "rules" as we should.

The idea of praying to the Father in Jesus' name raises the question: Are we to pray only to the Father and not to the Son or the Spirit? Jesus invites his disciples to pray to him (John 14:13–14; Matt 11:28). Nevertheless, Jesus also taught his disciples to pray to our Father, and while we are not bound to the exact words of the Lord's Prayer, that initial direction must be taken seriously. Only three times after

Jesus' ascension—in the rest of the New Testament—is prayer addressed directly to Jesus. In the vast majority of cases, prayer is addressed to the Father. While it is not at all improper to address the Son or the Spirit, ordinarily prayer will be addressed to the Father with gratitude to the Son and dependence on the Spirit.[229] Packer uses an interesting rule of thumb. "I pray to the Father through the mediation of the Son and the enabling of the Holy Spirit. I may speak also to the Son and the Spirit directly when this is appropriate: that is, when I am praying about something that Scripture specified as the direct concern of either."[230]

Fear—Prayer Is the Heart Engaged in Loving Awe

We know that the heart should be "engaged" in prayer. Prayer must not be only a recitation of words. "These people honor me with their lips, but their hearts are far from me" (Matt 15:8). One important sign of an engaged heart is awe before the greatness of God and before the privilege of prayer. The Westminster Larger Catechism says that prayer should engage the affections, and with "due apprehensions" of God's power, majesty, and grace.[231]

No one today thinks of drawing near to God as being traumatic and lethal. Yet when Moses asked to draw near and see God's glory, God refused because, he said, it would kill Moses (Ex 33:18–23). God allowed Moses only to see his "back" or "outskirts" and said he would cover Moses with his hand so that he would be protected from God's holiness and wouldn't die. Moses is protected *from* God *by* God. That's the gospel. But in John 1:18, we learn that in Jesus Christ we behold God's glory. How is that possible? Because in Christ our sins are covered. We are hidden in the hollow of God's hand, as it were, in Jesus (Col 3:1–3). This doesn't mean we can ever take lightly the privilege of approaching "the throne," however. It is an astonishing right to do so—won at unimaginable cost. This is what we are doing when we pray in Jesus' name, and we need to remind ourselves of what is happening every time we pray. We should take time and meditate on this truth until it thrills us.

"Loving awe" conveys that we should approach God with neither a sentimental or casual familiarity nor a stilted, remote formality. Many of the best books on prayer over the years counsel that, before beginning prayer and meditation, we take ourselves in hand and wake ourselves up to the magnitude of what is going to happen. One suggested we make the following speech to ourselves:

> God is here, within these walls; before me, behind me, on my right hand, on my left hand. He who fills immensity has come down to me here. I am now about to bow at His feet, and *speak* to Him. . . . I may pour forth my desires before Him, and not one syllable from my lips shall escape his ear. I may speak to him as I would to the dearest friend I have on earth.[232]

This "taking oneself in hand" can proceed by thinking briefly about some aspect of the theology of prayer. Remember, for example, that we are now adopted, loved children going to our Father. Or remember that we have a great High Priest and Advocate at the right hand of God, so we can approach the throne in confidence. Or remember that we have the Holy Spirit within us, prompting us and helping us to pray. This prepares the heart for prayer.

Helplessness—Prayer Is Accepting Weakness and Dependence

Norwegian author Ole Hallesby begins his short book *Prayer* by defining prayer as an attitude of mind and heart, characterized primarily as helplessness. "As far as I can see, prayer has been ordained only for the helpless. . . . Prayer and helplessness are inseparable. Only he who is helpless can truly pray."[233] Such prayer is just an outworking of gospel faith, because only the one who confesses complete spiritual bankruptcy can receive Christ's salvation. Augustine told Anicia that you cannot truly pray until you "account yourself desolate in the world."

This touchstone is intimately related to praying in Jesus' name, but it deserves its own heading because it is such an important, practical principle. Many people get into situations where they feel so destitute and helpless that they don't want to pray. Prayer, however, is made for those who have no other recourse, no other resort. In some ways prayer is simply connecting Jesus to your absolute helplessness, your sense of fragility and dependence. Evidence for this can be seen in Paul's teaching that the Spirit aids us when we feel so helpless we don't even know what to pray for. "The Spirit helps us in our weakness. We do not know what we ought to pray for, but the Spirit himself intercedes for us through wordless groans" (Rom 8:26). It almost seems that the help of the Spirit is triggered by our helplessness. To pray is to accept that we are, and always will be, wholly dependent on God for everything.

In fact, our helplessness can also be a source of confidence. The famous statement of Jesus to the church in Laodicea—"Behold, I stand at the door and knock. If anyone hears my voice and opens the door, I will come in and eat with that person, and they with me" (Rev 3:20)—is often used to call nonbelievers to have faith in Christ. However, an invitation to dining in ancient times was an offer of friendship. Jesus is calling believers to intimate communion with him—to prayer. Prayer, in this image, is a response to Jesus' knocking. We would not open to him if he did not come to us. Since no human heart naturally seeks God (Rom 3:11) or can come to God without his drawing (John

6:44), no one even thinks about praying unless God is prompting or leading us to pray by his Holy Spirit.

In short, if you want to pray, you don't have to be anxious about whether God will listen. You wouldn't even be feeling helpless and needy toward God unless he was at your side making you capable of feeling that way, leading you to think of prayer. When we feel most completely helpless, we should be more secure in the knowledge that God is with us and is listening to our prayer.

What Prayer Gives

Perspective—Prayer Reorients Your View toward God

Prayer in all its forms—adoration, confession, thanksgiving, and petition—reorients your view and vision of everything. Prayer brings new perspective because it puts God back into the picture. Merely addressing God verbally about our needs, fears, hopes, concerns, questions, perplexities, and sins almost immediately forces us to think differently about them.

One image for the reorientation of prayer is your going on a journey and getting to a higher elevation where you can see the terrain you are traversing as a whole, and realizing, "I'm farther along than I thought" or perhaps "I've made less progress than I thought." In prayer we may see that we are more loved and cared for than we had felt, and this diminishes our fears. Or we see that we are more foolish and self-absorbed than we thought, and prayer gets rid of our anger and self-pity.

A practical example of the reorientation of prayer is found in Psalm 73:17–20. Here we see a man filled with envy and resentment at the many people in life who abuse and exploit others and seem to never pay for it. They thrive while his own life is filled with troubles. Then what profit is there in serving God? "Surely in vain, I have kept my heart pure and have washed my hands in innocence. All day long I have been afflicted" (vv. 13–14).

Then he says, "I went into the sanctuary"—the equivalent of prayer—and "I discerned their end." He goes on to show how being in God's presence reminded him that God is in control of all life and history. Not only does sin eventually find us out in this life but there is a final judgment. Then he inserts a new image for the reorientation of prayer—it is like waking up from a dream to reality. "Like a dream when one awakes . . . you despise them as fantasies" (v. 20). In this case, prayer is like waking up from a nightmare to reality. We laugh at what we took so seriously inside the dream. We realize that all is truly well. Of course, prayer can have the opposite effect; it can puncture illusions and show us we are in more spiritual danger than we thought. It can also be like waking from a pleasant dream—to a more difficult reality. So prayer can lead us to shake ourselves and say, "Why was I so scared? This can't hurt me if God is with me!" It can also lead us to say, "Why was I so oblivious? How could I have justified this?" Prayer brings perspective, shows the big picture, gets you out of the weeds, reorients you to where you really are.

Strength—Prayer as Spiritual Union with God

"Prayer is a means to energy," writes J. I. Packer. "Spiritual alertness, vigor, and confidence are the regular spin-off from earnest prayer on any subject. The Puritans spoke of prayer as oiling the wheels of the soul."[234] P. T. Forsyth writes:

> Prayer brings with it, as food does, a new sense of power and health. . . . The life of every organism is but the con-

stant victory of a higher energy, constantly fed, over lower and more elementary forces. Prayer is the assimilation of a holy God's moral strength. We must work for this living. To feed the soul we must toil at prayer. . . . Prayer is the powerful appropriation of power, of divine power. It is therefore creative.[235]

When we become Christians we are said to be "united with Christ."[236] This means, among other things, that we are like branches grafted onto a vine, in order that the life of Christ the Vine might more and more appear in us (John 15:1ff). One of the ways this happens is through prayer.

At the end of Paul's letter to the Ephesians, he instructs them to "be strong in the Lord and in his mighty power" (Eph 6:10). He does not leave that as an abstract directive. He tells believers to put on spiritual "armor." Truth should be your buckler, righteousness your breastplate, the peace that comes from the gospel is your shoes or boots. Defend yourself with the shield of faith and the helmet of salvation. This metaphor and its subimages have been fruitfully expounded to thousands of congregations over the years. The basic idea is that all the benefits of Christ's salvation—pardon, peace, God's love for us—that have been objectively secured for us must be personally appropriated for daily life. The assurance of God's love, the promise of the Spirit's indwelling presence, the knowledge of our pardon, the access to his presence, the power to overcome our sinful habits—all these things are abstractions until they are inwardly received for our actual use. They must not only grip our heart but shape our life through the operation of God's Spirit.

How do we actually get ourselves ready for life's battles? How do we get strong in the Lord? How do we become so spiritually sensitive that we can discern what is really going on in complicated situations? How do we get the assurance of God's wisdom, love, and power so that we can turn to him and rest in him? At the end of the passage, Paul comes out of the metaphor and says, "And pray in the Spirit on all occasions with all kinds of prayers and requests. With this in mind, be alert and always keep on praying for all the Lord's people" (Eph 6:18). Many interpreters try to list prayer as one of the items in the armor, along with truth, righteousness, peace, faith, salvation, and the Word of God. That won't work, however, because every other item is likened to something like a helmet, sword, or breastplate. When he comes to the end, he just says pray, pray, pray in the Spirit, pray with alertness, pray all kinds of ways, pray all the time.

You can't get more basic than this. Prayer *is* the way that all the things we believe in and that Christ has won for us actually become our strength. Prayer is the way that truth is worked into your heart to create new instincts, reflexes, and dispositions.

Spiritual Reality—Prayer Seeks a Heart Sense of the Presence of God

Edmund Clowney writes: "God does not merely speak . . . he is present. Prayer is steeped in the awareness, often an awe-filled awareness, of the presence of God."[237] Through prayer our somewhat abstract knowledge of God becomes existentially real to us. We do not just believe in the glory of God; we sense his greatness. We do not just believe that he loves us; we find our hearts flooded with it.

The Westminster Larger Catechism says that one of the roles of the Holy Spirit in our lives is to help us pray "by working and quickening in our hearts (although not in all persons, nor at all times, in the same measure) those apprehensions, affections, and graces which are requisite for the right performance of that duty."[238] This is a remarkably balanced statement. Prayer is a duty—we must do it no matter what. However, engaged "affections"—a heart engaged in fear, wonder, and love—are necessary for the "right performance" of prayer. It is fitting, then, that our prayers not be distracted and coldhearted. That is not the best way to honor God.

Nevertheless, we do not have full command over our hearts. Even the Holy Spirit does not do so in all persons at all times and in equal measure. Eighteenth-century minister and hymn writer John Newton spoke of God's "sensible presence"—a feeling of his presence on our hearts—as a gift of God that we cannot dictate. He wrote, "The Lord sometimes withdraws his sensible influence, and then the buzzing of a fly will be an overmatch for our patience: at other times he will show us what he can do in us and for us."[239]

The Larger Catechism does not, however, counsel passivity in this. When discussing how Christians should receive the Lord's Supper, it says they should "affectionately meditate on his death and sufferings, and thereby stir up themselves to a vigorous exercise of their graces."[240] This means that we are to meditate on the truth until our heart's affections are stirred and we find ourselves desiring the service of God. What does the presence and reality of God look like in prayer? Remember that the Spirit does not help us with this in all times and in the same way; nevertheless, a striking example of what is possible is seen in the seventeenth-century spiritual classic *The Christian's Great Interest* by William Guthrie:

> It is a glorious divine manifestation of God unto the soul, shedding abroad God's love in the heart; it is a thing better felt than spoken of: it is no audible voice, but it is a ray of glory filling the soul with God, as He is life, light, love, and liberty, corresponding to that audible voice, "O man, greatly

beloved" (Dan 9:23). . . . It is that which went out from Christ to Mary, when He but mentioned her name—"Jesus saith unto her, Mary." . . . When He uttereth this one word "Mary," there was some admirable divine conveyance and manifestation made out unto her heart, by which she was so satisfyingly filled, that there was no place for arguing and disputing whether or no that was Christ.[241]

Guthrie says it is not an audible voice heard with the ears or a visible sight seen with the eyes. Yet it is a kind of voice and a kind of sight—a sense on the heart, not the physical senses. In prayer you can come into the presence of God.

Where Prayer Takes Us

Self-Knowledge—Prayer Requires and Creates Honesty and Self-Knowledge
We have already noted that prayer cannot begin without humility. Prayer, however, must eventually take us beyond a mere sense of insufficiency into deep honesty with ourselves. Honesty in prayer before an omniscient God would seem to be obvious, but instead we often mouth prayerful platitudes without taking the time or making the effort to expose to God and ourselves our deepest fears, hurts, flaws, and sins. "Prayer, true prayer, does not allow us to deceive ourselves. It relaxes the tension of our self-inflation. It produces a clearness of spiritual vision. . . . It saps our self-deception and its Pharisaism. . . . So by prayer we acquire our true selves."[242]

Not only does prayer require the confession of explicit sins and wrongdoing, we are also to uncover the inward postures, attitudes, perspectives, and inordinate desires that lead us to sins small and large.[243] It is a simple fact that the nearer we get to supreme beauty or intelligence or purity, the more we are aware of our own unsightliness, dullness, and impurity.

Calvin famously began his *Institutes* with the words, "Nearly all wisdom we possess, that is to say, true and sound wisdom, consists of two parts: the knowledge of God and of ourselves."[244] In other words, we cannot truly know God better without coming at the same time to know ourselves better. It also works the other way around. If I am in denial about my own weakness and sin, there will be a concomitant blindness to the greatness and glory of God. There is no greater example of this than Isaiah, who when he was given a vision in the temple of the holiness of God, said immediately in response, "Woe to me! I am ruined! For I am a man of unclean lips, and I live among a people of unclean lips, *and for my eyes have seen the King, the Lord Almighty*" (Is 6:5). It was because he'd seen the king in a new way that he saw himself in a new way. They must go together. If we are not open to the recognition of our smallness and sinfulness, we will never take in his greatness and holiness.

Edmund Clowney observes that prayer involves an honesty that has no real parallel in human relationships, because every human relation necessarily involves only a part of your personality. We relate differently to our spouse, our business partner, and a chance acquaintance on the street because each of our social roles expresses only a part of our personhood. Even our spouse sees only part of who we are. "In relation to God, however, we are 'naked and pinned down' (Heb 4:13). Our masks are gone, pretense is useless: the relationship is not partial, but total. All that we are stands related to our Maker and Redeemer."[245]

Trust—Prayer Requires and Creates
Restful Trust and Confident Hope

Just as prayer must combine awe and intimacy, it must also combine submission and "importunity." The final thought of every prayer must be for the help we need to accept thankfully from God's hand whatever he sends in his wisdom. Even children whose instincts are to resist their wills being crossed usually know deep down that they don't understand the world as their parents do. Our Father "alone knows what is best; granting our request might, in many cases, be our destruction."[246]

On the other hand, we are invited to specifically, intensely, and repeatedly make our needs known in prayer with confidence they will be heard. Norwegian author Ole Hallesby, in his classic book on prayer, talks of prayer as "work" and "wrestling."[247] Though we must always end prayers with "nevertheless, thy will be done," our prayers should nonetheless begin with great striving with God. Luther had the temerity to talk of importunate prayer as "conquering God."[248] Prayer is not a passive, calm, quiet practice.

A balance between these two required attitudes—restful trust and confident hope—is absolutely crucial. Under "requisites for prayer" in his systematic theology, Charles Hodge lists "importunity" and "submission" back-to-back. If we overstress submission, we become too passive. We will never pray with the remarkable force and arguments that we see in Abraham pressing God to save Sodom and Gomorrah (Gen 18:16–33), or Moses pleading with God for mercy for Israel and himself (Ex 33:12–22), or Habakkuk and Job questioning God's actions in history. However, if we overstress "importunity," if we engage in petitionary prayer without a foundation of settled acceptance of God's wisdom and sovereignty, we will become too angry when our prayers are not answered. In either case—we will stop praying patient, long-suffering, persistent yet nonhysterical prayers for our needs and concerns.

Hallesby likens prayer to mining as he knew it in Norway in the early twentieth century. Demolition to create mine shafts took two basic kinds of actions. There are long periods of time, he writes, "when the deep holes are being bored with great effort into the hard rock." To bore the holes deeply enough into the most strategic spots for removing the main body of rock was work that took patience, steadiness, and a great deal of skill. Once the holes were finished, however, the "shot" was inserted and connected to a fuse. "To light the fuse and fire the shot is not only easy but also very interesting. . . . One sees 'results.' . . . Shots resound, and pieces fly in every direction." He concludes that while the more painstaking work takes both skill and patient strength of character, "anyone can light a fuse."[249] This helpful illustration warns us against doing only "fuse-lighting" prayers, the kind that we soon drop if we do not get immediate results. If we believe *both* in the power of prayer *and* in the wisdom of God, we will have a patient prayer life of "hole-boring." Mature believers know that handling the tedium is part of what makes for effective prayers.

We must avoid extremes—of either not asking God for things or of thinking we can bend God's will to ours. We must combine tenacious importunity, a "striving with God," with deep acceptance of God's wise will, whatever it is.

Surrender—Prayer Requires and Creates
Surrender of the Whole Life in Love to God

Psalm 66:18 says, "If I had cherished sin in my heart, the Lord would not have listened." At first sight, this seems to mean that I can merit

God's answers to my prayer through greater moral purity. Of course, everything we have seen so far about the biblical theology of prayer to the Father in Jesus' name contradicts that idea. What does this mean, then? James talks about prayers that do not work because "you ask with wrong motives, that you may spend what you get on your pleasures" (James 4:3).

The idea is this. Just as faith in Christ cannot accomplish or merit our salvation but is necessary to receive it—so a commitment to put God first and love and follow him supremely is necessary before God can grant our prayers without harming us. If we are living lives in which God does not have our highest allegiance, then we will use prayer instrumentally, selfishly, simply to try to get the things that may be already ruining our lives.

This truth is behind the words of James 1:6–8, that when you pray "you must believe and not doubt. . . . That person [who doubts] should not expect to receive anything from the Lord. Such a person is double-minded and unstable in all they do." This throws many readers into great anxiety, because it looks on the surface as if James is saying we must have absolute psychological certainty in our minds as we petition God. That is not what he is talking about. He defines *doubt* in verse 8 as being "double-minded"—using the word *dipsychosis*, or literally "two psyches." J. I. Packer and Carolyn Nystrom explain this term with reference to Søren Kierkegaard's classic book title *Purity of Heart Is to Will One Thing*. It means not that you are perfect, or morally pure, or devoid of any uncertainty. It means you have made a decision that God is your God and you are going to ditch all competing concerns the moment you can discern them. It is to take hold of Psalm 73:25—"Whom have I in heaven but you? And earth has nothing I desire besides you." Packer adds, "Nothing, that is, that I would not consent to lose if adhering to God required it. It is a matter of wanting and valuing fellowship with [God] more than I want and value anything else in this world."[250]

At first blush, we may read the last paragraph and ask, "Who, then, can pray?" The right answer is "Every born-again believer without a single exception."[251] Real believers, though they are profoundly aware of how imperfectly they love God, nonetheless *want* to love him supremely. They may cry, "I do not do the good I want to do" and "while I delight in God's will in my inmost heart, I see so many impulses still within me that pull me away from that."[252] Romans 7 and other passages indicate that while Christians will always be capable of great lapses into sin and battles with doubt, there has been a fundamental change in their primary allegiance. This fundamental change is a requisite for prayer that is not shallow and selfish.

At this point we should remember Augustine's letter to Anicia. There he says, in short, that you should not begin to pray for all you want until you realize that in God you have all you need. That is, unless we know that God is the one thing we truly need, our petitions and supplications may become, simply, forms of worry and lust. We can use prayer as just another way to pursue many things that we want too much. Not only will God not hear such prayers (because we ask for things selfishly to spend on our lusts [James 4:2–3]), but the prayers will not reorient our perspective and give us any relief from the melancholy burden of self-absorption.

One of the most striking things John Calvin says about prayer is that it is the main way we receive everything there is for us in Christ: "It remains for us to seek in him, and in prayers to ask of him, what we have learned to be in him."[253] Think about it. We cannot receive Christ and believe on his name (John 1:12–13) except through prayer. Martin

Luther wrote that "all of life is repentance" and that is how we grow in grace. But that again is prayer. Our "chief end," says the Westminster Shorter Catechism, is "to glorify God and enjoy him forever." All these things are, at their essence, prayer.

At the end of time, history will culminate in a great banquet (Rev 19:9), but, as we have seen, we can eat with Jesus now. How? Through prayer. Commentators understand that Jesus' invitation to "hear his voice" and "open the door" so he can "come in and eat with that person, and they with me" (Rev 3:20) is an invitation to fellowship and communion with him through prayer. Prayer—though it is often draining, even an agony—is in the long term the greatest source of power that is possible.

PRAYER

What It Is

Work

Prayer is a duty and a discipline.

Word

Prayer is conversing with God.

Balance

Prayer is adoration, confession, thanks, and supplication.

What It Requires

Grace

Prayer is "In Jesus' name," based on the gospel.

Fear

Prayer is the heart engaged in loving awe.

Helplessness

Prayer is accepting one's weakness and dependence.

What It Gives

Perspective

Prayer reorients your view toward God.

Strength

Prayer is spiritual union with God.

Spiritual Reality

Prayer seeks a heart sense of the presence of God.

Where It Takes Us

Self-Knowledge

Prayer requires and creates honesty and self-knowledge.

Trust

Prayer requires and creates both restful trust and confident hope.

Surrender

Prayer requires and creates surrender of the whole life in love to God.

PART FOUR

Deepening Prayer

TEN

As Conversation:
Meditating on His Word

We have said that when we respond in trust to the Word of God, then prayer becomes a conversation with God. Many have written about the hyperactivity of today's contemporary society and our cultural attention deficit disorder that makes slow reflection and meditation a lost art. Nonetheless, if prayer is to be a true conversation with God, it must be regularly preceded by listening to God's voice through meditation on the Scripture.

Gateway to Prayer

Blessed is the one who does not walk in step with the wicked or stand in the way that sinners take or sit in the company of mockers, but whose delight is in the law of the Lord, and who meditates on his law day and night. That person is like a tree planted by streams of water, which yields its fruit in season and whose leaf does not wither—whatever they do

prospers. Not so the wicked! They are like chaff that the
wind blows away. Therefore the wicked will not stand in the
judgment, nor sinners in the assembly of the righteous. For
the Lord watches over the way of the righteous, but the way
of the wicked leads to destruction. (Ps 1:1–6)

The Psalms are the prayer book of the Bible, but it is noteworthy
that the first Psalm is not a prayer per se but a meditation—in fact, it
is a meditation *on* meditation. This Psalm's prime place is not an acci-
dent. Eugene Peterson points out that the Psalms are an edited book,
and Psalm 1 is the entrance to the rest. "The text [of the Psalms] that
teaches us to pray doesn't begin with prayer. We are not ready. We are
wrapped up in ourselves. We are knocked around by the world."
Psalm 1 is "pre-prayer, getting us ready." [254]

This is an important discovery. Many of us have a devotional life in
which we jump from fairly academic study of the Bible into prayer.
There is a "middle ground," however, between prayer and Bible study,
a kind of bridge between the two. While deep experiences of the presence and power of God can happen in innumerable ways, the ordinary
way for going deeper spiritually into prayer is through meditation on
Scripture. "If we pray without meditation," writes Edmund Clowney,
"our own communion with God becomes poor and distant."[255]

According to Psalm 1, meditation promises at least three things.
The first is stability. The person experienced in meditation is like a tree
rooted so that wind cannot blow it away. Notice that this tree is
planted by streams of water. Trees by streams do well even if there is
little rain. This is an image of someone who can keep going in hard,
dry times. We need to have the roots of our heart and soul in God at
such times, and meditation is the way to do that. The streams of water
represent the "law of the Lord," the Word of God, and to put roots

into the water is a metaphor for meditation.[256] Meditation, then, is what gives you stability, peace, and courage in times of great difficulty, adversity, and upheaval. It helps you stay rooted in divine "water" when all other sources of moisture—of joy, hope, and strength—dry up. By contrast, chaff—the husk around the seed or the kernel in grain—is very lightweight and in any little puff of breeze just blows away. Anything can move it. The way to avoid being chaff rather than a tree is through meditation on God's Word.

There is a note of realism here. Notice that the tree bears fruit only in season, yet it never loses its leaves. Meditation leads to stability—the tree is an evergreen!—but not to complete immunity from suffering and dryness. We must not always expect meditation to lead to uniform experiences of joy and love. There are seasons for great delight (spring-time blossoms?) and for wisdom and maturity (summertime fruit?). However, there are also spiritual wintertimes, when we don't feel God to be close, though our roots may still be firmly in his truth.

Meditation also brings the promise of substance, of character. Chaff cannot produce anything, while the tree can produce fruit. The reason for the difference is that the tree is a growing thing, and the chaff is not. Persons who meditate become people of substance who have thought things out and have deep convictions, who can explain difficult concepts in simple language, and who have good reasons behind everything they do. Many people do not meditate. They skim everything, picking and choosing on impulse, having no thought-out reasons for their behavior. Following whims, they live shallow lives. The people who meditate can resist pressure—but those who do not go along with the throng, chafflike, wherever it is going.

Meditation bears fruit, which in the Bible means character traits such as love, joy, peace, patience, humility, self-control (Gal 5:22ff). Real meditation, then, does not merely make us feel "close to God" but changes our life. As Old Testament scholar Derek Kidner observes, "The tree is no mere channel, piping water unchanged from one place to another, but a living organism which absorbs it, to produce in due course something new and delightful, proper to its kind and to its time."[257]

Finally, meditation brings *blessedness*—a very fulsome idea in the Bible. It means peace and well-being in every dimension. It means character growth, stability, and *delight* (Ps 1:2). Meditating on the law of the Lord, the Scripture, moves us through duty toward joy. The biblical promises for meditation are enormous.

Meditation and the Mind

When the first Psalm calls us to meditate, it uses a word that literally means "to mutter." It refers to the fact that, particularly in ancient times, the Scripture was recited aloud from memory. There is no better way to meditate on a verse and draw out all the aspects, implications, and richness of its meaning than to memorize it. Other words translated as "meditate" in the Psalms mean to ponder and question thoroughly (cf. Ps 77:3, 6, 12). To meditate is to ask yourself questions about the truth, such as: "Am I living in light of this? What difference does this make? Am I taking this seriously? If I believed and held to this, how would that change things? When I forget this, how does that affect me and all my relationships?" In every case, meditation means to use the mind intensely.[258]

Meditation on a text of the Bible assumes that, through study and interpretation, you already know something about what the text means. You can't reflect on or enjoy what you don't understand. To understand a section of Scripture means answering two basic questions about it. First, what did the original author intend to convey to his readers in this passage? Second, what role does this text play in the whole Bible; how does it contribute to the gospel message and move along the main narrative arc of the Bible, which climaxes in the salvation of Jesus Christ? These two questions are "hermeneutical"— their answers help you interpret the meaning of the text so you can then go on to meditate on the implications and applications of its truth.

Unless you first do the hard work of answering those questions about a text, your meditations won't be grounded in what God is actually saying in the passage. Something in the passage may "hit" you— but it may hit you as expressing almost the opposite of what the biblical author, inspired by the Spirit, was saying. When that happens, you are listening to your own heart or to the spirit of your own culture, not to God's voice in the Scripture. A great number of books advise "divine reading" of the Bible today, and define the activity uncarefully as reading "not for information but to hear a personal word of God to you." This presents a false contrast. It is certainly true that meditation personalizes the Word, but before we can meditate on what the text personally means to us and our time, we must first need to know as much as possible what the author meant to say to his readers when he wrote it. Martin Luther said that before he could turn a biblical text into praise, he first needed to understand it as "instruction," as truthful information.[259] In short, biblical meditation is founded on the work of sound biblical interpretation and study.

Biblical meditation does not empty the mind of rational thought. By contrast, consider "mantra meditation," one version of which was the popular Transcendental Meditation (or TM). In TM, participants repeat a word or phrase that first blots out other thoughts and then loses its own meaning. A recent study defined mantra meditation as "the repetition of a phrase in such a way that it transcends one to an effortless state where focused attention is absent."[260] The result is to become no longer aware of any words, ideas, images, or concepts—instead to become aware only of awareness itself. Beyond this lie other forms of consciousness that lead us toward a sense of being one with all that is, with God who is all things. As one Christian theologian observed, this is the opposite of the goal of Christian meditation. It is not the experience "of *knowing* God but . . . of *being* God."[261]

Christian meditation, however, is quite rational, even argumentative. "Why, my soul, are you downcast? Why so disturbed within me?" David says in Psalm 42, literally contending with his own heart. Mantra meditation seeks to suppress the analytical side of the mind. Christian meditation, however, stimulates our analysis and reflection—and centers it on the glory and grace of God.

Meditation and the Heart

Meditation on the Bible is more than just intense thinking. The Bible contains information, but it is more than that. It talks about itself as a living and active agent (Heb 4:12). The gospel, the message of the Bible, is said to be not just a word but a power (Rom 1:16; 1 Thess 1:5). When Paul talks about the Word of God "dwelling richly" within us (Col 3:16), he is clearly talking of something beyond mere assent to information. He is talking about "a deep and penetrating contemplation" that enables the Bible's message to have transforming power.[262]

Psalm 1's metaphors convey all this. Meditation is likened to tree roots taking in water. That means not merely knowing a truth but taking it inside and making it part of yourself. Meditation is spiritually "tasting" the Scripture—delighting in it, sensing the sweetness of the teaching, feeling the conviction of what it tells us about ourselves, and thanking God and praising God for what it shows us about him. Meditation is also spiritually "digesting" the Scripture—applying it, thinking out how it affects you, describes you, guides you in the most practical way. It is drawing strength from the Scripture, letting it give you hope, using it to remember how loved you are. To shift metaphors, meditation is taking the truth down into our hearts until it catches fire there and begins to melt and shape our reactions to God, ourselves, and the world.

An example of meditation is Psalm 103:1–2: "Praise the Lord, my soul; and all my inmost being, praise his holy name. Praise the Lord, my soul, and forget not all his benefits." Notice that David is not speaking directly to God, though he is aware of being in the presence of God. He is talking to himself, to his soul. He is taking truth down into his heart before the face of God. That is meditation. The "benefits" David lists are those of salvation—the forgiveness of sins; the reception of grace; and the infinite, unconditional love of God (Ps 103:3, 8–12). He is taking these biblical truths and driving them into his own heart until it is affected, delighted, and changed by them. He does this by chiding his heart that it tends to "forget" its salvation. That can't literally mean that David forgets he is a believer. It must mean, rather, that his *heart* forgets in that our instinctive responses and drives and emotions and attitudes do not connect themselves to the truths we profess. A Christian's meditation along these lines might go something like this:

> When I forget I am justified by faith alone—I give place to guilt and regret about the past. I therefore live in bondage to idols of power and money that make me feel better about myself.

When I forget I'm being sanctified through the presence of God's Holy Spirit—I give up on myself, stop trying to change.

When I forget the hope of my future resurrection—I become afraid of aging and death.

When I forget my adoption into the family of God—I become full of fears. I don't pray with candor. I lose my confidence. I try to hide my faults from God and myself.

Fixing the Mind

While there are many specific ways to meditate on a passage of Scripture, the British theologian John Owen believed there are three basic movements or stages within meditation.[263] Owen begins by distinguishing meditation from Bible study and from prayer proper. He writes:

> It is distinguished from the study of the word, wherein our principal aim is to learn the truth, or to declare it unto others; and so also from prayer, whereof God himself is the immediate object. But . . . meditation . . . is the affecting of our own hearts and minds with love, delight, and [humility].[264]

He goes on to explain the first stage, which is selecting and getting a clear view—"*fixing the thoughts*"—of a truth from the Bible:

> By solemn or stated meditation, I intend [first] the thoughts of some subject spiritual and divine, with the fixing, forcing, and ordering of our thoughts about it. . . . [It

is] the actual exercise of the mind, in its thoughts, meditations, and desires, about things spiritual and heavenly. . . .
They mind them by fixing their thoughts and meditations
upon them.

There are many traditional ways to get such a clear view of a text. One
is to read the biblical text slowly, answering four questions: What does this
teach me about God and his character? About human nature, character,
and behavior? About Christ and his salvation? About the church, or life in
the people of God? So, for example, we might read John 2:13–22, about
Jesus driving the money changers out of the temple:

When it was almost time for the Jewish Passover, Jesus went
up to Jerusalem. In the temple courts he found people sell-
ing cattle, sheep and doves, and others sitting at tables ex-
changing money. So he made a whip out of cords, and drove
all from the temple courts, both sheep and cattle; he scat-
tered the coins of the money changers and overturned their
tables. To those who sold doves he said, "Get these out of
here! Stop turning my Father's house into a market!" His
disciples remembered that it is written: "Zeal for your house
will consume me." The Jews then responded to him, "What
sign can you show us to prove your authority to do all this?"
Jesus answered them, "Destroy this temple, and I will raise
it again in three days." They replied, "It has taken forty-six
years to build this temple, and you are going to raise it in
three days?" But the temple he had spoken of was his body.
After he was raised from the dead, his disciples recalled what
he had said. Then they believed the scripture and the words
that Jesus had spoken.

What do we learn about God from this passage? We might see that God cannot be taken lightly, that he is holy. In his presence, his "house," it matters how we live. What do we learn about who we are and how we should live? It might strike us how important it is to concentrate on him during worship, and not daydream about other affairs. We might also meditate on what it means to be highly committed, to be "zealous" for God in other areas of life. What do we learn about Christ and his salvation? Jesus is not only predicting his resurrection here, but he is also claiming that *he* is the ultimate temple, the bridge over the chasm between God and humankind. What do we learn about being the people of God? We see how important it is to learn the Scripture, even though it may take time and patience to understand and rejoice in its teaching.

Another fruitful approach to meditation is to ask application questions. Look within the passage: for any personal examples to emulate or avoid, for any commands to obey, for any promises to claim, and for any warnings to heed. Let's use these questions on another passage from the Gospel of John (1:29–42):

> The next day John saw Jesus coming toward him and said, "Look, the Lamb of God, who takes away the sin of the world! This is the one I meant when I said, 'A man who comes after me has surpassed me because he was before me.' I myself did not know him, but the reason I came baptizing with water was that he might be revealed to Israel." Then John gave this testimony: "I saw the Spirit come down from heaven as a dove and remain on him. And I myself did not know him, but the one who sent me to baptize with water told me, 'The man on whom you see the Spirit come down and remain is the one who will baptize with the Holy

Spirit.' I have seen and I testify that this is God's Chosen One."

The next day John was there again with two of his disciples. When he saw Jesus passing by, he said, "Look, the Lamb of God!" When the two disciples heard him say this, they followed Jesus. Turning around, Jesus saw them following and asked, "What do you want?" They said, "Rabbi" (which means "Teacher"), "where are you staying?" "Come," he replied, "and you will see." So they went and saw where he was staying, and they spent that day with him. It was about four in the afternoon. Andrew, Simon Peter's brother, was one of the two who heard what John had said and who had followed Jesus. The first thing Andrew did was to find his brother Simon and tell him, "We have found the Messiah" (that is, the Christ). And he brought him to Jesus.

Jesus looked at him and said, "You are Simon son of John. You will be called Cephas" (which, when translated, is Peter).

Here we see an example to emulate. John the Baptist is a teacher with loyal disciples, but he knows that any human being's highest loyalty should be to Jesus, so he deliberately sends his disciples away to him, and they go. We too should be sure not to make any human relationship more important than our relationship with Christ. We also see a command, namely to "behold," to believe and embrace Jesus as the Lamb of God. We must trust Jesus as our atoning sacrifice, our Passover lamb, the one through which our sins can be forgiven. There is a promise here too, namely "Come, and you will see." Following Jesus is a process. He does not give us all we want right away. Jesus calls us to come now and commit to him and as time goes on we will "see" and learn wondrous things. There is even a mild warning implied here. If we do come to Jesus and commit to be his disciples, we will "see," but it will also disrupt our lives and change us, as Jesus says to Simon when he tells him he will receive a new name. We won't be the same.

Another approach to meditating on the Scripture, especially with a short passage, is to take one crucial verse and think through it by emphasizing each word. Ask what each word uniquely contributes to the meaning of the text, or what meaning would be lost from the statement if that particular word were removed. Consider Mark 1:17 and meditate by putting stress on each word. "*Follow* me, and I will make you to become fishers of men." This means we are not to be students merely absorbing information but disciples aligning our entire lives with Christ. "Follow *me*, and I will make you to become fishers of men." Jesus doesn't say merely "obey this" but "obey and follow *me*." While we do have to obey Jesus' word, in the end Christianity is a personal, intimate relationship with him. There must be warmth and fellowship with him, not mere ethical compliance. "Follow me, and I *will* make you to become fishers of men." It's a promise, an assurance that he will change us. "Follow me, and I will make you to *become* fishers of men." However, it will be a process. We should not be impatient. See how each word reveals some other aspect of the directive that would be missed without meditating on that specific expression.

Another way to fix the mind on the truth of the passage is to paraphrase the verse in your own words. Read the verse(s) and close the Bible and try to restate it. Then look back at the passage and you will see how much you missed. Do this until you are satisfied with your paraphrase. This kind of meditation forces you to think more deeply about the text than you would otherwise. If you realize you don't really know what a word or concept means, take time to study and find out. Putting it in your own words—your own heart language—will send it down into your inner being more easily.

As we observed before, a final way to meditate on a text is to memorize it. This tool of learning was a time-honored method used far more in the past than it is today, and that is a pity. Memorization can be particularly fruitful and in some ways combines the other approaches. As you work on remembering the exact words, particular meanings will strike you that otherwise you would have missed, and many insights will simply flow in unbidden along the way. Also, memorized texts often come to you spontaneously during the day when you realize how it applies directly to a particular situation you are in. It is not for nothing that memorization is called "learning by heart." Indeed it is, and that leads us to the second movement within meditation.

Inclining the Heart

After engaging the mind, John Owen says the second part of meditation is inclining the heart. After engaging the mind to clearly see what we are being taught about God, Christ, salvation, eternity, and our own state, we must then seek to incline the heart until its hope and joy more fully rests in those things.

Owen describes this as "the inclination, disposition, and frame of . . . all . . . affections" so that the heart "adheres and cleaves unto spiritual things . . . from the love and delight . . . in them and engagement unto them."[265] This is what Owen's contemporary Richard Baxter called "soliloquy." It means seeing how God's truth should be affecting you, your life, and all your relationships—and then pleading and preaching to your heart until it connects to the truth and begins to turn away from its false hopes and to change its attitudes, feelings, and commitments. Baxter speaks of self-exhortation, by which he means to "plead thyself from a clod to a flame; from a forgetful sinner and a lover of the world, to an ardent lover of God; from a fearful coward to a resolved Christian; from an unfruitful sadness to a joyful life; in a word, till thou hast pleaded thy heart from earth to heaven."[266]

How do you do this practically? One way is Martin Luther's approach. After fixing the truth in the mind as instruction, he asks how it shows you something about the character of God for which you can praise him, something wrong about yourself for which you can repent, and something that is needed for which you can petition him. In each case, Luther is working the truth into his relationship to God, to himself, and to the world.

Luther is de-abstracting the scriptural truth, refusing to regard it in a detached way, plunging himself into it, and pushing it into his soul to see how that truth should change him. There's an old saying that the difference between abstract knowledge and real wisdom is that "wisdom is knowledge with the knower left in." It is taking the truth into all your relationships. It is to ask, "What does this mean for my relationship to God? to myself? to this or that person or group? to this or that behavior or habit? to my friends, to the culture?"

Another way of discerning how a truth can change you is to look more deeply at yourself. Ask yourself what wrong thoughts result in you when this truth is forgotten. Then consider the excessive and hard-to-control feelings that result when it is not fully believed and embraced. Ask how a loss of orientation to this truth may lead to inordinate hopes for something else to give you what only God can give you. Consider what actual sins and wrongdoings might result from a failure to grasp and appreciate this truth. Be concrete—Is there something you must stop doing because of it? Is there something you should start doing?

A final way you can discern how a scriptural truth should change you is by considering the timing of your insight. Why might God be showing this to you *today*? What is going on now in your life to which this would be relevant?

These questions are very searching, and the process of answering them is often moving but not necessarily pleasant. As you work a truth in, you may be convicted, humbled, and troubled, or calmed and comforted, or excited and filled with uncontainable joy. Meditation aims here—at the heart. Owen writes forcefully on this:

> If we settle for mere speculations and mental notions about Christ as doctrine, we shall find no transforming power or efficacy communicated unto us thereby. But when, under the conduct of spiritual light, our affections do cleave unto him with full purpose of heart, our minds fill up with thoughts and delight in him—then virtue [change in character] will proceed from him to purify us, increase our holiness, strengthen our graces, and to fill us sometimes with joy unspeakable and full of glory.[267]

It is not right, says Owen, to settle for mere mental assent to doctrines about Jesus, because that does not honor him. There should be "love, trust, delight, and longing after the full enjoyment of him" (1 Peter 1:8).[268] The only way to get that is to study the Word, meditate to the point of delight (Ps 1:2), and then experience inward love and joy and also life-change. Owen calls this the way to arrive at the "just [or proper] temperature of a state of spiritual health." It is when the amount of our "knowledge of the glory of God in Christ" is answered proportionately by the affections of the heart.[269] That is, all that we know theologically must be "accessed" by our heart with all the joy, peace, self-control, love, durability, patience, and graciousness that it should produce in a human being.

Enjoying or Crying Out

John Owen quickly adds that once we have fully meditated—working out the truth and then working it into the heart—the immediate results may vary. A heart experience of the truth will be "according to the various degrees of it—for some have more and some have less." What, then, is the third stage of meditation? It depends on where we are along a spectrum (the "various degrees") between two poles.

It may be that the heart senses the presence of God and the realities of his salvation in a moving way. Owen calls us, then, to stop and savor it. He uses the old word *gust* to talk about an experience of spiritual sweetness and satisfaction:

> In this gust and relish lies the sweetness and satisfaction of spiritual life. Speculative notions about spiritual things, when they are alone, are dry, sapless, and barren. In this gust we taste by experience that God is gracious, and that the love of Christ is better than wine, or whatever else hath the most grateful relish unto a sensual appetite. This is the proper foundation of that "joy which is unspeakable and full of glory."[270]

That is what David spoke of when he said, "One thing . . . I seek . . . to gaze on the beauty of the Lord" (Ps 27:4), and "My whole being longs for you. . . . I have seen you in the sanctuary and beheld your power and glory. Because your love is better than life, my lips will glorify you. . . . I will be fully satisfied as with the richest of foods" (Ps 63:1–5).

Like Martin Luther—who knew that sometimes the Holy Spirit begins immediately to "preach to you" and sometimes he does not— Owen is quite realistic. He admits that sometimes, no matter what we do, we simply cannot concentrate, or we find our thoughts do not become big and affecting, but rather we feel bored, hard, and distracted. Then, Owen says, simply turn to God and make brief, intense appeals for help. Sometimes that is all you will do the rest of your scheduled time, and sometimes the very cries for help serve to concentrate the mind and soften the heart. He writes: "When, after this preparation, you find yourselves yet perplexed and entangled, not able comfortably to persist in spiritual thoughts unto your refreshment . . . cry and sigh to God for help and relief."[271] Even if your meditations give you only a "renewed gracious sense of your own weakness and insufficiency," that is by no means a waste of time. It is bringing you into greater touch with spiritual reality. Then, he adds, our expressions of grief at the sense of God's absence are themselves ways to show love to God, and they will not go unappreciated by him.[272]

He advises to end the time and come back to it tomorrow. "Constancy in [this] duty will give ability for it. Those who conscientiously abide in its performance shall increase in light, wisdom, and experience, until they are able to manage it with great success."[273] Perhaps Psalm 1 again gives us some help on this subject. The one who meditates is like a tree. Trees don't grow overnight. Meditation is a sustained process like a tree growing its roots down toward the water source. The effects are cumulative. You must stick with it. We must meditate *"day and night"*—regularly, steadily.

According to Owen, meditation means analyzing the truth with the mind; bringing it into the feelings, attitudes, and commitments of the heart; and then responding to the degree to which the Holy Spirit gives illumination and spiritual reality. We could say that meditation before prayer consists of thinking, then inclining, and, finally, either enjoying the presence or admitting the absence and asking for his mercy and help. Meditation is thinking a truth *out* and then thinking a truth *in* until its ideas become "big" and "sweet," moving and affecting, and until the reality of God is sensed upon the heart.[274]

Meditating on the Incarnate Word

Psalm 1 tells us the godly man or woman meditates on the *law of the Lord*. This phrase refers to the entire Scripture, but particularly with a view to its normative character. It is our "rule of faith and practice." It shows us the will of God for our lives, and this raises an important practical issue. How can anyone who truly meditates on the will of God in the Word find it delightful? Look at Jesus' meditations on the Ten Commandments in the Sermon on the Mount. He thinks through the meaning of "thou shalt not commit adultery" and concludes it means that merely lusting after someone other than your spouse is a sin (Matt 5:27–30). He meditates on the commandment "thou shalt not kill" and draws out the implication that we cannot even be resentful of our neighbor (Matt 5:21–22). How can anyone truly think intensely about the law of the Lord and not fall into despair?

The answer is to look at the central figure of the entire written Word, the one the gospel of John calls "the Word made flesh" (John 1:14)—Jesus Christ, the ultimate expression and communication of God. This will lead us to look at how Jesus himself regarded the Scripture.

Jesus was the great Meditator. He is the one who delights in doing God's will. Hebrews 10:7 quotes Psalm 40:8 as the words of Jesus: "I delight to do your will . . . your Law is within my heart." He is the one who prays day and night (Luke 5:16, "Jesus often withdrew to lonely places and prayed"; 6:12, "He went to a mountainside and prayed all night"; 9:18, 28; 11:1; 22:39–40, "As usual"). He is the one who, when he looks to God, experiences delight (Luke 3:21–22, "As he was praying, heaven opened and the Holy Spirit descended and a voice said—'you are my Son'"). He is the one who meditated so profoundly on Scripture that he virtually "bled" Scripture, quoting it instinctively in the most extreme moments of his life. He combats each of the assaults of Satan with "It is written" (Matt 4:1–11). He quotes Psalm 22:1 even as he dies: "My God, my God, why have you forsaken me?" (Matt 27:46). That is how he stood firm. That was how he was truly a tree "ever green," using the Word of God even when enduring the infinite agony of the cross. Do you want to be able to endure even the greatest pain? Put your roots into Scripture as he did.

Yet Jesus is not simply a good example. If that were all he was to us, his life would crush us with guilt, since no one could meditate on the Scripture as he does. He is, thank God, infinitely more than that. He is not just an exemplar within Scripture, he is the one to whom all the Scripture points, because the main message of the Bible is salvation by grace through Jesus (Luke 24:27, 44). The Bible is all about him. Moses wrote of him, and Abraham rejoiced to see his day (John 5:46, 8:56).

The written Word and its law can be a delight because the incarnate Word came and died for us, securing pardon for our sins and shortcomings before God's law. You *can't* delight in the law of the Lord without understanding Jesus' whole mission. Without him, the law is nothing but a curse, a condemnation, a witness against us (Gal 3:10–

11). He obeyed the law fully for us (2 Cor 5:21), so now it is a delight to us, not an everlasting despair.

Jesus is supremely the one also on whom we meditate, because he *is* the meditation of God. He is God's truth become "real," made concrete, and applied. He is the one who enables us to stand in the Judgment Day. He is the one who gives us the fruit of the Spirit (Gal 5:22ff). We must both meditate on him and with him, and then, not only will Psalm 1 come to life in new ways, but we will become unshakable trees, as he was. Richard Lovelace wrote:

> It is an item of faith that we are children of God; there is plenty of experience in us against it. The faith that surmounts this evidence and that is able to warm itself at the fire of God's love, instead of having to steal love and self-acceptance from other sources, is actually the root of holiness. . . . We are not saved by the love we exercise, but by the love we trust.[275]

When Lovelace speaks of warming oneself "at the fire of God's love," he is describing what it means to meditate on the righteousness we have in Christ through his sacrificial death. If we don't meditate on that until our hearts are hot with assurance, we will "steal love and self-acceptance" from worldly achievements, beauty, and status.

Meditate on Jesus, who is the ultimate meditation of God. Look at him loving you. Look at him dying for you. Look at him rejoicing in you. Look at him singing over you (Zeph 3:17). Look at all that, and he will be a delight to you, and then the law will be a delight to you, and you will be like a tree planted by streams of water. You'll bear your fruit in season, and no matter what will happen, your leaf will not wither.

ELEVEN

As Encounter: Seeking His Face

Prayer is a conversation that leads to encounter with God. As we have seen, the Westminster Larger Catechism acknowledges that this "working and quickening in our hearts" does not take place "in all persons, nor at all times, in the same measure."[276] Nevertheless, that is our goal. In John Owen's treatment of meditation, the third stage anticipates a character-forming experience of God's presence and reality.

John Calvin argues that Jesus' gifts for his people are not experienced by so many of them. That enjoyment, he says, can happen only through "communion with Christ" and "the secret energy of the Holy Spirit, by which we come to enjoy all his benefits."[277] Later he adds: "For the Word of God is not received by faith as if it flits about in the top of the brain, but when it takes root in the depth of the heart."[278] We must not settle for an informed mind without an engaged heart.

All this leads naturally to ask: What kind of experience should be expected and how should it be sought?

Being Rich but Living Poor

Calvin's idea—that we have blessings in Christ we don't experience—is expressed also in the great prayer by Paul in Ephesians 3.

> I kneel before the Father. . . . I pray that out of his glorious
> riches he may strengthen you with power through his Spirit
> in your inner being, so that Christ may dwell in your hearts
> through faith. And I pray that you, being rooted and estab-
> lished in love, may have power, together with all the Lord's
> holy people, to grasp how wide and long and high and deep
> is the love of Christ, and to know this love that surpasses
> knowledge—that you may be filled to the measure of all the
> fullness of God. (Eph 3:14, 16–19)

Paul prays for his readers "that Christ may dwell in your hearts through faith" (v. 17) and that they would "know this love" of Christ (vv. 18–19). Finally, he prays that they would be filled with "all the fullness of God" (v. 19). Those are Paul's three main petitions.[279]

These Ephesian readers, however, were all Christian believers, and Paul teaches elsewhere that if you don't have the Spirit and Christ resident in your life, you are not a Christian at all. In Ephesians 2, Paul goes on at length about how all his readers have been united with Christ and united with others who have Christ in them. In Ephesians 1, he teaches that by being united with Christ, they *already* have the fullness of God in them (Eph 1:22–23). All this leads us to ask: Isn't Christ already living in Christians? Don't they already know his great sacrificial love? How can anyone be a Christian otherwise? Why is he asking God to give Christians things they must surely already have?

There can be only one answer. At one level, Christians have these things. At another level, they haven't experienced them.[280] It is one thing to know of the love of Christ and to say, "I know he did all that." It is another thing to *grasp* how wide and long and high and deep is the love of Christ. What Paul is talking about is the difference between having something be true of you in principle and fully appropriating it, using it, and living in it—in your "inner being" (Eph 3:16) or "in your heart" (v. 17).

It is possible for Christians to live their lives with a high degree of phoniness, hollowness, and inauthenticity. The reason is because they have failed to move that truth into their hearts and therefore it has not actually changed who they are and how they live.

Blaise Pascal was a Christian believer and philosopher, and one of the great minds of history. When he died it was discovered that he had sewn into the inner lining of his coat the description of an experience he had had one night. It read: "In the year 1654, Monday, twenty-third November, from about half past ten in the evening until half an hour after midnight . . . FIRE . . . God of Abraham, God of Isaac, God of Jacob, and not of the philosophers and of the learned. Certainty. Certainty. Feeling. Joy. Peace." Pascal was not talking about a sight of literal flames but of an experience of the presence of God—what fire in the Bible so often represents. He had believed in God, but when he said he had met the God of Abraham, Isaac, and Jacob—not the "God of the philosophers"—he meant he now knew in the heart what he had known in the abstract.[281] Another, less famous example is Dwight L. Moody, a prominent Chicago minister and evangelist in the late nineteenth century. He wrote: "One day in the city of New York—oh what a day!—I cannot describe it, I seldom refer to it; it is almost too sacred an experience to name. . . . I can only say that God revealed himself to me, and I had such an experience of his love that I had to ask him to stay his hand."[282] It wasn't that Moody was not a Christian or that he had never known Christ's love and presence. Perhaps we could say that the objective reality of who he was in Christ and the inward subjective experience came together. For a moment he lived as the person he actually was.

These are well-known cases of unusually intense spiritual encounters. But don't write them off too quickly as exceptional. Paul would not be praying something for each of his Ephesian readers to have a nearly unattainably high, rare occurrence. In Ephesians 3, he is praying that by the Spirit's power we may have our hearts and affections engaged and shaped by the truths of the faith we hold in the mind. Such a sense of the heart can come in many degrees, from a mild and gentle warming to an explosive epiphany. It does not have to be an experience we write down and think about the rest of our lives, though such gifts are welcome. What *is* common to all these moments is that you sense the power of what you have been given in Christ so that your attitudes, feelings, and behavior are altered. Imagine you get a notice that someone left you some money, but for various reasons, you assume it is a very modest amount. You get busy and don't get around even to checking on it for quite a while. Finally, you do so and are thunderstruck to discover it was a fortune, and you had not been doing anything with it. You were actually rich but had been living poor. This is what Paul wants his Christian friends to avoid, and only through encounter with God in prayer can they avoid it.

This may be where you are. You are in him. You are adopted into the Father's family. You have the very divine life in you, the Holy Spirit. You are loved and accepted in Christ. You know about these things, and yet at another level you don't know them, you don't grasp them. You are still dogged by your bad habits, often anxious or bored or discouraged or angry. You may have many specific problems and issues that need to be faced and dealt with through various specific means. Yet the root problem of them all is that you are rich in Christ but nevertheless living poor.

"The Truth Begins to Shine"

What does it mean to speak of spiritual experience in the inner being? What is the "inner being"? It is the same thing as the heart, the center of both our personal consciousness and our most fundamental faith commitments.[283] This is where the truths we know about Jesus with our mind can fail to register. We may mentally assent to the idea of Jesus' love for us, yet our hearts are committed to finding love through popular acclaim. In such a case the inner being has not been affected by what the mind believes. The Spirit must prepare it to be reshaped and formed by the truth. How does that happen?

The Spirit creates an inner spiritual sensitivity to gospel truth. Paul says, "I pray that out of his glorious riches he may strengthen you with power through his Spirit in your inner being, so that . . . [you may] grasp how wide and long and high and deep is the love of Christ." This word *grasp* is important—it is more than just to "believe." It means to get a secure hold on something.

Photography used to require film that was made sensitive to light by treating it with chemicals. The camera shutter opened and in came light, bouncing off an object such as a tree. The chemically treated film "grasped" the image of the tree, and there the image remained. The film was permanently impressed with and changed by the tree. Imagine, however, that there is some failure to put the film through the proper chemical treatment. Then the shutter opens and the light comes in, but the film isn't sufficiently sensitive to receive a clear image, if any image at all. The light makes no difference to the film whatsoever.

Paul's prayer suggests that Christians need the Spirit's "chemical treatment," a spiritual sensitizing, or the truths we mouth and assent to will make no real difference in how we live. If you are exposed to the "light" of the Christian truth that God is holy, and if the Holy Spirit has sensitized your heart, then you not only respond with emotion—with tears or trembling or joy—but you permanently change the way you live and behave in the world. When your feelings and behaviors are affected, you have, to a degree, *grasped* a particular truth about God. The light comes in and makes permanent impressions.

No one has expressed this better than Jonathan Edwards in his great sermon "A Divine and Supernatural Light." At the heart of the sermon is his famous illustration of honey. There are two ways to know that honey is sweet, he says. You can know it with the rational mind, and you can also know it with the sensing tongue. You can know that honey is sweet because people tell you about it and you believe them, but when you actually taste the sweetness of honey yourself, you know fully—mentally as well as experientially.

When you move from just mentally knowing about the sweetness of honey to directly tasting it, you may say something like this: "I knew it was sweet, but I really didn't realize what that meant. *I knew but I didn't know.*" Edwards concludes that, in the same way, "there is a difference between having an opinion that God is holy and gracious, and having a sense of the loveliness and beauty of that holiness and graciousness on the heart."

You may say, "I really believe in God, I really believe that Jesus died on the cross. I have no doubts about that." Edwards can respond that you may not have had any doubts at all about honey being sweet either. You could have talked to a hundred people who told you it was. You could have read scientific reports that proved it was sweet and pleasant to the human palate. You could have been quite sure about it without having tasted it yourself.

Honey is one thing, however, and God is quite another. Knowing God is not optional, and this is what Paul is praying for. He asks that the Holy Spirit will sensitize our hearts so that we taste these truths, spiritually speaking, or—as he says in Ephesians 1:18, when he prays that "the eyes of your heart may be enlightened"—that we see them, spiritually speaking. When the Spirit is doing his work, the truths of the Word and gospel lift us up, move us, strike us, maybe melt and compel us. That is what happens to us instead of our saying, "Okay, I know all that." There's an old hymn that uses this kind of sensory language:

> When once Thou visitest the heart,
> Then truth begins to shine,
> Then earthly vanities depart,
> Then kindles love divine.[284]

Knowing the Father

There is another phrase in Paul's prayer that helps us understand the nature of spiritual experience. Paul begins by saying that he "kneels before the Father" (Eph 3:14). To kneel was not the normal prayer posture for Christians and Jews, and so to "bow the knee" was an act of special reverence.[285] Paul may be taking particular notice of the fact that God is, indeed, now our *Father*. In Romans 8, Paul calls the Spirit who helps us to pray the "spirit of sonship," who leads us to pray "*Abba*, Father" (v. 15). He goes on to say that the heart of the Spirit's ministry to us is to "testify with our spirit"—to assure us inwardly—

"that we are God's children" (v. 8:16). So another aspect of communion with God is a deeper understanding and the appropriation of our family relationship with the Father.

When the Holy Spirit comes upon Jesus at his baptism, he hears a voice say, "This is my Son, in whom I am well pleased. You are my Son, and I delight in you." In the same way, Romans 8:16 tells us that the Spirit bears witness to our hearts that we are children of God. Part of the mission of the Spirit is to tell you about God's love for you, his delight in you, and the fact that you are his child. These things you may know in your head, but the Holy Spirit makes them a fiery reality in your life.

Thomas Goodwin, a seventeenth-century Puritan pastor, wrote that one day he saw a father and son walking along the street. Suddenly the father swept the son up into his arms and hugged him and kissed him and told the boy he loved him—and then after a minute he put the boy back down. Was the little boy more a son in the father's arms than he was down on the street? Objectively and legally, there was no difference, but subjectively and experientially, there was all the difference in the world. In his father's arms, the boy was *experiencing* his sonship.

When the Holy Spirit comes down on you in fullness, you can sense your Father's arms beneath you. It is an assurance of who you are. The Spirit enables you to say to yourself: "If someone as all-powerful as that loves me like this, delights in me, has gone to infinite lengths to save me, says he will never let me go, and is going to glorify me and make me perfect and take everything bad out of my life—if all of that is true—why am I worried about anything?" At a minimum this means joy, and a lack of fear and self-consciousness.

In Ephesians 5:18, Paul says, "Don't be drunk with wine but be filled with the Spirit." Remember the disciples on Pentecost. They went out and spoke the gospel in public with such a wonderful lack of self-consciousness that some thought they had had too much to drink (Acts 2:13). But their boldness was unlike being drunk in the most important respect. Alcohol is a depressant—it deadens parts of the rational brain. The happiness you may feel when you are drunk comes because you are less aware of reality. The Spirit, however, gives you joyful fearlessness by making you *more* aware of reality. It assures you that you are a child of the only One whose opinion and power matters. He loves you to the stars and will never let you go.

Grasping the Love

Paul asks the Holy Spirit to give "power to grasp." The word *grasp* means "to wrestle" or it could mean "to capture," as in capturing a city in battle. It means to jump on somebody, overpower him, wrestle him to the ground, and knock him out. At first it seems a very strange word to use when talking about the love of God, but Paul is talking about meditating and pondering something until you break through, until, as we say, it "hits" you. The breakthrough will happen, of course, only with the Spirit's empowering help.

How does that happen? It is through the Spirit's blessing of our meditation on the saving work of Jesus. I believe that in Ephesians 3 we are given a case study of this. Why does Paul spell it out, calling us to consider the width and breadth and depth and height of Christ's love? He is proposing a way to meditate and inviting us to do it. Let's take up his invitation.

How *wide* is the love of God? Think of Isaiah 1:18: "Though your sins are like scarlet, they shall be as white as snow." Scarlet is the color of blood. This was God's way of saying through Isaiah, "Even if you have killed somebody, even if you have blood-guilt, blood on your hands, my love is wide enough to enfold and embrace you. It doesn't matter who you are or what you have done. It doesn't matter if you *have* killed people. If Jesus Christ died on the cross so that you are saved by *grace* alone, then my love is infinitely wide. It is wide enough for you."

How *long* is the love of God? Jesus says in John 10, "I know my own. I give them eternal life . . . and no one can pluck them out of my hand." In Philippians 1:6, Paul says to the Christians, everybody he is writing to at Philippi, "I am convinced . . . that he who began a good work in you *will* carry it on to completion until the day of Christ Jesus." Not "may." *Will.* His love is infinitely long. And when did his love begin? We are told in the book of Revelation that the Lamb of God was slain before the foundation of the world. God put his love on you in the depths of time, and he will never remove it from you. Why? Because salvation is by grace. It is not by works. It is not given to you because of what you do. It has begun in the depths of time and will last into eternity. It is infinitely long.

The reason that the love of God in Christ is infinitely wide and infinitely long is because it is infinitely *deep*. How *deep* is the love of God? Without Jesus Christ, talk about the "depth of God's love" would be simply an abstraction. Without Jesus Christ, God could send you sixty volumes, with every page saying, "I love you deeply, I love you deeply, I love you deeply," but it would still be an abstract concept, not a life-changing reality. To genuinely understand the depths of God's love you must know the depths to which Jesus Christ went in order to love *you*. How deep did he go? "My God, my God, why hast thou forsaken me?" That is hell. He was thrown into the deepest pit anybody ever went into, and he went in voluntarily. He went down and down and down—to *the depths*. Because of the gospel, you can know that God's love is infinitely wide and infinitely long because it was infinitely deep.

God's love is also infinitely *high*. What is the *height* of God's love? In John 17, Jesus says, "Father, [about us] I want them to have the glory we have had before the creation of the world." In 1 John 3:2, it says, "Beloved, we do not know what we will be like. But we know we will be like him, because when we see him, we will see him as he is." That is the height of God's love. He is going to give us the same thing that fills his heart with infallible joy from all eternity. He is going to show us his glory, and he is going to give us that glory.

Can you think of anything higher than that? That is where Jesus' love is taking us.

What have we just done? We just did a brief meditation. We meditated on the dimensions of Christ's love. If, as we do that, the Spirit gives us some power to grasp it, we will encounter God. That will change the way we see all of life and how we behave in this world. Spiritual experience consists of luminous truth and profound assurance of God's fatherly love.

Yet there is another way to speak of it.

The Face of Christ

David says, "Your face will I seek" (Ps 27:8). God is, of course, omnipresent—he is everywhere (Ps 139:7–12). What does it mean, then, to seek his face and to "draw near" if he is everywhere already? When we speak to someone, we don't look at and address his or her kneecaps or feet or back or stomach. We address the person to his or her face. The face is the "relational gate" into a person's mind and heart. To seek God's face is not to find some place in space where God is located. Rather, it is to have our hearts enabled by the Holy Spirit to sense his reality and presence. "The Lord spoke to you face to face out of the fire on the mountain" (Deut 5:4; cf. Gen 32:30; Num 6:25–26). People are called by God to "pray and seek my face" (2 Chron 7:14). To lose a sense of God's presence is to lose God's face (Ps 13:1), and to seek his face is to seek communion with him, a real interaction with God, sharing thoughts and love.

In the Old Testament, however, we are told that no one can see God's face and live (Ex 33:20). Despite this, the beginning of John's gospel tells us that Jesus, the Word of God, became flesh and "we beheld his glory" (John 1:14). Because of his shed blood and forgiveness, we can have a nearness to God that was not possible before. Jesus' person and work is the breakthrough for any who want to draw near and seek God's face.

John Owen gave great attention to 2 Corinthians 3:18—"And we all, who with unveiled faces contemplate the Lord's glory, are being transformed into his image with ever-increasing glory which comes from the Lord, who is the Spirit"—in connection with 2 Corinthians 4:6, where Paul says that God has given us "the light of the knowledge of God's glory displayed in the face of Christ." Throughout Owen's writing, he returns continually to the subject of what has been called the beatific vision. The term describes the direct sight of the glory of God. This is what the redeemed will have in heaven fully, by sight, and what believers have now on earth partially, by faith and not yet with our literal eyes. While Catholic theologian Thomas Aquinas made this the centerpiece of his thought, very few Protestant theologians have touched on it at all. Yet Owen "is doggedly insistent that meditating upon the beatific vision is a vital practice for all Christians to cultivate," because "our Christian life and thinking should be oriented toward the hope of the beatific vision, and shaped by the foretaste we receive of it here and now."[286]

Owen did not understand "beholding the glory of God in the face of Jesus Christ" to be either an esoteric subject or something only for certain highly spiritual kinds of people. With great force he argued that no one "will ever behold the glory of Christ by *sight* hereafter who doth not in some measure behold it by *faith* here in this world."[287] This raises the stakes on prayer and meditation to high levels. Owen held that, unless you learn how to behold the glory of Christ, you are not actually living a truly Christian life in this world.

What does "beholding" Christ's glory mean, according to Owen? It is important that "we rest not in the notion of this truth [of Christ's glory as] . . . a bare assent of the doctrine of it." He rightly observed that, when Paul spoke of *beholding* Christ's glory, he could not be talking of mere belief that Jesus was glorious. Rather, "the affecting power of it upon our hearts is that which we should aim at. . . . Doth it not fill and satiate . . . with joy, rest, delight . . . and ineffable satisfaction? . . . It is our present view of the glory of Christ which is our initiation thereunto, if we are exercised in it, until we have an experience of its transforming power in our souls."[288]

To behold the glory of Jesus means that we begin to find Christ beautiful for who he is in himself. It means a kind of prayer in which we are not simply coming to him to get his forgiveness, his help for our needs, his favor and blessing. Rather, the consideration of his character, words, and work on our behalf becomes inherently satisfying, enjoyable, comforting, and strengthening.[289] Owen insisted that it was crucial that Christians be enabled to do this. He reasoned that if the beauty and glory of Christ do not capture our imaginations, dominate our waking thought, and fill our hearts with longing and desire—then something else will. We will be "continually ruminating" on *some*thing or some things as our hope and joy. Whatever those things are, they will "frame our souls" and "transform us into their likeness." If we don't behold the glory of God in the face of Christ, then something else will rule our lives. We will be slaves.[290]

Some years ago I spoke to a man who had gone to church all his life, but he was nevertheless a particularly fearful and anxious person. Under especially clear gospel preaching, however, he came to see that all his life he had basically been a moralist, assuming God would hear his prayers and save him because of his decency and ethical life and inner sincerity. In this view of things, God was someone with whom he had to negotiate in order to get the kind of life he wanted. Then through the gospel he realized the scope and depth of his self-centeredness, spiritual willfulness, and sin. He came to see that it was impossible to overcome this in God's eyes with his spotty record of good works. He also realized how unmerited God's love for him was, and how much this grace cost Jesus on the cross. For the first time in his life—he began to be attracted to this God. He gradually began to find his joy *in* God. Prayer became not just a time of going through his list of requests but also a time of adoration, confession, and simply enjoying God.

As God became more and more his heart's joy, he began to find himself becoming less anxious, more courageous. "In the past, it seemed so saccharine and unreal to say 'God is my treasure.' But now that he actually is becoming that to me—I just can't worry as much about money as I used to."

The choice is ours. If we want to be sure to experience this vision by sight hereafter, we must know it by faith now. If we want freedom from being driven by fear, ambition, greed, lust, addictions, and inner emptiness, we must learn how to meditate on Christ until his glory breaks in upon our souls.

Keeping Truth and Experience Together

John Owen's balance is striking.[291] He is unabashedly experiential. The term he uses for this is to be "spiritually minded." He writes: "Let us not mistake ourselves. To be spiritually minded is not to have the notion and knowledge of spiritual things in our minds; it is not to be constant, no, nor to abound, in the performance of duties: both which may be when there is no grace in the heart at all." That is, you can have all the sound doctrine possible and be fastidiously performing your ethical and religious duties according to biblical principles and have "no grace in the heart at all." What is the essence of real Christianity? He adds immediately: "It is to have our minds really exercised with delight about heavenly things, the things that are above, especially Christ himself as at the right hand of God."[292] Owen promotes what could be called a radically biblical mysticism. It comes through meditation on Scripture, on theological truth, on the gospel—but it must break through to real experience of God.

Because of his concern to keep spiritual experience tied to the Scripture, Owen was wary of the tradition of mysticism that developed in the medieval church. In his only book on prayer, Owen devotes a full chapter to assessing the Catholic contemplative tradition. He begins with a startling statement of the importance of encounter with God:

> The spiritual intense fixation of the mind, by contemplation on God in Christ, until the soul be as it were swallowed up in admiration and delight, and being brought unto an utter loss, through the infiniteness of those excellencies which it doth admire and adore . . . are things to be aimed at in prayer, and which, through the riches of divine condescension, are frequently enjoyed.[293]

Here is a writer who is not afraid of spiritual experience. Indeed, as we have seen, he teaches that regular delight in God and experiences of sweetness and love are the only ways to avoid being dominated at a practical level by false gods and enslaving passions and drives. Yet he is critical of the Catholic tradition because the Bible is not sufficiently emphasized as the main material for meditation and contemplation.

At one point Owen lays down a principle about the relationship of truth to experience. He writes: "Where light leaves the affections behind, it ends in formality and or atheism; where affections outrun light they sink into the bog of superstition, doting on images and pictures or the like."[294]

By "light" Owen means our knowledge of right teaching or doctrine. Our doctrinal and biblical knowledge cannot "leave the affections behind." If we believe with our minds that God is holy, we must also come to find his holiness enjoyable and satisfying just to praise it. If we believe the great God of the universe really loves us, it should make us emotionally unshakable in the face of criticism, suffering, and death. In short, we must be able to existentially *access* our doctrinal convictions. If doctrinal soundness is not accompanied by heart experience, it will lead eventually to nominal Christianity—that is, in name only—and eventually to nonbelief. The irony is that many conservative Christians, most concerned about conserving true and sound doctrine, neglect the importance of prayer and make no effort to experience God, and this can lead to the eventual loss of sound doctrine. Owen believes that Christianity without real experience of God will eventually be no Christianity at all.

Still, there is a danger in the other direction. "Affections can outrun light," which leads us not to unbelief but to "superstition, doting on images and pictures or the like." Here, Owen particularly has in mind many elements of the medieval church's mystical tradition. It is possible to use techniques of meditation and imagination to create changes in consciousness that are not tied at all to the reality of who God is. For example, it can be an extraordinarily powerful experience to vividly imagine Jesus walking into your room and speaking words of affirmation and assurance to you. Or you can imagine him coming into some past incident in your life, intervening, defending you, and embracing you. In such an exercise it would be easy to put words in Jesus' mouth that directly contradict his teaching in the Bible. Or, as we have seen, repeated words and phrases can bring about changes in consciousness, and trancelike states.

In Owen's chapter on Roman Catholic contemplative prayer, he lists many criticisms. He charges that the experience of perfect peace and calm, utterly undisturbed by feelings of either anger or desire, comes from the Neoplatonic philosophers like Plotinus. But Jesus prayed with vehement cries (Heb 5:7). The love of God does not extinguish desire but fulfills it. Owen argues that wordless prayer, while sometimes occurring, is never prescribed or seen as an ideal. In Luke 11, Jesus told his disciples to use words. In 1 Corinthians 14, Paul urged Christians to "pray with the mind" in words.

Another problem for Owen is that emphasis on ascetic techniques—which are conceived as rungs in a ladder from purgative, lower forms of prayer (such as petition and confession) to higher forms—can obscure the truth of God's grace. Prayer becomes a regimen by which one prepares oneself to be worthy of the vision. It also becomes elitist, something only monastics and others can do because it requires hours a day and complicated techniques. Last, Owen argues that in much mystical prayer there is a loss of orientation to the centrality of Christ's mediation between us and the Father. Much of the language of the medieval tradition talks about direct experience of God in his essence.

This tends to leave to one side the gospel and his saving work. For Owen, that is deadly. It means the experiences people are having are psychological. They are not contacting the real God, who reveals himself personally only through Christ.[295]

Nevertheless, despite his deep concerns, in the end Owen concludes: "It is better that our affections exceed our light from the defect of our understandings, than that our light exceed our affections from the corruption of our wills."[296] That's a remarkable thing for a Puritan to say. If we are going to be imbalanced, better that we be doctrinally weak and have a vital prayer life and a real sense of God on the heart than that we get all our doctrine straight and be cold and spiritually hard. In his treatise *Spiritual-Mindedness*, there is a passage speaking to this concept that is worth quoting at some length:

> In your thoughts of Christ, be very careful that they are conceived and directed according to *the rule of the word*, lest you deceive your own souls, and give up the conduct of your affections unto vain imaginations. . . . [But] we are not to forego our duty [to contemplate Christ] because other men have been mistaken in theirs, nor part with practical, fundamental principles of religion because they have been abused by superstition. . . . Yet I must say that I had rather be among them who, in the actings of their love and affection unto Christ, do fall into some irregularities and excesses in the manner of expressing it . . . than among those who, professing themselves to be Christians, do almost disavow their having any thoughts of or affection unto the person of Christ.[297]

Modern Roman Catholic writers like Hans Urs von Balthasar have acknowledged the difficulty of holding the "exterior Word" of the

Bible together with the "interior, indwelling Word" of the Spirit.[298] Von Balthasar concedes that the Catholic mystical tradition tends to rely too much on the inward, passing very quickly into a tranquil beholding, while Protestants are better at studying the Scripture in order to hear God, and then to wrestle with and respond to him. He counters, however, that Protestants, for their part, have too weak an understanding of the indwelling Spirit to lead them to profound experience. He thinks they settle for mere doctrinal knowledge.[299] As we have seen, it is true that many Protestants are hesitant about spiritual experience. Nevertheless, the best Protestant theologies of the Holy Spirit are more than adequate for the task, as Owen's massive treatises and robust spiritual theology attest.

Cautions and Appreciation

John Owen's critique of what he considers unbiblical mysticism goes hand in hand with appreciation for those who intensely desire—as the medieval mystics did—to be swallowed up by the glory of God. Owen did not shrink from saying that we *should* desire a "contemplation on God in Christ, until the soul be as it were swallowed up in admiration and delight." Yet his criticism is sharp of those who do not ground this contemplation in the Word and in the gospel of grace.

I believe Owen could have been more generous in granting at points the similarity of his own descriptions of spiritual experience with many of the descriptions by the mystics. Yet on the whole Owen is correct and strikes the rare and right balance, even preferring—slightly!—engaged affections over sound doctrine.

With this in mind, I think Protestants who find the biblical mysticism of a John Owen or a Jonathan Edwards appealing should read the medieval mystics with appreciation but also plenty of caution.[300] In the article "Why Should Thoughtful Evangelicals Read the Christian Mystics?" church historian Carl Trueman points out that medieval Catholic spirituality embraces what he (and I) consider a massive error—the belief that Jesus is resacrificed in the Mass and thus our pardon from sin was not completely "finished" nor our future glory guaranteed by Christ's death on the cross. This leads to many of the distortions in medieval mysticism that Owen points out: the idea that you can purge and qualify yourself for higher experiences, the strong impression that you can connect to God directly, and a general lack of use of the gospel itself in prayer.

Nevertheless, Trueman says of the medieval mystics, "There is a sense of God's holiness and transcendence in these works that is significantly absent from much modern writing and thinking about God. . . . What makes them mystics is their sensitivity to their very smallness and insignificance before the vastness of God who, in himself, is unknowable and who has chosen to reveal himself in the fragile forms of human words and human flesh. If the theology often leaves much to be desired, it would seem that the answer is not to reject the ambition of the mystics but to combine this ambition with appropriate theology."[301]

In the Garden of Eden, we sinned and lost the face of God. This was the greatest disaster possible, because we were designed to live in the unique, perfect, marvelous light of his countenance. We have wandered empty and destitute. Moses realized that, in the beatific vision of the face of God, all his longings would be fulfilled. He asked to see it—but his sin was a barrier. In Jesus that barrier is taken away and we can begin to see, though only partially and by faith, the light of the glory of God in the face of Christ. When we meditate and pray the gospel and its attendant truths into our hearts with the power of the Spirit, those longings are slowly satisfied, and other things in life become gifts rather than gods, and we slowly but surely and radically change in our character and in all our relationships. Augustine expressed it perfectly in the *Confessions*. He realized that all the things he loved were in God, the headwater of all streams of desire:

> But what do I love when I love you? Not the beauty of any body or the rhythm of time in its movement; not the radiance of light, so dear to our eyes; not the sweet melodies in the world of manifold sounds; not the perfume of flowers, ointments and spices; not manna and not honey; not the limbs so delightful to the body's embrace: it is none of these things that I love when I love my God.
>
> And yet when I love my God I do indeed love a light and a sound and a perfume and a food and an embrace—a light and sound and perfume and food and embrace in my inward self. There my soul is flooded with a radiance which no space can contain; there a music sounds which time never bears away; there I smell a perfume which no wind disperses; there I taste a food that no surfeit embitters; there is an embrace which no satiety severs. It is this that I love when I love my God. (*Confessions* 10.6.8)

PART FIVE

Doing Prayer

TWELVE

Awe: Praising His Glory

There are three basic kinds of prayer to God. There is "upward" prayer—praise and thanksgiving that focuses on God himself. We could call this the "prayer of awe." Then there is "inward" prayer—self-examination and confession that bring a deeper sense of sin and, in return, a higher experience of grace and assurance of love. That is the prayer of intimacy. Finally, there is "outward" prayer—supplication and intercession that focuses on our needs and the needs of others in the world. This prayer requires perseverance and often entails struggle. Through the next three chapters, we will look in turn at each of these fundamental forms of prayer.

The Alpha Prayer

In Jesus' instruction on prayer, the Lord's Prayer, praise comes first. In what ways is praise primary? Praise motivates the other kinds of prayer. The more we attend to God's perfect holiness and justice, the more readily we will see our own flaws and confess them. Seeing God's greatness also leads to supplication. The more we sense his majesty and the more we realize our dependence on him, the more readily we will go to him for every need. We could say that awe-filled adoration of God corrects the other forms of prayer.

Years ago I was preaching on the Lord's Prayer and commented—rather offhandedly—that since adoration comes before asking for "daily bread," we need to spend time thanking and praising God for who he is before we go to our prayer list of needs. One woman in my congregation took this to heart and a couple of weeks later related what a difference the advice had made. "Before," she said, "I would run right to my prayer list and the more I went through all the problems and needs, the more anxious and burdened I would get. Now I've started spending time thinking about how good and wise he is, and how many prayers he's answered of mine in the past. And when I get to my own needs—now I find I can put them in his hands and I feel the burden coming *off* me rather than on me." I never forgot her testimony, because she had taken a principle I barely understood myself and had appropriated it in her life.

Praise and adoration are the necessary preconditions for the proper formulation and motivation of all the other kinds of prayer. This doesn't mean we can never go immediately to petition or confession, but it means that, in our overall prayer life, praise and adoration must have a prime place.

The Health of Praise

Another reason for the primacy of praise is that it has such power to heal what is wrong with us and create inner spiritual health.

One of the most influential modern essays on praising God is "A

Word about Praising" in C. S. Lewis's book *Reflections on the Psalms*.[302]
Lewis begins recounting a problem he had with many of the Psalms,
namely that God so often calls people to praise him. "We despise the
man who demands continued assurance of his own virtue, intelligence,
or delightfulness," Lewis responded. It almost seemed as if God were
saying, "What I most want is to be told that I am good and great."[303]

As time went on, Lewis began to reflect on why we praise anything
at all. What do we mean, for example, when we say that a picture, a
piece of music, or a book is "admirable"? We mean that people *ought*
to admire those things, and if they do not, they will lose out and miss
something wonderful. This began to help Lewis understand the calls
to praise God. If God is the great object of admiration behind all other
beauties and magnificence, then to praise and admire him would be
"simply to be awake, to have entered the real world," while not doing
so would be to become far more profoundly crippled than those who
are blind, deaf, and bedridden.[304]

That was not all he discovered. "The most obvious fact about
praise—whether of God or anything—strangely escaped me." He had
never noticed that all enjoyment spontaneously overflows into praise
unless "shyness or the fear of boring others is deliberately brought in
to check it." When you find anything great or enthralling, you have an
almost visceral, instinctive need to praise it to others and get others to
recognize it. "Listen to this!" you say to your friend. "I can't wait for
you to read it! You'll absolutely love it." "Isn't it great? Isn't it wonderful?" Why, when we have had our imaginations captured by something, do we unavoidably *need* to do this? Lewis answered:

> I think we delight to praise what we enjoy because the praise
> not merely expresses but completes the enjoyment; it is its
> appointed consummation. It is not out of compliment that

lovers keep on telling one another how beautiful they are; the delight is incomplete until it is expressed. . . . This is so even when our expressions are inadequate, as of course they usually are. But how if one could really and fully praise even such things to perfection—utterly "get out" in poetry or music or paint the upsurge of appreciation which almost bursts you? Then indeed the object would be fully appreciated and our delight would have attained perfect development.[305]

This insight was a breakthrough for Lewis, and it has been the same for many who have read his chapter, including me. It reveals that we must praise God or live in unreality and poverty. We cannot merely believe in our minds that he is loving or wise or great. We must praise him for those things—and praise him to others—if we are to move beyond abstract knowledge to heart-changing engagement.

Learning to praise, then, changes us. Lewis couldn't help but notice that

the humblest, and at the same time most balanced and capacious minds, praised most, while the cranks, misfits, and malcontents praised least. The good critics found something to praise in many imperfect works; the bad ones continually narrowed the list of books we might be allowed to read. The healthy and unaffected man, even if luxuriously brought up and widely experienced in good cookery, could praise a very modest meal: the dyspeptic and the snob found fault with all. Except where intolerably adverse circumstances interfere, praise almost seems to be inner health made audible.[306]

The Reordering of Our Loves

Why would praise and adoration have such an effect on us? It is because, of the three kinds of prayer—adoration, confession, supplication—praise is the one that directly develops love for God, and if St. Augustine is right, what we love is basically what we are.

James K. A. Smith, in his book *Desiring the Kingdom: Worship, Worldview, and Cultural Formation*, points to several models of human personality and identity. In contrast to them all, he chooses an Augustinian model—"I Am What I Love."[307] As Augustine puts it in his commentary on 1 John, "Such is each one as is his love."[308] Our most fundamental identity and life behavior is a function of what we love.

Augustine taught that all people seek happiness, and they attach themselves to things they believe will make them happy. That attachment is experienced as love. The main human problem, however, is that, because of sin, we misidentify what will make us happy. As we have discussed before, the result is disordered loves—loves "out of order." We either love what we ought not to love, or we fail to love what we ought to love, or we love more what we should love less, or love less what we should love more.[309] If a man loves making money more than doing justice, he will exploit his workers and employees. If he loves his career more than his children, his family relationships will break down.

The ultimate reason for our misery, however, is that we do not love God supremely. As Augustine so famously put it in prayer, "You have made us for yourself, and our hearts are restless until they find their rest in you" (*Confessions* 1.1.1). That means, quite simply, if you love anything at all in this world more than God, you will crush that object under the weight of your expectations, and it will eventually break your heart. For example, if your spouse and his or her love of you is more important to you than God's love, then you will get far too angry and despondent when your spouse is failing to give you the support and affection you need, and you will be too afraid of your spouse's anger and displeasure to tell the truth. Only if God's love is the most important thing to you will you have the freedom to love your spouse well.

Elaborating on this idea later in his *Confessions*, Augustine wrote:

> Wherever the soul of man turns, unless towards God, it cleaves to sorrow, even though the things outside God and outside itself to which it cleaves may be things of beauty. (*Confessions* 4.10.15)[310]

Smith, following Augustine, argues that our ultimate loves are constitutive of our identity. They determine "that to which we are fundamentally oriented, what ultimately governs our vision of the good life, what shapes our being-in-the-world . . . and makes sense of all our penultimate desires and actions."[311] The things we love individually not only determine our character, but what a society loves collectively shapes its culture. This latter idea was the heart of Augustine's great work *City of God*. He believed societies are the mutual associations of individuals united by what they love in common.

What does this mean? Smith's entire book is committed to the thesis that to change people most profoundly, we must change what we worship. Thinking, arguments, and beliefs are crucial as means of moving the heart, but ultimately we are what we adore. We are what captures our imagination, what leads us to praise and to compel others to praise it. Our inordinate anger, anxiety, and discouragement result from disordered loves. Our relational problems result from disordered loves, and our social and cultural problems as well. What can re-engineer our very inner being, the structure of our personality? What can create healthy human community? Worship and adoration of God. We must love God supremely, and that can be cultivated only through praise and adoration.

The Importance of Thanks

Many people talk about "praise" and "thanksgiving" as being two kinds of prayer, and there certainly are important distinctions that should be kept in mind so that we can be careful to do each one. Ultimately, however, thanksgiving is a subcategory of praise. Thanksgiving is praising God for what he has done, while "praise proper" is adoring God for who he is in himself. Psalm 135 calls us to praise the Lord, and Psalm 136 to give thanks, and yet close inspection shows how the two tend to overlap. Psalm 135 praises God for having delivered Israel from slavery in Egypt, and Psalm 136 thanks God for being loving and good. Thanksgiving for a blessing automatically draws our mind toward the attributes and loving purposes of the God who has done the blessing. Praise for God's love and goodness transforms effortlessly into thanksgiving for all the examples of his goodness in our life.

If we are going to make headway in the work of praise and thanksgiving, we need to know what we are up against. Confession and repentance are often driven by circumstances. We fall or fail and we are burdened with guilt and shame—so we pray fervently. Supplication and intercession are also driven by circumstances. A friend or family member gets a diagnosis of cancer, or our career looks like it is about to take a bad turn—so we pray fervently. In these cases the prayers are fueled by the external circumstances and our sense of helplessness.

When good things happen to us, we would expect that they would provoke thanks and praise in the same way that bad things cause petition and supplication. Yet that is not the case. In Romans 1:18–21, Paul is describing the character of human sin. He writes: "For although they knew God, they neither glorified him as God nor gave thanks to him." That sounds rather anticlimactic. That's the essence of sin—that we don't "give thanks"? Is that such a big deal? Yes, it is.

Think about plagiarism for a moment. Why is plagiarism taken so seriously? It is claiming that you came up with an idea yourself when you did not. It is not acknowledging dependence, that you got the idea from someone else. Plagiarism is a refusal to *give thanks* and give credit and is, therefore, a form of theft. It not only wrongs the author of the idea—it also puts you in a vulnerable position, because you are not capable of producing such ideas yourself in the future.

Do you see, then, why God takes this seriously? *Cosmic* ingratitude is living in the illusion that you are spiritually self-sufficient. It is taking credit for something that was a gift. It is the belief that you know best how to live, that you have the power and ability to keep your life on the right path and protect yourself from danger. That is a delusion, and a dangerous one. We did not create ourselves, and we can't keep our lives going one second without his upholding power. Yet we hate that knowledge, Paul says, and we repress it. We hate the idea that we are utterly and completely dependent on God, because then we would be obligated to him and would not be able to live as we wish. We would have to defer to the one who gives us everything.

Therefore, because the sin in our hearts makes us desperate to keep control of our lives and to live the way we want, we cannot acknowledge the magnitude and scope of what we owe him. We are never as thankful as we should be. When good things come to us, we do everything possible to tell ourselves we accomplished that or at least deserve it. We take the credit. And when our lives simply are going along pretty smoothly, without a lot of difficulties, we don't live in quiet, amazed, thankful consciousness of it. In the end, we not only rob God of the glory due him, but the assumption that we are keeping our lives going robs *us* of the joy and relief that constant gratitude to an all-powerful God brings.

We have a problem with thanks and praise, and yet praise is the alpha prayer—the one kind of prayer that properly motivates, energizes, and shapes the others. What will we do about our problem?

The Habit of Praise

If thanks and praise are more contrary to our hearts than other kinds of prayer, how can we develop better habits of mind? There are three ways I can think of, and they are indebted to three British Christian writers.

First, we should learn to do what C. S. Lewis speaks about in his book on prayer, *Letters to Malcolm.* He deliberately tries to see all pleasures as "shafts of the glory as it strikes our sensibility. . . . I have tried . . . to make every pleasure into a channel of adoration." By "pleasure" Lewis means things as diverse as a beautiful mountain valley, delicious food, a great book, or a piece of music. What does it mean to make every pleasure into adoration? He quickly points out that, while we should give God thanks for every pleasure, Lewis means something more. "Gratitude exclaims . . . 'How good of God to give me this.' Adoration says, 'What must be the quality of that Being whose far-off and momentary coruscations are like this!' *One's mind runs back up the sunbeam to the sun.*"[312] He learns to instinctively think "What *kind* of God would create this, give me this?" He concludes that while he doesn't succeed in always keeping this discipline, it has enriched both his joy in everyday life and his concentrated times of prayer. He says we "shall not be able to adore God on the highest occasions if we have learned no habit of doing so on the lowest."[313]

The second way to develop the habit of adoration comes from the great sixteenth-century English Reformer Thomas Cranmer, the author of the original Book of Common Prayer. The "collects" or corporate prayers that Cranmer wrote for the book followed a general structure.

1. The address—a name of God
2. The doctrine—a truth about God's nature that is the basis for the prayer
3. The petition—what is being asked for
4. The aspiration—what good result will come if the request is granted
5. In Jesus' name—this remembers the mediatorial role of Jesus

We see this structure in Cranmer's famous collect for the service of Holy Communion.

1. Almighty God,
2. unto whom all hearts are open, all desires known, and from whom no secrets are hid,
3. cleanse the thoughts of our hearts by the inspiration of thy Holy Spirit,
4. that we may perfectly love thee, and worthily magnify thy holy name,
5. through Jesus Christ our Lord, Amen.

See how the prayer moves from a grounding in God's nature (why we can ask) to the petition (what we want) to the aspiration (what we will do with it if we get it). It is remarkable how this pattern combines praise with petition, sound theology with deep aspirations of heart, and concrete goals for our daily life.[314]

One of the ways to cultivate this same maturity in prayer is to write your prayers to God in a journal and follow this basic design until it becomes a habit. Eventually, you will find that when praying aloud or praying privately, you will instinctively start any petition by looking at God himself and appealing to that as you cry out to him. That's what it means to call on his *name*, on who he is.

The last guide is Matthew Henry, a Welsh Presbyterian minister of the late seventeenth century. Best known for his commentary on the whole Bible, he also wrote the book *A Method for Prayer*. The book is an encyclopedic digest of the prayers in the Bible—from short ones to long ones—categorized under the headings: Praise, Confession, Petition, Thanksgiving, and Intercession. Within each chapter the prayers are also clustered into subheadings, and I have found that these subheadings can be extremely useful. Choose one of the headings, then look at a few of the biblical passages beneath it, and, finally, put the prayer in your own words. This is an effort to help us do with the whole Bible what Luther proposes we do with the Lord's Prayer—turn it into our prayer.

Here are a list of my own headings, based heavily on Henry's, without the biblical passages. These may suggest ways to spend your allotted time in praise and thanksgiving.[315] Say these to God, addressing him directly as "you"; and all this will be praises.

Adoring God

- God is transcendently and infinitely bright, blessed, and beautiful. He is self-existent—depending on nothing for his being. Instead, all things are dependent on him. He is an infinite and eternal Spirit, the only perfect One, the God of absolute glory and importance.

- God's perfections are matchless and without comparison. Those perfections include his eternal and unchanging character; his presence everywhere; his perfect knowledge of all things; his perfect, unsearchable wisdom; his absolute, irresistible power and sovereignty over all that happens; his unspotted moral purity, beauty, and holiness; and his justice—his inexorable judgment that will ultimately put all things right.

- God is a Creator God, the maker, protector, sustainer, and ruler of all creation. He is a God of truth, a speaking God with whom we may have a personal relationship. He is the covenant God, who is faithful to his promises, who has bound himself to us that we might bind ourselves to him. He is the triune God, one and yet three, Father, Son, and Holy Spirit. He is not only our King but our Friend and Spouse. Our hearts were made for him to be our only joy.

Thanking God

- For the ways he gives and sustains our physical life. For making us in his image, capable of knowing, loving, serving, enjoying him and other relationships; for preserving our lives thus far—bringing us through injuries and sicknesses so that we are alive today; for the supports and comforts that make our lives enjoyable, pleasant, and bearable; for the successes we have received, goals attained, and for the blessings we weren't wise enough or capable of achieving but which he sent anyway.

- For the ways he gives and sustains our spiritual life. For the plan of salvation itself, and how the Father, Son, and Holy Spirit planned it from the deeps of eternity; for Christ emptying himself of his glory for us; for his teaching and character that reveal to us the beauty of holiness; for Jesus' death on our behalf, paying for our sins, fulfilling all the requirements, bringing us into a new covenant relationship with God through grace; for the Holy Spirit, for his power and presence in our lives enabling us to understand God's truth, know his love and glory, be conformed to Christ's character, and serve others with his gifts; for the Word of God, the Scripture—for its wisdom and truth, and its power; for the church, its congregations and leaders, who have shaped and formed us, who have helped us grow in faith, hope, and love; for the Christian friends who have given us so much; for the assurance of our salvation, that we can rest in the hope of future resurrection and living with him forever; for being able to *know* that, no matter what, everything will be all right.

- For the particular mercies bestowed on us. Ways God has been patient with us; ways he has helped us change and break bad habits and patterns of thought, heart attitude, and practice; ways he has protected us from the fuller consequences of our own blindness and foolishness; ways he has revealed himself to us, giving us communion with him; ways he has answered our prayers; ways he has walked with us through pain and suffering.

The Omega Prayer

The last Psalms of the Psalter are all praise, and the final one—Psalm 150—speaks about praise in the strongest terms.

Praise the Lord.
Praise God in his sanctuary;
praise him in his mighty heavens.
Praise him for his acts of power;

praise him for his surpassing greatness.
Praise him with the sounding of the trumpet,
praise him with the harp and lyre,
praise him with timbrel and dancing,
praise him with the strings and pipe,
praise him with the clash of cymbals,
praise him with resounding cymbals.
Let everything that has breath praise the Lord.
Praise the Lord.

Why does the Psalter end in unbroken praise? Eugene Peterson believes that, just as all prayer is framed by praise, in the end, all prayer should and will end in praise. He writes:

> All [true] prayer, pursued far enough, becomes praise. Any prayer, no matter how desperate its origin, no matter how angry and fearful the experiences it traverses, ends up in praise. It does not always get there quickly or easily—the trip can take a lifetime—but the end is always praise. . . . There are intimations of this throughout the Psalms. Not infrequently, even in the middle of a terrible lament, defying logic and without transition, praise erupts. . . .
>
> Psalm 150 does not stand alone; four more hallelujah psalms are inserted in front of it so that it becomes the fifth of five psalms that conclude the Psalter. These five hallelujah psalms are extraordinarily robust. . . . [This means] no matter how much we suffer, no matter our doubts, no matter how angry we get, no matter how many times we have asked in desperation "How long?," prayer develops finally into praise. Everything finds its way to the doorstep of praise. *This is not to say*

that other prayers are inferior to praise, only that all prayer pursued far enough, becomes praise. . . . Don't rush it. It may take years, decades even, before certain prayers arrive at the hallelujahs, at Psalms 146–150. Not every prayer is capped off with praise. In fact, most prayers, if the Psalter is a true guide, are not. But prayer is always reaching toward praise and will finally arrive there.

So . . . our lives fill out in goodness. Earth and heaven meet in an extraordinary conjunction. Clashing cymbals announce the glory. Blessing. Amen. Hallelujah.[316]

C. S. Lewis says that a lack of praise of God is a lack of reality, and praising him helps us enter the real world and enjoy him more fully. This gives us an exciting, concrete vision of the future. Lewis argues that the more perfectly we can praise an object, the greater our enjoyment, and "the worthier the object, the more intense this delight would be." What will happen when, in heaven, we are able to love and delight in the triune God, the greatest of all beings, and "simultaneously at every moment to give this delight perfect expression"? What will that be like? The answer is that "that soul would be in supreme beatitude." In order, then, to understand heaven and the future for believers:

We must suppose ourselves to be in perfect love with God— drunk with, drowned in, dissolved by, that delight which, far from remaining pent up within ourselves as incommunicable, hence hardly tolerable, bliss, flows out from us incessantly again in effortless and perfect expression, our joy no more separable from the praise in which it liberates and utters itself than the brightness a mirror receives is separable from the brightness it sheds. The Scotch catechism says: "a

man's chief end is to glorify God and enjoy Him forever."
But we shall then know that these are the same thing. Fully
to enjoy *is* to glorify. In commanding us to glorify him, God
is inviting us to enjoy Him.[317]

That is an overwhelming vision of our future, and it enables us to
almost experience the beatific vision. It sounds lofty, but it is the most
practical of truths.

You believe in a loving God. Then along comes criticism, or rejection
(say, a relationship breaks up), or some failure that's a blow to your reputation in some realm. Anyone in such a situation will feel quite crestfallen
and downcast. But there is a difference between being discouraged and
being devastated, between sliding into despondency and not being able
to function. If God's love is an abstraction, it is of no consolation. But if
it is a felt and lived reality through prayer, then it buoys you up.

Do you ever notice that if you are doing a task, and you hear voices
or music or other sounds on audio only, you can tune it out? If, however, you are trying to do a task, and you are trying to watch something on video, it is almost impossible to tune out the video. That is
what prayer does—it takes something you believe about God that is
ignorable and detached from how you live your life and makes it vivid.
Prayer encounter with God takes the love of God, the greatness of
God, the power of God, the wisdom of God—which most of us experience only on audio—and puts it on video. Prayer plunges us into the
fullness of who he is, and his love becomes more real than the rejection or disappointment we are experiencing. Then we can handle our
problems, and we can hold our heads up again.

What could be more practical than that?

THIRTEEN

Intimacy: Finding His Grace

Free Forgiveness; Infinite Cost

God forgives. For contemporary people, who often have a one-dimensional view of God as a spirit of love, this doesn't seem all that remarkable. For the prophets and authors of the Hebrew Scriptures, however, the fact of God's forgiveness was an awesome, barely-to-be-believed wonder.[318] God is "a God of pardons" (Neh 9:17) who is "merciful and forgiving" (Dan 9:9), and yet this divine mercy must not be taken for granted. Exodus 34:6–7 says that God "maintains love to thousands, and forgives wickedness, rebellion and sin. Yet he does not leave the guilty unpunished."

These two assertions—one following the other—are startling to contemporary readers. God is forgiving yet also is so holy that he cannot let injustice and wickedness go unpunished. The two points are in themselves very clear, but how they fit together is not explained in these passages. At the very least, Exodus 34:6–7 reveals that God's forgiveness is neither simple nor expected. This is why David says in Psalm 130:3–4, "If you kept a record of sins, O Lord, who could stand? But with you there is forgiveness, *therefore you are feared*." David does not say, "Of course you are forgiving, Lord—that's your job." He trembles with amazement that the God of the universe, to whom we owe everything, would forgive rebellion and sin. The prophet Micah says it even more majestically:

> Who is a God like you, who pardons sin and forgives the transgression? . . . You do not stay angry forever but delight to show mercy. . . . You will tread our sins underfoot and hurl all our iniquities into the depths of the sea. (Mic 7:18–19)

The conundrum of Exodus 34:6–7 is actually the tension that drives the plot of the entire Old Testament. God relates to people by way of a covenant—a solemn and binding yet highly personal and intimate relationship. Both parties swear faithfulness to the other. "You will be my people, and I will be your God" (Ex 6:7). Despite the many covenant ceremonies and vows, the history recorded in the Bible is an account of individuals and communities continually breaking their promises and obligations to God. We would expect that this would mean God's covenant is null and void. The people's unfaithfulness should disqualify them from God's blessing. We would expect God to simply cut them off. Yet there are numerous statements throughout the Old Testament that somehow God will nevertheless remain faithful, that he will forgive and restore us (Jer 31:31–34; Ezek 36:24–29). Throughout the pages of the Hebrew Bible we face this question: Is our covenant relationship with God conditional, based on our obedience to him, or is it unconditional, based on his love for us? In the end, will his holiness and justice be more fundamental than his love and mercy, or will it be the other way around? Will he punish us or forgive us? The seeming contradiction of Exodus 34:6–7 expresses this suspenseful mystery, this great tension. How will it be solved?

The authors of the New Testament point out the answer to all the riddles of the Old. "God presented [Jesus] as a sacrifice of atonement, through the shedding of his blood. . . . He did this . . . so as to be just and the one who justifies those who have faith in Jesus" (Rom 3:25–26). Is the covenant with God conditional because God is just, or unconditional because God is our justifier? Because of the great saving work of Jesus Christ, the answer is—both. When Jesus died on the cross he took our curse for our unfaithfulness, so that we could receive the blessing he earned through his perfect faithfulness (Gal 3:10–14). Jesus fulfilled the conditions of the covenant so we can enjoy the unconditional love of God. Because of the Cross, God can be both just toward sin and yet mercifully justifying to sinners.

It is not surprising that everywhere in the New Testament Jesus is seen as the source of that most improbable of gifts, that of divine forgiveness. His blood is shed for forgiveness (Matt 26:28), he ascended to God's right hand to grant forgiveness (Acts 5:31), and the message with which he sends his disciples out into the world is to "preach repentance and forgiveness of sins" (Luke 24:47). Paul concludes, "In him we have redemption through his blood, the forgiveness of sins" (Eph 1:7).

Only against the background of the Old Testament, and the great mystery of how God could fulfill his covenant with us, can we see the freeness of forgiveness *and* its astounding cost. It means that no sin can now bring us into condemnation, because of Christ's atoning sacrifice. It also means that sin is so serious and grievous to God that Jesus had to die. We must recognize both of these aspects of God's grace or we will lapse into one or the other of two fatal errors. Either we will think forgiveness is easy for God to give, or we will doubt the reality and thoroughness of our pardon.

Both mistakes are spiritually deadly. To lose our grip on the costliness of forgiveness will result in a superficial, perfunctory confession that does not lead to any real change of heart. There will be no life-change. To lose our grip on the freeness of forgiveness, however, will lead to continued guilt, shame, and self-loathing. There will be no relief. Only when we see both the freeness and the cost of forgiveness will we get relief from the guilt as well as liberation from the power of sin in our lives.

Remembering the Freeness of Forgiveness

Jesus Christ paid for our sin. Sin's condemnation can no longer fall on we who have repented and believed in him (Rom 8:1). If we forget this, we turn confession into a grueling, self-punishing penitence rather than gospel repentance.

Martin Luther challenged the authorities of the church to debate his Ninety-Five Theses, which he nailed to the door of the Castle Church in Wittenberg, Germany, in 1517. The first was "our Lord and Master Jesus Christ . . . willed the entire life of believers to be one of repentance."[319] At first glance this appears to be saying that Christians never make any progress, that they are always asking forgiveness for repeated failures. Actually, he was saying the opposite, namely that repentance is the *way* we make progress in the Christian life. It is the key to growing deeply and steadily into the character of Jesus.

In Luther's view the gospel of free justification—that we are saved and accepted through Christ apart from any of our good works or efforts—changes the nature of repentance. When we forget the free-ness of grace, the purpose of our repentance becomes the appease-ment of God. When we aren't sure that God loves us in Christ, then confession and repentance become a way of keeping on God's good side with expressions of sorrow that we hope impress him with our sincerity and move him to take pity on us. If that is what repentance becomes, it is self-righteous and will be bitter all the way to the bottom. It will lead only to a forced compliance of the will, not a change of view, motivation, and heart.

Luther denounced this kind of legalistic repentance as self-righteous because it is essentially an attempt to atone for our own sin. It can become a kind of self-flagellation, even a self-crucifixion, through which we try to convince God (and ourselves) that we are so truly unhappy and regretful that we deserve to be forgiven. This is not confession in Jesus' name, but in our own name. We try to earn God's mercy through our own inner suffering of conscience. Through the gospel, however, we learn that Jesus has suffered for our sin. We do not have to make ourselves suffer to merit God's forgiveness. We simply receive the forgiveness earned by Christ.

The apostle John writes that if we confess our sins, God is "faithful and just and will forgive us our sins" (1 John 1:9). It doesn't say that if we confess our sins, God forgives because he is merciful (though that is, of course, also true). It says he forgives when we confess because he is *just*. In other words, it would be unjust of God to deny us forgiveness because Jesus earned our acceptance, as John goes on to immediately point out. "If anybody does sin, we have an advocate with the Father—Jesus Christ, the Righteous One. He is the atoning sacrifice for our sins" (1 John 2:1–2a). All those who are in Christ must and will be forgiven. Why? He has taken the punishment and paid the debt for all their sins. It would be unjust of God—and unfaithful to his covenant with us—to receive two payments on the same debt, so it would be unjust for him not to forgive us. This profound assurance and security transforms repentance from being a means of atoning for sin into a means of honoring God and realigning our lives with him.

Legalistic repentance is destructive. Paul talks about gospel repentance "that leads to salvation and leaves no regret," which is contrasted with "worldly sorrow [that] brings death" (2 Cor 7:10). In moralistic religion our only hope is to live a life good enough to require God to bless us. Every instance of repentance in this view of things is traumatic and unnatural—because it serves only to (we think) win back God's favor through our misery. Without a firm grasp of our free justification, we will admit wrongdoing only under great duress, only as a last resort. We will focus on the behavior itself and be blind to the attitudes and self-centeredness behind it. We will also take as little blame as possible, reciting all the mitigating circumstances to ourselves and others. When we do try to repent in this legalistic frame of mind—since we can never be sure if we have been abject enough to merit God's favor—we can never experience the release and relief of resting in Jesus' forgiveness.

I remember once meeting with a man who was in deep distress over an extramarital affair, which had taken place years before. He had kept it secret from his wife, who later had stood by him during his very serious illness and through some career reversals. She was now dead. He did not think God forgave him. I asked him why not. Although he had lived a life crushed with guilt, he explained that he did not think he had repented with enough humiliation to be forgiven. I proposed to him that he ask forgiveness not only for the affair but also for having a less than fully contrite heart. He looked at me in surprise, and wondered if God could forgive such a thing. Why, I responded, would Jesus have died only for extramarital affairs and not for hard hearts? This led to a breakthrough. When he realized Jesus paid the penalty also for the sin of his hard heart, he felt his hard heart begin to melt. A deeper awareness of the freedom of his grace—a grace not conditioned on perfectly penitent emotions—brought release and relief and, ironically, more profound and fully grateful humility before God.

This is all in Martin Luther's first Wittenberg thesis. If we know we are loved and accepted in spite of our sins, that makes it far easier to admit our flaws and faults. It gives us the deep spiritual and psychological security necessary to be quick to admit when we have been wrong. This softens almost all conflicts, since getting admissions of wrong is no longer like pulling teeth. This simplifies many personal problems, because when we have taken a wrong course of action, we are more readily able to see it and turn back. Most of all, we can more immediately and more often go to God with our sins, confess them, remember Jesus' sacrificial death, and relive in miniature the joy of our salvation. While there always is some bitterness and grief in repentance, deeper realizations of sin lead to greater assurances of his grace. The more we know we are forgiven, the more we repent; the faster we grow and change, the deeper our humility and our joy.

Remembering the Costliness of Forgiveness

It is wrong, then, to conceive of confession as an arduous process of self-purgation. The freeness of our forgiveness in Christ corrects that mistake. Yet it is just as wrong to take forgiveness lightly and to forget the cost of how it was obtained. I once heard a sermon by D. Martyn Lloyd-Jones in which he said that forgiving sin was the greatest problem that the just and holy God ever faced. He immediately surrounded this statement with the required caveats. Of course God is all-powerful and sovereign. However, he went on, all sins are like debts that must be paid. To forgive a debt means that *you* absorb the cost and bear the payment. Our great debt and sin against God required an infinite payment, and the only way God could forgive us was to bear it himself. Therefore, God the Father sent God the Son to take our punishment, who with the Father sent God the Spirit into our hearts to both show us and help us receive that costly forgiveness.

Why does this matter? If you forget the costliness of sin, your prayers of confession and repentance will be shallow and trivial. They will neither honor God nor change your life. British theologian John R. W. Stott, in his book *Confess Your Sins*, admits that many Christians routinely confess their sins. Yet most people do not find that their confessions change them. They usually go right back to the same bad patterns of attitude and behavior again and again.

Stott argued that confessing our sins implies the forsaking of our sins. Confessing and forsaking must not be decoupled, yet most people confess—admit that what they did was wrong—without at the same time disowning the sin and turning their hearts against it in such a way that would weaken their ability to do it again.[320] We must be inwardly grieved and appalled enough by a sin—even as we frame the whole process with the knowledge of our acceptance in Christ—that it loses its hold over us.[321]

When I was a pastor in a small town in the South in the 1970s, I counseled a married couple in my church. The husband had a problem with uncontrolled anger, and he often spoke very cruelly to his wife. When we first started meeting, he took the situation very lightly. Within his own peer group and subculture, many men were much more abusive than he was. After all, he reasoned to himself, he never hit his wife or threw things or broke things in his rages. I tried to make him see the seriousness of the situation, but he was unconvinced. Finally, his wife moved out. He came to me in a panic, now eagerly taking all my advice on how to make changes and reconcile with her. He insisted that he was ready to repent. He followed the counsel and she moved back in, but after a few months, his abusive language returned, and she left for good. It was clear that, while he was unhappy with the consequences of his behavior, he never saw the wrongness of the behavior in itself. He therefore never truly repented of his sin toward her.

This is a classic demonstration of Stott's principle. It is possible to merely assent that something is a sin without getting the new perspective on it and experiencing the new inward aversion to it that gives you the power and freedom to change. Put another way, there is a false kind of repentance that is really self-pity. You may admit your sin, but you aren't really sorry for the sin itself. You are sorry about the painful consequences to you. You want that pain to stop, so you end the behavior. It may be, however, that there hasn't been any real inward alteration of the false beliefs and hopes, the inordinate desires, and the mistaken self-perceptions that caused the sin. For example, this husband did not come to grips with his misplaced pride and insecurity, and his need for exaggerated deference and respect from women. His "repentance" was completely selfish, caring only about his pain and not about the grief he was causing his wife and God. He was only sorry about himself, not about the sin.

Stott therefore argues that real repentance should have these two components—admitting and rejecting. We begin by admitting the sin for what it is, but then "secondly, we forsake it, rejecting and repudiating it. . . . [This is to] adopt a right *attitude* towards both God and the sin itself."[322] For a biblical example, Stott looks to the greatest of all the penitential Psalms, in which David not only admits his sin but says, "Against you, you only, have I sinned" (Ps 51:4). He was not denying he had wronged human beings—of course he had. However, he was bringing himself to see that when he trampled on people, he was offending the God who had made them. Leviticus 6:2 shows the principle well when it says: "If anyone sins and is unfaithful to the Lord by deceiving a neighbor. . . ." David was bringing his heart to see that "all sins are first and foremost a defiance of the holy laws of God."[323]

Another case study illustrating these two parts to repentance is Psalm 32. First, there is simple *honesty*. "I acknowledged my sin to you" (v. 5a). David says he "did not cover up my iniquity" (v. 5b). There are many ways to cover up our sin. We may justify or minimize it by blaming circumstances and other people. However, real repentance first admits sin as sin and takes full responsibility. True confession and repentance begins when blame shifting ends.

David does not stop here, however. He says, "Do not be like the horse or the mule, which have no understanding but must be controlled by bit and bridle or they will not come to you" (v. 9). The mule does not love you enough to come to you just because you want it to come. It must be controlled through rewards and punishments. It will come only if you can make it worth its while. It will come only for *its own* sake, not for yours. David repents not like a mule—not just because circumstances have forced him to. He repents because he understands what sin is in the eyes of God, and in love wants to please his Lord. Just as real repentance begins only where blame shifting ends, so it also begins where self-pity ends, and we start to turn from our sin out of love for God rather than mere self-interest.

David does not grovel obsequiously before a tyrant; he affirms that "the Lord's unfailing love surrounds the one who trusts in him" (v. 10). This is a reference not to God's love in general but to his *chesedh*, his promised, covenantal, steadfast love. Christians, of course, have a far greater resource for grateful joy than David did. He knew the general promise of God to be faithful to us (Gen 15). We, however, know the infinite cost and depth of God's faithfulness, because we see Jesus Christ dying on the cross for us.

David, then, not only admits his actions to sin, he finds the attitudes of the heart that led to the wrongdoing and loads them, as it were, with thoughts about God's greatness and steadfast love until the motives for willfulness and selfishness begin to weaken and erode. He admits sin with the mind and forsakes sin with the heart.

John Owen on Killing Sin

It is only natural to ask, "But isn't this 'forsaking' a kind of wallowing in guilt?" Aren't we supposed to see ourselves as freely justified and loved children in God's family? Yes, but to be a child of God is not only to rest secure in his love—it is also to want to please and resemble our Father. This means that when we sin, we will take every opportunity to seek God's pardon for displeasing him, and we also will take pains to pursue hearts that will not displease him again so readily in the future. We won't simply admit sin but will forsake it, as Stott says. But how do we do that?

John Owen's short classic on this subject has the forbidding title *The Mortification of Sin. Mortification* is an old word for killing something. It is to weaken sin at the motivational level by meditating on God's holiness and love in Christ, and other biblical doctrines, and then seeing our specific sin in their light. That process makes the sin itself look unattractive to us. We come to see its folly and evil in this true light and find ourselves more able to resist it in the future.

This can only happen, Owen writes, if we aim to move beyond seeing only the *danger* of sin—its consequences—and find ways to convince our hearts of the *grievousness* of sin—how it dishonors and grieves the one to whom we owe everything. If we think just of the danger and then confess, we will find that our repentance is self-oriented and we will end up returning to the same character flaws and patterns of wrongdoing again and again.[324] Instead, Owen urges us to identify our habitual sin patterns and load them with "spiritually alive" thoughts about God and salvation that are poison to the sin habits.[325] What are those thoughts?

Owen brings out a remarkable range of doctrines to use on ourselves, to weaken sin's hold on us. He urges us to think of the intimacy we now have with the Father and the Holy Spirit, the justice of the Law, the costly sacrifice of Christ, the glory and transcendent majesty of God, and the patience of the Lord toward us.[326] He shows how we can meditate on each of these biblical truths in such a way that we find the fears, selfishness, pride, and willfulness within us diminishing, as fungus and mildew die under the warm rays of the sun. He does not give us a program template to be used by all. Instead, he calls us to learn the ways of our own hearts and to devise spiritual soliloquies—ways of talking or even preaching to our own hearts, using biblical truths in ways that especially weaken our particular false beliefs and wrong attitudes. Owen gives us some remarkable speeches—clearly taken from his own prayer life—showing vividly how "mortification" actually goes on in the heart.[327] Owen's model soliloquies never say, "I must stop this or I'm going to be punished," which nourishes the self-centeredness of sin even as you think you are repenting. Rather, they say things like "How can I treat Jesus like this—who died so I would never be punished? Is this how I treat the one who has brought me into this unconditionally loved state? Is this how I treat him after all he's done? Will I fail to forgive when he died to forgive me? Will I be anxious over the loss of money when he gave himself to be my security and true wealth? Will I nurse my pride when he emptied himself of his own glory to save me?"

While Owen shows that it is possible to weaken sin by meditating on a great variety of biblical doctrines, he privileges the truths at the heart of the gospel. He says efforts to stop sin that come from "convictions from the law" will only temporarily stop "particular sins," but those who seek to weaken sin "by the spirit of the gospel" will change the whole person—mind, will, and affections.[328] Owen is saying here that mortification arising from *only* the convictions of the law—that is, from a belief that we can save ourselves through our own efforts—cannot really change a sinful heart. It can only squelch behavior temporarily through external pressure. It is the truths of the gospel—Jesus' dying love, his unconditional commitment to us, his costly sacrifice, our adoption into God's family—that make the sin itself hateful in our eyes.[329]

This God-centered way of confessing and forsaking sin is a powerful instrument of change. Fear of consequences changes behavior through external coercion—the inner impulses remain. However, a desire to please and honor the one who saved you and who is worthy of all praise—that changes you from the inside out. The Puritan author Richard Sibbes, in his classic *The Bruised Reed*, says that repentance is not "a little bowing down our heads . . . but a working our hearts to such a grief as will make sin [itself] more odious unto us than punishment."[330]

Self-Examination and Repentance

Confession should not be done simply as a response to a sin about which you are already aware and convicted. Our prayer life is the place where we should examine our lives and find the sins that otherwise we would be too insensitive or busy to acknowledge. We should have regular times of self-examination, using guidelines that come from biblical descriptions of what a Christian *should* be. Martin Luther, as we have seen, advised regular or even daily meditations on the Ten

Commandments. His method of meditation included thinking out the way in which you have been violating each commandment in deed or attitude of heart. This kind of self-examination requires a good grasp of what each of the commandments forbids and enjoins. Many of the catechisms of the Reformation, such as the Heidelberg Catechism and the Westminster Larger and Shorter Catechisms, provide long, specific lists that will help you confess your sins. Another guide for self-examination could be the fruit of the Spirit listed in Galatians 5:22–24. This would require that you study and understand what each of the spiritual fruits are, whether love, joy, patience, humility, self-control, or some other. You must have a good idea of what each fruit looks like in life and also what its absence looks like. Once you have your own outline of all this through study, you could apply Luther's meditation method to each of the fruits and so conduct a good spiritual checkup and self-examination.

For example, the eighteenth-century British evangelist George Whitefield once wrote, "God give me a deep humility, a well-guided zeal, a burning love and a single eye, and then let men or devils do their worst!"[331] Those four features make a good summary of a vital Christian life. Here is how we could turn the four features into a daily self-examination.

Deep humility. **Examination:** Have I looked down on anyone? Have I been too stung by criticism? Have I felt snubbed and ignored? **Consider the free grace of Jesus** until I sense (a) decreasing disdain, since I am a sinner too, and (b) decreasing pain over criticism, since I should not value human approval over God's love. In light of his grace, I can let go of the need to keep up a good image—it is too great a burden and is now unnecessary. I reflect on free grace until I experience grateful, restful joy.

A well-guided zeal. **Examination:** Have I avoided people or tasks that I know I should face? Have I been anxious and worried? Have I failed to be circumspect, or have I been rash and impulsive? **Consider the free grace of Jesus** until there is (a) no cowardly avoidance of hard things, since Jesus faced evil for me, and (b) no anxious or rash behavior, since Jesus' death proves that God cares and will watch over me. It takes pride to be anxious, and I recognize I am not wise enough to know how my life should go. I reflect on free grace until I experience calm thoughtfulness and strategic boldness.

A burning love. **Examination:** Have I spoken or thought unkindly of anyone? Am I justifying myself by caricaturing someone else in my mind? Have I been impatient and irritable? Have I been self-absorbed, indifferent, and inattentive to people? **Consider the free grace of Jesus** until there is (a) no coldness or unkindness, as I think of the sacrificial love of Christ for me, (b) no impatience, as I think of his patience with me, and (c) no indifference, as I think of how God is infinitely attentive to me. I reflect on free grace until I feel some warmth and affection.

A "single" eye. **Examination:** Am I doing what I do for God's glory and the good of others, or am I being driven by fears, need for approval, love of comfort and ease, need for control, hunger for acclaim and power, or the fear of other people? (Luke 12:4–5). Am I looking at anyone with envy? Am I giving in to even the first motions of sexual lust or gluttony? Am I spending my time on urgent things rather than important things because of these inordinate desires? **Consider how the free grace**

of Jesus provides me with what I am looking for in these other things.

Perhaps the most life-giving and crucial part of repentance is found in using the joy and benefits of the gospel to *both* convict *and* assure you at the same time. For example, prayers of repentance for pride, for coldness and a lack of love, and for anxiety and mistrustfulness could sound like this:

O Lord, I fall into *pride*, but on the cross you made yourself of no reputation and gave up all your power and glory— for me! The more I thank you and rejoice that you did that, the less I need to worry about my own honor and reputation, about whether people are approving of me or not.

O Lord, I fall into *coldness and irritability*, but in the garden just before you died, you were so gentle and affirming of us even when we went to sleep on you. On the cross you were giving yourself for people who abandoned you or mocked you. The more I thank and rejoice that you did that for me, the more it melts away my hardness and makes me able to be patient and attentive to people around me.

O Lord, I fall into *anxiety and fearfulness*, but you faced the most astonishing dangers for me. You were torn to pieces, so bravely, for me, so I could be utterly loved and eternally safe in you. If you were courageous for me facing those overwhelming cosmic evils, I know you are with me now. Therefore, I can be steady as I face my problems.

Jesus Can Get the Spot Out

When Jesus turned the water into wine at Cana, he used great stone jars as the vessels for his miracle. The jars were used for the rites of ceremonial purification prescribed by Jewish law (John 2:6–8). The washings and the sprinklings were all ways in which the Jewish ceremonial system conveyed a crucial truth—that no one of us is what we should be, that we all know shame and guilt, and that we must do something to cleanse ourselves of the dirt and stain of sin before going into God's presence. By putting his wine in such jars, Jesus was saying symbolically that he came to bring the reality to which all the ceremonial rites pointed—final atonement and cleansing from sin.

There may be no more gripping depiction of the agony of guilt than the tortured speeches of Lady Macbeth. Having helped her husband with the murders of Duncan and Banquo, her mind breaks under the shame and guilt of what she has done. She sees spots of blood on her hand. "Out, damned spot! . . . who would have thought the old man to have had so much blood in him." She smells blood and sees the stain on her hand and no effort on her part can remove the stain. That's a picture of the human race, of course. We know we are stained, we sense it, but beating ourselves up and doing good works can't eradicate it. The stain seems indelible. "All the perfumes of Arabia will not sweeten this little hand. Oh, Oh, Oh!" Nothing she can do will get the spot out.

Jesus, however, says that he can do it. He died on the cross to get out the spots and stains that we cannot remove ourselves. That's why we must stop trying to cleanse ourselves through self-punishment, or to get a sense of cleanness by living in denial about our sin. Instead, we must go to him in prayer, looking to his work on the cross, and both admit and forsake our sin.

FOURTEEN

Struggle: Asking His Help

Strenuous Petition

A third form of prayer is supplication—asking God for things for yourself, for others, and for the world. The primal prayer is a cry for help. "Listen to my prayer. From the ends of the earth I cry to you, I call as my heart grows faint" (Ps 61:1–2). This kind of prayer looks rather simple and straightforward, hardly the sort of prayer that requires much instruction to do it well. However, looks can be deceiving.

The New Testament book of James says: "You do not have because you do not ask God. [And] when you ask you do not receive, because you ask with wrong motives, that you may spend what you get on your pleasures" (James 4:2–3). One way petitionary prayer can actually do us harm is if we see it as a means to say to God, "*My* will be done." We are prone to indulge our appetites, telling God in no uncertain terms how he should run the universe. Such prayer neither pleases God nor helps us grow in grace.

Prayer can avoid obvious arrogance, however, and still be manipulative. Many requests to God are like Friedrich Heiler's "ritual prayer"—they are ways of procuring blessings from the deity through compliance with elaborate forms and practices. They are meant to put God in the supplicant's debt. They do not seek God's face, grace, and glory so much as power to get things from him. It is quite easy in prayer, even natural, to ask wrongly.

Yet it is possible, in the face of all these necessary warnings about asking amiss, to be too timid. Prayer is not merely a way to get inward peace—it is also a way to look outward and participate with God in his work in the world. Donald Bloesch says, "Prayer is not simply peti-tion, but *strenuous* petition. It is . . . active pleading with God. It con-sists not merely in reflection on the promises of God but in taking hold of these promises" (cf. Isa 64:7). Paul asks the Roman Christians to "join me in my struggle by praying to God for me" (Rom 15:30). Prayer has been called "rebellion against the world's evil *status quo*." Indeed, it is listed as a weapon in the spiritual warfare against the forces of darkness (Eph 6:12).

It is quite natural in prayer to ask wrongly or not at all. We must learn to ask, and to ask rightly.

The Power of Prayer

The Bible is filled with promises about the power of prayer in the af-fairs of history. In the New Testament book of James, the author points out that Elijah, "a man like us," prayed away the rain in Israel and then prayed it back as a way to confront a corrupt ruler. James concludes that prayer can "have great power and produce wonderful results" (James 5:16). John Calvin, famous for his views of predestina-tion and God's sovereignty, makes some remarkable statements about prayer based on James's teaching. He says:

It was a notable event for God to put heaven, in some sense, under the control of Elijah's prayers, to be obedient to his requests. By his prayers, Elijah kept heaven shut for two years and a half. Then he opened it, and made it suddenly pour with a great rain, from which we may see the miraculous power of prayer.[332]

Calvin is both bold and yet careful in his language. He says that prayer "in some sense" affected the weather conditions in Israel. Obviously, in the ultimate sense, God is in charge of everything that occurs—our prayers could not possibly wrest control of any part of the universe away from God. However, it is part of God's goodness and appointment that he allows the world to be susceptible to our prayers. How he does this—how he maintains control of history and yet still makes human prayer and action responsible within history—is one of the most practical mysteries of the Bible. In Nehemiah 4, the Jews were rebuilding the wall of Jerusalem when they learned that they were going to be attacked by their enemies. What did they do? "We prayed to our God and posted a guard day and night to meet the threat" (Neh 4:9). In Isaiah 38, King Hezekiah was dying and the prophet Isaiah told him so. Then Hezekiah prayed and the Lord replied, "I have heard your prayer . . . I will add fifteen years to your life" (Is 38:5). And yet, when Isaiah brings this message to the king, he also tells him to prepare a hot dressing and apply it to the infection in order to recover (Is 38:21).

Why call this a "practical" mystery? The teaching is that our prayers matter—"we have not because we ask not"—and yet God's wise plan is sovereign and infallible. These two facts are true at once, and how that is possible is a mystery to us.[333] We feel that if God is completely in control then our actions don't matter—or vice versa. But think how practical this is. If we believed that God was in charge and our actions meant nothing, it would lead to discouraged passivity. If on the other hand we really believed that our actions changed God's plan—it would lead to paralyzing fear. If *both* are true, however, we have the greatest incentive for diligent effort, and yet we can always sense God's everlasting arms under us. In the end, we can't frustrate God's good plans for us (cf. Jer 29:11).

It is a tremendous truth. God deigns to hear prayer. He allows the world to be "in some sense" under the control of the power of prayer. Thus is prayer powerful and effective.

Austin Phelps makes this point in a chapter in his volume on prayer. He tells of Ethelfrith, the pagan Saxon king of Northumbria, who had invaded Wales and was about to give battle. The Welsh were Christians, and as Ethelfrith was observing the army of his opponents spread out before him, he noticed a host of unarmed men. When he asked who they were, he was told that they were the Christian monks of Bangor, praying for the success of their army. Ethelfrith immediately realized the seriousness of the situation. "Attack them *first*," he ordered.

Phelps goes on to say that the non-Christians of the world often have more respect for the "sturdy reality" of prayer than we do. The power of prayer "is no fiction, whatever [we] may think of it."[334] If prayer is so powerful, how should we use it?

How We Should Ask

How shall we use this powerful aspect of prayer? We have seen that it is possible to ask wrongly, or to be too timid to ask. How can we proceed? I believe the Westminster Shorter Catechism gives us an excellent, nuanced guideline. We are to lift our desires to God with a view to his wisdom. The catechism puts it like this:

> Q. 98. What is prayer?

> A. Prayer is an offering up of our desires unto God, for things agreeable to his will, in the name of Christ, with confession of our sins, and thankful acknowledgement of his mercies.

We are indeed to ask God to fulfill desires—let's not shrink back from that. The Psalms are filled with examples of worshippers pouring out their hearts' desires to God.

Yet the catechism assumes our desires can be not only sinfully disordered but also perfectly well-intentioned though mistaken. We may think a particular request will help us or others, but if God were to grant it, we would later realize to our horror and grief that we had been wrong. Therefore, as a guard against both selfish motives as well as our shortsightedness we ask God to fulfill our requests with things "agreeable to his will." We are to ask God for things that fulfill *both* our desires *and* his will and wisdom (John 14:13–14; 1 John 5:14). It is natural to ask, "But how do we know what those things are?" The answer is, of course, that we don't always know. We pray for those things as we can best envision them and with a new open-mindedness, a willingness for God to do something different. J. I. Packer gives us at least three ways this works out.

It means, to begin with, that when we petition God, "we should lay before God, as part of our prayer, the reasons why we think that what we ask for is the best thing."[335] This is an insightful and practical idea. Packer mentions that many older Christian writers talk about "arguing" with God in prayer, which does not mean they assumed their wisdom or will was greater than God's. Rather, by "arguing" they meant "telling God why what we have asked for seems to us to be for the best, in light of what we know God's own goals to be."[336] This means embedding theological reasoning in all our prayers. It means that rather than simply running down a quick list of things we want, we should reflect on what we want in light of all we know from the Scripture about the things that delight and grieve God, in light of what we know about how his salvation works and what he wants for the world. Those who practice this discipline find that it helps them revise—sometimes deepening, sometimes lessening—their desires and purposes. It also gives greater power to our prayers so that when we are done we find we have really cast our burdens on God (Ps 55:22; 1 Peter 5:7) and can go out into our lives relieved of their weight.

Another implication of the catechism's guideline, according to Packer, is that when we make our needs known, we will explicitly tell God "that if he wills something different [than what we are asking] we know it will be better and it is that (rather than the best we could think of) that we really want him to do."[337] To try to say such words to God from our hearts, especially when we are asking for something we very desperately want, reshapes our hearts. If we find we cannot say something along these lines, it is a signal that we are dealing with one of Augustine's "disordered loves," a heart idol, a rival for God himself in our inmost being. It should trigger a great deal of self-examination. If we don't do such work, we will find ourselves enslaved to paralyzing emotions and out-of-control behavior.

If we can speak those words from the heart we will find, again, it calms our hearts. We can leave our concerns with God, knowing that he will hear them and act on them when and as is best. There is a peace and confidence that comes from such praying that cannot be experienced any other way. Here, of course, we are facing the perennial question—if God has a plan and he is in charge, why pray at all? The best answer is that, ultimately, "there is no such thing as unanswered prayer from a child of God."[338] Why not?

We have the assurance that God, our heavenly Father, always wants the best for his children. Therefore, as John Calvin writes, "God grants our prayer, [even if] he does not always respond to the exact form of our request," and later he says, "even when he does not comply with our wishes, [he] is still attentive and kindly to our prayers, so that hope relying upon his word will never disappoint us." In short, God will either give us what we ask or give us what we would have asked if we knew everything he knew.

More than that, however, we know as we pray for good things that we already have the ultimate good thing. In God himself we have the headwaters and source of all we desire, even if one of the tributaries of our joy, something in this world that we love, goes dry. "For though all things fail us, yet God will never forsake us, who cannot disappoint . . . since all good things are contained in him and he will reveal them to us . . . when his Kingdom will be plainly manifested."[339]

This is the "safety catch" on prayer—without it, wise people would never pray again. We can be sure that, if we ask for something that wouldn't be best for us, God won't give it to us. We must have the assurance that he will answer the basic desire but find a form and mode that isn't harmful. Abraham asked God to give the son he already had—Ishmael—God's special blessing rather than the son he did not yet have—Isaac. "If only Ishmael might live under your blessing!" (Gen 17:18). God responded no and yes. No, it is Isaac, not Ishmael, who was God's chosen one to bring his covenant people and salvation into the world. Nonetheless, God says of Ishmael, "I *will* make him into a great nation. But my covenant I will establish with Isaac" (Gen 17:20–21).

In my years training for the ministry, I was trying to become the kind of person who could be a preacher and pastor. When I entered seminary I was in a relationship with a woman who subsequently wanted to break up with me. So I prayed fervently: "O Lord, I can't do this without her. I really need her. Please don't break up this relationship." In hindsight, it was a misguided prayer. It is a good thing the relationship broke up because I later married Kathy, but that is not how I felt at the time. Did God deny my prayer? Yes but no, because there was at the core of the prayer a desire for God to give me a ministry partner. This was the implicit request. Then there was the mistaken part: "This is the woman who will help me."

The Spirit, even when you do not know how to pray, takes your core prayer and prays as you should be praying before the throne (cf. Rom 8:26). When you struggle in prayer, you can come before God with the confidence that he is going to give you what you would have asked for if you knew everything he knows. He does care, and he loves you boundlessly.

Lifting up our desires with a view to God's wisdom has one more effect on our petitions that we have not mentioned. We must ask ourselves "what we ourselves might need to do to implement answers to our prayers."[340] To some degree the answers to many of our petitions would be facilitated by changes in *us*, but we usually do not take time to consider this as we pray. We should discipline ourselves to connect each petition to what we know about God, but we should also ask ourselves what our petition tells us about our own motives, our own loves, and even our own sins and weaknesses.

For all of these reasons Packer is concerned about how many Christians tend to pray from long "prayer lists." The theological thinking and self-reflection that should accompany supplication takes time. Prayer lists and other such methods may lead us to very speedily move through names and needs with a cursory statement "if it is your will" without the discipline of backing up our requests with thoughtful reasoning. Packer writes that "if we are going to take time to think our way into the situations and personal lives on which our intercessions focus," we may not be able to pray for as many items and issues. "Our amplifyings and argumentation will [then] lift our intercessions from the shopping list, prayer-wheel level to the apostolic category of what Paul called 'struggle'" (Col 2:1–3).[341]

Two Purposes of Petitionary Prayer

We are seeing the necessary balance of two purposes of petitionary prayer—to put the world right ("thy kingdom come") and to align our hearts with God ("thy will be done"). Neither of these should get the upper hand or our supplications will become either too shrill and frantic or too passive and defeatist. We must make our desires known—and also rest in his wisdom. These elements come back-to-back in the Lord's Prayer, and we also see them together in Jesus' own great prayer in Gethsemane: "If it is possible, may this cup be taken from me. Yet not as I will, but as you will" (Matt 26:39).

One is *external*. Through our petitions, God effects the circumstances of history (James 5:16b–18). He will work justice in the world through our prayers (Luke 18:7–8). There are many things that he says he will not give or effect until we ask (James 4:2b). When we do ask, he will give us above and beyond what we have asked for (Eph 3:20). He will begrudge us no good thing that we ask for (James 1:6). All of this means we should pray assertively and confidently. We should be like Hezekiah, who took the threatening letter from the Assyrian king and "spread it out before the Lord" (Is 37:14), offering a mighty prayer for protection. We have a God who runs the universe and is also our heavenly Father. Therefore, Jesus says we should pray with "shameless audacity" (Luke 11:8). The Greek word here is remarkable—it ordinarily means "rudeness or impertinence." Even though we are, the author of Hebrews says, to "worship God acceptably with reverence and awe" (Heb 12:28), we nonetheless are to assertively spread our concerns before God.

On the other hand, we see that the second goal of petitionary prayer is *internal*. Through our petitions, we receive peace and rest. Just as physical sleep is "giving up control," so petition is giving up control, a resting and trusting in God to care for our needs. We must pray not only with shameless assertiveness but, at the same time, with a restful submissiveness, a confidence that God is wiser than we are and wants the best for us.

We see these two purposes of petitionary prayer near the very beginning of the Psalter. Psalm 4 is an evening prayer, oriented toward accepting what has happened that day and reflecting on it in light of God. Psalm 5 is a morning prayer, oriented toward asking God to change the status quo in the world. It is quite straightforward, asking God for protection from murderers and liars who are threatening harm (Ps 5:4–6). Nevertheless, before the assertiveness of Psalm 5 comes the submissive, heart-at-rest prayer of Psalm 4:4–8.

> Tremble and do not sin; when you are on your beds, search your hearts and be silent. Offer the sacrifices of the righteous and trust in the Lord. Many, Lord, are asking, "Who will bring us prosperity?" Let the light of your face shine on us. Fill my heart with joy when their grain and new wine abound. In peace I will lie down and sleep, for you alone, Lord, make me dwell in safety.

Notice how David, the Psalmist, achieves the goal of an evening prayer. "In peace I will lie down and sleep." The purpose of evening prayer is seen in the phrase "in *peace*." Evening prayer aims to give the soul the same peace spiritually that a night's sleep gives the body physically. The soul and the body rest better if they do it together. A troubled soul will lead to fitful sleep, and the body won't fully get what it needs.

The prayer that says "thy will be done"—the heart-at-rest prayer—is not primarily a prayer of praise or of repentance. It is primarily a prayer of petition in which the needs and concerns that burden us are prayed into the hands of God so our souls do not go weighed down into the night's sleep.

How does David get his heart at rest? In Psalm 4 we see a form of "self-communing" or meditation, David working on his own heart. "Fill my heart with joy when their grain and new wine abound" (Ps 4:7). He is saying something like this: "If I have the privileges of the gospel—assurance of and access to the love and grace and friendship of God, then all other prosperity and treasure pales by comparison." Years ago, the young Jonathan Edwards wrote a sermon with the following outline:[342]

1. Our bad things will turn out for good (Rom 8:28),
2. Our good things can never be taken away from us (Ps 4:6–7), and
3. The best things are yet to come (1 Cor 2:9).

If, as we lay our requests before God, we find ourselves sinking deeper into despondency, anger, or self-pity, it is because we have failed to really do this kind of heart work.

What We Should Ask For

From biblical examples we see three sorts of petitions: asking, complaining, and waiting. These are overlapping and not discrete categories, but it is nonetheless helpful to consider each one.

There are ordinary prayers for our own needs and those of others. Praying for our "daily bread," for ourselves, should cover the full range of what we need spiritually, emotionally, and materially. It means praying for freedom from our besetting sins and temptation, for clarity and energy to do our daily work well, for protection from injuries and sickness, for the financial means to support ourselves and our family. It includes asking, above all, for communion and fellowship with God.

Prayer for others and for the world has been called intercessory prayer. This includes the needs of family members and friends as well as opponents and even enemies. Be sure to remember to pray for individuals you meet during the day who are suffering or in difficulty. There are many places in the Bible that encourage prayer for the sick (cf. James 5:15). It means praying for faith for those around you who don't know Christ and especially for those who seem to be searching spiritually. It also means prayers in general for both the church and the world. For the church, pray for its vitality and protection and faithfulness. For the world, pray for peace rather than war and strife, for prosperity rather than poverty and hunger, for freedom rather than tyranny and slavery, for the virtue of leaders and the health of societies.

Another category of petitionary prayer that looms large in the Bible has traditionally been called a lament when it appears in the Psalms. This is the prayer of someone in suffering and difficulty, who is wrestling with God's will, perhaps questioning his ways, and seeking help to understand and endure.[343] J. I. Packer comes right out and calls this kind of petition "complaining." He admits that no one likes people who whine and complain, but he points out that in the Bible, when "bad things happen to good people . . . they complain with great freedom and at considerable length to their God. And Scripture does not seem to regard these complaining prayers as anything other than wisdom."[344] He goes on to note that the plaintive question to God, "How long?" is asked almost twenty times in the prayers of the Psalms, and is almost a technical sign of this kind of complaining prayer.[345]

There are a variety of circumstances that appropriately evoke prayers of lament and complaint. There are prayers in the face of opposition, when individuals or forces are betraying or persecuting us (cf. Ps 13, 55). Then there are prayers addressing deprivation, particularly of one's health or of material goods (cf. Ps 6, 38). Finally, there are prayers of isolation, when the one praying is either far from home or has lost or has been deserted by family and friends (cf. Ps 39, 79).[346]

There is also a kind of lamentation prayer we find in the Psalms that cuts across the other categories. Psalms 39 and 88 can reasonably be called pitch-darkness prayers. Sometimes the sense of God and of hope is completely gone. In most "Psalms of discouragement," such as Psalms 42–43, we see the psalmist taking himself in hand and deliberately walking out of his despondency, but Psalm 88 begins and ends in darkness. Sometimes, Christians can feel they are in spiritual darkness for a very long time.

Why are lamentation and complaint usually left out of contemporary books on prayer? The reasons are many. Historian Ronald K. Rittgers, in his book *The Reformation of Suffering*, points out how both the medieval Catholic Church and Lutheran Reformers minimized the legitimacy of lament, because they believed it was important that Christians exhibit to God an unflinching, joyful acceptance of his will.[347] This can be, of course, a subtle legalism, a way of securing God's favor by being good and not complaining. Another reason lamentation is absent from Christian thinking and practice today is the consumerist character of so much contemporary religion. Most people in Western societies today who believe in God see him as obliged to arrange things for our benefit if we live a good enough life according to our own chosen standards. This is, in Christian Smith's now famous phrase, the worldview of "moralistic, therapeutic deism."[348] This soft contemporary moralism, along with an older, more rigid legalism, combines to dismiss complaint as a valid form of prayer.

J. I. Packer addresses this error head-on. As a British man, he writes that "Northern European–influenced culture has historically embraced the stiff-upper-lip ideal of human behavior, and habitually looks down on people who voice personal complaints in public as morally inferior weaklings." He argues that this fits more with the legacy of Platonism than with a biblical understanding of the person. Platonists believed in a mind-body dualism, in which the reasoning mind was supreme, while the emotions were part of the body. It was believed that we must control and squelch our emotions for the smooth working of our rationality. The Bible, by contrast, sees the heart and its loves, hopes, and faith commitments as the seat of both reasoning and feeling. We are to offer and submit both our thoughts and our feelings in prayer to God. Packer concludes: "Complaints . . . are integral to this new, regenerate life of communion and prayer . . . so complaint will be, or at least should be, a recurring element in the praying of the born again."[349]

A third and last broad category for petitionary prayer is often called "waiting on God." In a famous parable of prayer, Jesus tells of an oppressed widow who "kept coming" to a judge "with the plea, 'Grant me justice against my adversary.'" Jesus concludes, "And will not God bring about justice for his chosen ones, who cry out to him day and night?" (Luke 18:1–8). The point of Jesus' parable is twofold. We should be confident that God will hear us, but we should also be extremely patient with God's timing. We should be willing to pray with temerity and perseverance, waiting months or years for God to answer some things. "The Lord is not slow in keeping his promise, as some understand slowness" (2 Peter 3:9) means, quite simply, that our time frames are not in touch with ultimate reality. Our perspective on timing compared with God's is analogous to a two-year-old's with an adult's. God has good reasons for making us wait a long time to see some prayers answered.

However, it usually requires years of experience in petitionary prayer to get the perspective necessary to see some of the reasons for God's timing. In some cases we realize that we needed to change before we were able to receive the request rightly or without harming ourselves. In other cases it becomes clear that the waiting brought us the thing we wanted and also developed in us a far more patient, calm, and strong temperament. There are other nuances and beauties to God's wise schedule that we can just barely glimpse.

Jesus' Unanswered Prayer

We have already argued that there is, in the end, no such thing as "unanswered prayer." This, however, will seem a facile formulation to people who have prayed to God to keep a loved one alive and then found that the person dies nonetheless. Some requests that God turns down are shattering. After such an experience, how can we maintain the confidence to pray again? How can we really believe that God is hearing and responding to us, if he denies such desperate, heartfelt requests?

When we look at David's Psalms, we see that David maintained his confidence in prayer despite many deep disappointments in life and despite many denied requests, such as when his infant son died (2 Sam 12; Ps 51). How did David maintain the heart to pray after that? He had his helps. He had his experiences with God over the years in which God saved him again and again, and he also had revelations of the Spirit of God in his heart. We who live after Christ and who believe the gospel, however, have even greater resources for assurance that God will hear our petitions. We know God will answer us when we call because one terrible day he did *not* answer Jesus when *he* called.

Jesus prayed in Gethsemane that the "cup" of suffering on the cross be taken from him, yet his request was turned down. On the cross itself he cried out, "My God," but he was forsaken (Matt 27:46). How could that be? Jesus was the perfect man—he served God with all his heart, soul, and mind, and loved his neighbor as himself (Mark 12:28–31) and so completely fulfilled the law of God. Elsewhere in the Psalms it says: "If I had cherished sin in my heart, the Lord would not have listened" (Ps 66:18).

Sinners deserve to have their prayers go unanswered. Jesus was the only human being in history who deserved to have all his prayers answered because of his perfect life. Yet he was turned down as if he cherished iniquity in his heart. Why?

The answer, of course, is in the gospel. God treated Jesus as *we* deserve—he took our penalty—so that, when we believe in him, God can then treat us as Jesus deserved (2 Cor 5:21). More specifically, Jesus' prayers were given the rejection that we sinners merit so that our prayers could have the reception that he merits. That is why, when Christians pray, they have the confidence that they will be heard by God and answered in the wisest way. When Jesus taught his disciples on prayer, he gave them this illustration:

> Which of you fathers, if your son asks for a fish, will give him a snake instead? Or if he asks for an egg, will give him a scorpion? If you then, though you are evil, know how to give good gifts to your children, how much more will your Father in heaven give the Holy Spirit to those who ask him! (Luke 11:11–13)

Jesus is saying something wonderful and powerful. If earthly fathers, who are sinful, ordinarily want to make their children happy, *"how much more"* committed is our perfect heavenly Father to our well-being and happiness? That means there has never been a parent on earth who wants joy for his or her children as much as your Father in heaven wants joy for you, his child. There has never been a human father who wanted to answer his child's petitions as much as God wants to answer yours. Yet we know that God is not only loving but holy and just. How can he shower blessings down on sinful people who deserve the opposite? The answer is that Jesus got the scorpion and the snake so that we could have food at the Father's table. He received the sting and venom of death in our place (cf. 1 Cor 15:55; Heb 2:14–15; Gen 3:15).

We know that God will answer us when we call "my God" because God did not answer Jesus when he made the same petition on the cross. For Jesus, the "heavens were as brass"; he got the Great Silence so we could know that God hears and answers.

We should ask God for things with boldness and specificity, with ardor, honesty, and diligence, yet with patient submission to God's will and wise love. All because of Jesus, and all in his name.

FIFTEEN

Practice: Daily Prayer

A History of Daily Prayer

Paul said we should "pray without ceasing" (1 Thess 5:17), meaning that we should, if possible, do everything all day with conscious reference to God (1 Cor 10:31). There should be background music of thankfulness and joy behind every incident in our day, audible only to us (Col 3:16–17). This kind of spontaneous and constant prayer during the day should be a habit of the heart. We will never develop it, however, unless we take up the discipline of regular, daily prayer.

Daily prayer has been a biblical practice from time immemorial. "Three times a day [Daniel] got down on his knees and prayed, giving thanks to God" (Dan 6:10). The Christian medieval practice of *horae canonicae,* the daily, fixed hours of prayer—also called the Daily Office—was said to be grounded in Jesus' challenge to his sleeping disciples, "What, could ye not watch with me one hour?" (Matt 26:40). In the monasteries multiple services of daily prayer were held. Alan Jacobs, however, argues that the seven daily fixed times of monastic prayer—Matins (midnight), Lauds (3 A.M.), Prime (6 A.M.), Terce (9 A.M.), Sext (noon), None (3 P.M.), Vespers (6 P.M.), and

Compline (9 P.M.)—were eventually proven to be physically insupportable. Many of the monastic orders either decreased the number of services or distributed responsibility for the various prayer times to different brothers or sisters.[350]

When the Protestant Reformation came to Great Britain, the Reformer Thomas Cranmer was faced with the question of how to help ordinary people with a full day of work do daily prayer. He was also concerned about how medieval prayer practices, so tied to an extremely detailed liturgical calendar of holy days, provided people only snatches of short, daily Bible passages appropriate for the holy day. He believed it prevented people from becoming acquainted with the entire Bible. In his preface to the first Book of Common Prayer of 1549, Cranmer argued that the earliest church fathers made sure that "all the whole Bible (or the greatest parte thereof) should be read ouer once in the yeare" in the regular services and prayers of the church.[351]

His solution was to first eliminate the numerous prayer times throughout the day except Morning Prayer (Matins) and Evensong. Then he provided, at the very beginning of his prayer book, a "Kalendar" in which four chapters of the Bible were to be read daily—two for Morning Prayer and two for Evensong. As Cranmer notes in his introduction to the Bible reading calendar, this meant that the entire Old Testament was read through once and the New Testament twice in a year, with the exceptions of chapters filled with genealogies, parts of Leviticus, and parts of the book of Revelation.[352] In addition, Cranmer prescribed immersion in the Psalms. This too was an adaptation of clerical practice for laypeople. While the monastics with their seven daily services could get through the Psalms every week, Cranmer outlined a schedule by which all 150 Psalms could be read morning and evening and completed in a month.[353]

The result was a new and brilliant reworking of an ancient form. It was a Protestant Daily Office with a greater focus on the systematic reading of the Scripture. It called for twice-daily prayer that could be conducted either in community or privately. It provided both written prayers of adoration, confession, and thanksgiving and space for free-form prayers of petition, as well as a plan for the consecutive reading of books of the Bible, which has been called *lectio continua*.

This Protestantizing of daily prayer was also attempted by non-Anglican churches, though Presbyterians, Congregationalists, and others put less emphasis than did Cranmer on written prayers. John Calvin, however, prepared five brief, simple model prayers to be used for each of the five times of the day he advised Christians to pray,[354] calling for prayers to be offered "when we arise in the morning, before we begin daily work, when we sit down to a meal, when by God's blessing we have eaten, and when we are getting ready to retire."[355] Most Protestant churches, though, settled into a pattern of morning private prayer and evening family prayer. Presbyterian minister Robert Murray M'Cheyne's famous annual Bible reading calendar, developed in Scotland in the early nineteenth century, included two chapters in the morning to accompany private prayer and two in the evening with the family.[356] In addition, the Reformed free churches practiced con-gregational Psalm singing rather than morning and evening Psalter readings, in order to work the Psalms deep into the hearts and minds of people.[357]

In more modern times the practice of a single, daily "Quiet Time" was considered mandatory for two or three generations of Christian college students. In the 1930s and '40s, British and Australian evan-gelical leaders produced a short booklet entitled *Quiet Time: A Practical Guide for Daily Devotions*. It was first published by InterVarsity Press in the United States in 1945.[358] The thirty-page booklet subsequently became a million-copy seller and shaped and influenced at least fifty years of evangelical books and guides thereafter.[359]

Quiet Time spends a good deal of its short length insisting that daily devotion is a discipline that requires a very deliberate act of the will. It advises finding a quiet place and composing our spirits with the thought that God himself seeks to meet with us. It instructs us to use a journal to write down the results of our Bible study, after which we are to conclude with a relatively similar amount of time in prayer. The only period of time specified is twenty minutes, which is referred to as a minimum.

At the heart of the most practical part of *Quiet Time* is a summary of some of the prayer practices of George Mueller (1805–98), a well-known German Baptist minister and founder of orphanages, who lived most of his life in England. Mueller was noted for his prayer life, which he described in some of his autobiographical writings. He was particularly concerned to meditate on Scripture as a means of warming his heart and leading it into prayer. In this Mueller was following Martin Luther's lead. His method of meditation was also a classic. He had a set of questions that he asked of a text, which echoed Luther's own. *Quiet Time* listed them prominently:

> Is there any example for me to follow?
> Is there any command for me to obey?
> Is there any error for me to avoid?
> Is there any sin for me to forsake?
> Is there any promise for me to claim?
> Is there any new thought about God Himself?[360]

After Bible study and meditation, prayer is outlined as first approaching God in confession of our sins, then responding with thanks

and praise for our salvation via the cross. After praise comes intercession for others and finally petition for our own needs.[361]

Doing Daily Prayer Today

The late-twentieth-century evangelical Quiet Time tended to play
down the more experiential aspects of prayer. Interpretive Bible study
was stressed, including outlining a passage and paraphrasing it, and
looking for literary structures of composition. One daily devotional
called us to ask of a passage: "Are there any recurring thoughts exem-
plified by repeated use of the same word, phrases, contrasting words
or thought? . . . What is the direction of the passage—specific to general or general to specific—in the subject matter?"[362] This takes a good
deal of practice, and it is difficult to imagine it happening in a very few
minutes every morning. The effect was to promote a method of daily
inductive Bible study aimed more at interpreting the text than at meditation and experience of God. After this kind of Bible study came
prayer, but this more cognitive study did not lead very naturally to
adoration. Prayer, then, was dominated by petitions for needs and
confession of sins.

Many have found the traditional evangelical Quiet Time—with its
emphasis on interpretive Bible study and petitionary prayer—to be
too rationalistic an exercise. In response, and with desire for greater
experience of God, many Protestants have turned to more Catholic
and Eastern Orthodox traditions, including *lectio divina*, contemplative prayer, and fixed hours of liturgical prayer.

One of the most successful contemporary reworkings of ancient
fixed-hours prayer has been the volumes by Phyllis Tickle, *The Divine
Hours*. Tickle usefully puts short Psalm and Scripture readings, hymn

verses, ascriptions, and prayers all on the same page for easier reference than traditional Divine Office guides offer. However, her work resists several of Cranmer's Protestant innovations to daily prayer. She calls for three or four daily times of prayer rather than two, and she moves away from the systematic, consecutive Bible reading associated with Cranmer, Calvin, and other churches of the Reformation.[363]

Tickle's encouragement of written prayers is not, however, counter to Reformation practice. While some non-Anglican ministers, such as John Bunyan, were vehemently opposed to all written prayer forms,[364] some of Bunyan's contemporaries, such as John Owen, believed that prescribed prayer forms could be useful if they were written by godly "persons from their own experience and the light of Scripture."[365] Such prayers can be heart affecting and give stimulation and guidance to our own prayers.[366]

It remains for us, then, to find ways of daily prayer and devotion. In general, I think we need to move beyond traditional twentieth-century evangelical devotional practice as well as the current restoration of medieval prayer forms. No reader of this book will be surprised by now to hear me say that I think we could learn more from the prayer practices of Protestant theologians of the sixteenth, seventeenth, and eighteenth centuries. If we look back to those writers as we have been doing throughout this book, I see several important changes to make.

I believe prayer should be *more often* than the classic once-daily Quiet Time. Luther, as we have seen, believed prayer should be twice a day, while Calvin advised prayer to be brief and even more often. To frame the day, there seems to be unanimity from the Christian past in all its branches that we should turn our thoughts to God at set times more than once during a twenty-four-hour period. I agree with most Protestant churches that twice a day is good, though we cannot be too insistent on one schedule. I personally find morning and evening prayer the best for me, but I also try to sometimes practice a brief, midday "stand-up" time of focused prayer to reconnect to my morning prayer insights.

I believe daily prayer should be *more biblical*, that is, more grounded in systematic Bible reading and study and in disciplined meditation on passages. My reasons for this conviction have been laid out at length in this book. Cranmer's Bible reading plan for the year is no longer in most current Common Prayer books used around the world, but it can be found in reprints of the 1549 and 1552 books. M'Cheyne's Bible reading calendar, readily available in many forms on the Internet and elsewhere, takes you through the Bible at various paces, depending on the time you have to give. In any case, systematic, consecutive reading of the Bible should precede or accompany prayer.

Daily prayer in private should be *more interwoven with the corporate prayer* of the church. Calvin wanted Christians to learn private prayer from the public prayers and the Psalm singing in gathered worship.[367] Luther wrote that he prayed twice a day, either by hurrying to his room "or, if it be the day and hour for it, to the church where a congregation is assembled."[368] This shows how important it was for the great teachers of the church that our prayer life not be completely privatized. It is right and necessary that we learn to pray not merely from reading the Psalms and the rest of the Bible but by hearing and reading the prayers of the church. Many churches today, especially those with what is called contemporary worship, give congregants almost no help with prayer at all in this way. The only prayers congregants hear are "spontaneous" expressions of worship leaders, or the final prayer of the preacher at the end of the sermon. Time-tested and carefully considered prayers are not provided as they were in times past. This means that many Christians today will have to search out such prayers, and that is where Cranmer's matchless "collects" as well as other resources, such as Phyllis Tickle's *The Divine Hours* or Arthur Bennett's *The Valley of Vision*, can be helpful.[369]

Finally, daily prayer should include meditation, not just Bible study, and in general we should be much *more expectant of experience in the full range*. We should expect more struggle and complaint and "darkness of soul" but also more awe, intimacy, and experience of God's spiritual reality. John Owen is quite clear that if the affections of the heart are not engaged in prayer, real character change and growth in Christ-likeness is impossible. We cannot settle for less.

A Pattern for Daily Prayer

The most practical question of all, then, is "How do you actually spend time in prayer?" A helpful book, *My Path of Prayer*, contains a series of very short essays by a number of Christian leaders, many recounting their main pattern for daily prayer.[370] One of the contributors, Selwyn Hughes, provided this description of his own prayer life. He prayed as soon as he could after rising in the morning. He read a passage of Scripture and meditated on it, including a Psalm if there was time. He then took a moment to "still his mind" and remind himself both of God's presence and of the privilege and power of prayer. Then, he began to pray, always beginning with adoration, praise, and thanksgiving to God. After this, he writes, he moved to "pray for my personal spiritual condition," and by this he meant self-examination, confession, and repentance. Then he did what we have called petitionary prayer for himself, for those he knew, for the church, and for the world. Finally, he says, he would end by again stilling his mind and heart to be sure he had heard from God what he especially wanted him to learn from this time of meditation and prayer.[371]

This account is striking for not being very original. It is surprisingly similar to the descriptions of daily prayer we have seen by many teachers, including Martin Luther. Therefore, I think we can outline a pattern for daily prayer with some confidence that it will serve many people, always remembering that neither the details nor the order I am providing is written in stone, the Bible, or any particular religious tradition. I suggest this framework—evocation, meditation, Word prayer, free prayer, and contemplation.

Evocation. To evoke means "to bring to mind," though it also can include *in*vocation, calling on God. There is almost universal agreement that prayer should be started by "thinking over who it is that you will be addressing, what he has done to give you access to himself . . . how you stand related to him . . . [and] the truly breathtaking fact that through his Word and Spirit the Lord Jesus is building a friendship with you."[372] One of the ways to do this is to recap in your mind the Trinitarian theology of prayer. God is your Father now, and he is committed to your good. Jesus gives you access to the throne of the universe because he is your mediator, advocate, and priest. The Holy Spirit is God himself within you prompting and helping you to pray, so you can know that if you are praying, God is listening.

Briefly ponder verses that speak to you about these truths, many of which have been discussed earlier in the book. Or you could read one of the traditional Psalms used in worship for entering God's presence, such as Psalm 95. Another method is to take one of the tested prayers of the church, such as one of Thomas Cranmer's collects, to use as a kind of invocation to begin your time of prayer.[373] Take no more than a couple of minutes for what we are calling evocation.

Meditation. To respond to God in prayer, we must listen to his

Word. This means taking time to meditate on some portion of the Bible as a bridge into prayer. This is not something that usually enriches our prayer life overnight. It is much easier to move into meditation after Bible reading the more you have read and come to understand the Bible over the years. Serious study of the Bible is something that must be done in order to grow as a Christian, but it is a mistake to spend most of your daily time with God in an in-depth interpretive Bible study. It leaves you little time and perhaps no inclination to meditate and pray.

For those starting out in the Christian life, therefore, it would be best to set aside some regular time—apart from daily prayer—for serious study of the Bible. That way the Bible gradually becomes less and less of a strange, confusing jumble of ideas, and it becomes easier to read and meditate on it every day. One way to do this kind of serious study is to read through the entire Bible once, slowly, perhaps reading a chapter a day and covering it in three years or so, and using a short, good one-volume commentary such as the *New Bible Commentary*, 21st Century Edition, to do so, taking notes in a journal as you go.[374] While doing this study, you can earmark some chapters for further reflection. Then, in daily prayer, you can turn to those chapters for the reflective reading and meditation we have been discussing. The actual order in your daily devotion would then be like this: first evocation, then Bible reading and meditation, and then on to prayer.

Word prayer. From Martin Luther we get an important step in daily prayer that is often overlooked. After meditating on the Scripture, Luther takes time to "pray the text" before moving on to more free-form prayer. Meditation, as we have said, is not prayer per se. It is a form of reflection and self-communing. When the psalmist says, "Return to God, O my soul," he is doing this kind of heart inclining that is meditation. However, if you use Luther's approach to meditation—discovering something in the text as a basis for praising, repenting, and aspiring—then the meditation itself can be immediately turned into a prayer. The Psalms too have a form such that they can quite easily be turned into prayers and prayed back to God. "Praying the Psalms" is an important and time-honored way to do Word prayer. (See below for a few more thoughts on this.)

Luther's favorite way to pray a text of Scripture has been treated earlier. He advises that the person praying take the Lord's Prayer and paraphrase each petition in his or her own words, filling it out with the concerns on his or her heart that day. I believe this is perhaps the single best way to bridge from the Word into prayer because, of course, the Lord's Prayer is Jesus' own comprehensive model. I advise doing this at least once a week as part of this step in your daily prayer pattern.

Free prayer. *Free prayer* means simply to pour out your heart in prayer. Nevertheless, nearly all sound guides remind us to give thought to balance our prayers among the three forms—adoration and thanksgiving, confession and repentance, petition and intercession. This balance does not need to be wooden, though it can be a good discipline to move through them habitually in some order that works well for you. Here is also where prayer lists filled with causes and concerns can be of help, so long as we remember J. I. Packer's warning that petitionary prayer is only life changing and powerful if we do not rapidly run down a "grocery list" but instead lift each cause to God with theological reasoning and self-examination.

Especially for beginners, it can be very helpful to use the older volume by Matthew Henry, *A Method for Prayer, with Scripture Expressions, Proper to Be Used Under Each Head*.[375] As we noted earlier, Henry digs out of the Scripture hundreds of actual prayers and then organizes and classifies them under subheadings of the larger headings of praise, confession, petition, thanksgiving, intercession, and conclusion. If you feel your own times of free-form prayer have stalled, Henry's book affords an almost endless amount of grist for the mill.

Contemplation. We have spent a great deal of time talking about what we do and do not mean by *contemplation*. Edwards described contemplation as times when we not only know God is holy, but when we sense—"see" and "taste"—that he is so in our hearts. Luther described it as a time in which he finds himself getting "lost" in some aspect of God's truth or character. In the original German he says literally that sometimes when he is going through his prayer regimen, he discovers that "his thoughts go for a walk." Thoughts about God become "big" and affecting. Then he stops and takes time to follow the lead of the Spirit. He writes:

> It often happens that I lose myself . . . in one petition of the Lord's Prayer, and then I let all the other six petitions go. When such rich good thoughts come, one should . . . listen to them in silence and by no means suppress them. For here the Holy Spirit himself is preaching and one word of his sermon is better than thousands of our own prayers. . . . [So] if the Holy Spirit should come and begin to preach to your heart, giving you rich and enlightened thoughts . . . be quiet and listen to him.[376]

As we saw when considering John Owen's teaching on meditation, we should not assume that after all is done, we will necessarily find our heart and affections engaged and the Holy Spirit opening our thoughts in new ways as Luther describes. That is not the norm for most people most times. We may begin and end our time of prayer with a sense of spiritual dryness or even of God's absence. In that case, this final moment of "contemplation" would simply mean to take the best thought we received about God, then praise and thank him for it and for who he is, and finally ask God sincerely to come near and show us his face in his good time.

What follows are two plans for daily prayer, one more full and challenging and one simpler for those starting out. Don't be intimidated by these plans. Follow the steps in the outline—approaching (evocation), meditation, Word prayer, free prayer, contemplation—without feeling the need to do all the specific proposals or answer all the questions within each part. Prayer will grow and draw you in.

A PATTERN FOR DAILY PRAYER

Morning Prayer (25 minutes)

APPROACHING GOD

Ask him for his presence and help as you read and pray. Choose from one of these scriptural invocations: Psalm 16:8; 27:4, 9–10; 40:16–19; 63:1–3; 84:5–7; 103:1–2; 139:7–10; Isaiah 57:15; Matthew 11:28–30; John 4:23; Ephesians 1:17–19; 3:16–20.

BIBLE READING AND MEDITATION

(Keep in mind that no one can do all of the following in any one session of meditation and prayer.)

To study the passage: Read it three or four times. Then make a list of everything it says about God (Father, Son, and Holy Spirit); list anything that it tells you about yourself; and finally, list any examples to be followed, commands to be obeyed (or things that need to be avoided), and promises to claim. When this is all done, choose the verse and truth that is most striking and helpful to you. Paraphrase the thought or verse in your own words.

To meditate on the passage: Write down answers to the following questions:

What does this text show me about God for which I should praise or thank him?

What does the text show me about my sin that I should confess and repent of? What false attitudes, behavior, emotions, or idols come alive in me whenever I forget this truth?

What does the text show me about a need that I have? What do I need to do or become in light of this? How shall I petition God for it?

How is Jesus Christ or the grace that I have in him crucial to helping me overcome the sin I have confessed or to answering the need I have?

Finally: How would this change my life if I took it seriously— if this truth were fully alive and effective in my inward being? Also, why might God be showing this to me now? What is going on in my life that he would be bringing this to my attention today?

PRAYER

Pray each of the meditations—adoration, confession, petition, and thanksgiving for Jesus and his salvation.

Pray for your needs and pressing concerns.

Take a final moment just to enjoy him and his presence.

Evening Prayer (15 minutes)

APPROACHING GOD

Ask him for his presence and help as you read and pray.

BIBLE READING AND MEDITATION

Read a Psalm, eventually working through the Psalter twice a year.

PRAYER

Turn the Psalm into a prayer and pray it back to God.

Think over your day and confess where you sinned or failed to respond as you should have.

Think over your day and pray for people you met or heard about who have needs or are in difficulty.

Pray for some of the more urgent and important needs on your heart.

A Starter Plan for Daily Prayer
(15 minutes)

APPROACHING

Think of the privilege of prayer. Realize God is present. Ask him to help you pray.

MEDITATION

Read a Scripture passage. Discern one or two truths you learn there. Choose the one that most impresses you and write it in a sentence. Now ask: How does this truth help me praise God? How does it show me a sin to confess? How does it show me something to ask God for?

WORD PRAYER

Now turn the answers to the three questions into a prayer— adoration, petition, and supplication.

FREE PRAYER

Pray about whatever needs are on your heart. Also spend time thanking God for the ways you see him working in your life and caring for you.

CONTEMPLATION

Take a moment to thank and admire God for what he has showed you today. End with a note of praise.

Praying the Psalms

From earliest times, the Christian church adopted the Psalms of the Old Testament to be its prayer book. A famous letter from the great fourth-century African theologian Athanasius to Marcellinus makes this clear. He wrote: "Whatever your particular need or trouble, from this same book [the Psalms] you can select a form of words to fit it, so that you . . . learn the way to remedy your ill." Athanasius goes on to argue that the Psalms show us how to praise God, repent for sins, and be thankful, in each case giving us "fitting words" to do so. Finally, he concludes: "Under all the circumstances of life, we shall find that these divine songs suit ourselves and meet our own souls' need at every turn."[377] There is no situation or emotion a human being can experience that is not reflected somewhere in the Psalms. Immersing ourselves in the Psalms and turning them into prayers teaches our hearts the "grammar" of prayer and gives us the most formative instruction in how to pray in accord with God's character and will.

What does it mean to pray the Psalms or turn them into prayer?

There are innumerable ways to do it, but here are some methods that have profited many.[378] One has been called verbatim praying. Many of the Psalms are already written as prayers direct from the author to God, so we can simply "pray the words as they lay." Psalm 90 works well for this method: "Lord, you have been our dwelling place. . . . Before the mountains were born or you brought forth the whole world, from everlasting to everlasting you are God."[379]

The second, perhaps most common way to pray, is to paraphrase and personalize the Psalm. Luther's example of how to paraphrase and elaborate on the petitions of the Lord's Prayer fits here as well. When paraphrasing Psalm 59 where it begins, "Deliver me from my enemies, O God," it may be that we do not have any human opponents dedicated to killing us or destroying our lives. The New Testament, however, talks about our enemies "the world, the flesh, and the devil" (1 John 2:16; Rev 12:9). You can paraphrase this to talk about temptations you are facing or other spiritual traps that it would be easy to fall into.[380]

A third basic kind of Psalm praying is sometimes called responsive praying.[381] Many Psalms are long or consist more of teaching than praying and are not in the form of prayer. So in this method we take themes and statements and let them stimulate adoration, confession, and supplication. This essentially uses Luther's kind of biblical meditation on the Psalm. We must not be rigid about any of these methods. Many Psalms lend themselves more to one or the other, but as time goes on, the person praying them does not even think about what method he or she is using. You can move back and forth between methods or come up with hybrids too.

For an example, let's select the following five verses from Psalm 116 (vv. 1–2, 7, 17–18):

I love the Lord, for he heard my voice;
he heard my cry for mercy.
Because he turned his ear to me,
I will call on him as long as I live. [vv. 1–2]
Return to your rest, my soul,
for the Lord has been good to you. [v. 7]
I will sacrifice a thank offering to you
and call on the name of the Lord.
I will fulfill my vows to the Lord
in the presence of all his people. [vv. 17–18]

We might pray the verses like this:

Verses 1–2: *I love you, Lord, for when I asked for mercy, you gave it to me. Lord, you have done it again and again. And for that, Lord, I will never stop depending on you— never. There's nowhere else I can go, nowhere else I should go.* (Paraphrase prayer)

Verse 7: *O Lord, my heart does not rest in your goodness, it is never consoled as deeply as it should be by your grace. It is too restless. Help me to know you—let your goodness be so real to my heart that it is completely at rest.* (Responsive prayer)

Verses 17–18: *I will sacrifice a thank offering to you, and call on the name of the Lord. I will live a life consistent with my baptism, with my membership in your church. I won't do this on my own, but in the community of your people.* (Verbatim prayer, slightly paraphrased)

Much of the sweetness and beauty of the Psalms lies in how they point us to the Messiah to come—Jesus Christ. Their power for our prayer life can be unlocked if we learn to pray the Psalms with Jesus in mind. How can we do that?

To begin with, we should remember that Jesus would have actually sung and prayed the Psalms through his entire life. As you consider a particular Psalm, imagine how he would have thought about it, knowing who he was and what he came to do. When we come to a "lament," we usually think of it in reference to suffering or feelings we are having. Remember, however, what Jesus suffered. When you come to a Psalm of refuge, remember that we "hide" in Jesus and he forgives and cleanses us from our sins, which is our truest danger.[382]

Finally, there are a number of very obviously Messianic Psalms that give us particularly rich views of Christ. They include the following: the enthroned Messiah (Ps 2, 110), the rejected Messiah (Ps 118), the betrayed Messiah (Ps 69, 109), the dying and rising Messiah (Ps 22, 16), the heavenly bridegroom of his people (Ps 45), and the triumphant Messiah (Ps 68, 72).[383] These are opportunities to simply consider the greatness and beauty of Jesus, to adore and rest in him.

Where Are You?

I often ask Christians to evaluate their situation with regard to prayer by using a metaphor. Imagine that your soul is a boat, a boat with both oars and a sail. In this case here are four questions:

Are you "sailing"? Sailing means you are living the Christian life with the wind at your back. God is real to your heart. You often feel his love. You see prayers being answered. When studying the Bible, you regularly see remarkable things and you sense him speaking to you. You sense people around you being influenced by the Spirit through you.

Are you "rowing"? Rowing means you are finding prayer and Bible reading to be more a duty than a delight. God often (though not always) seems distant, and the sense of his presence is fairly rare. You don't see many of your prayers being answered. You may be struggling with doubts about God and yourself. Yet despite all this, you refuse self-pity *or* the self-righteous pride that assumes you know better than God how your life should go. You continue to read the Bible and pray regularly, you attend worship and reach out and serve people despite the inner spiritual dryness.

Are you "drifting"? Drifting means that you are experiencing all the conditions of rowing—spiritual dryness and difficulties in life. But in response, instead of rowing, you are letting yourself drift. You don't feel like approaching and obeying God, so you don't pray or read. You give in to the self-centeredness that naturally comes when you feel sorry for yourself, and you drift into self-indulgent behaviors to comfort yourself, whether it be escape eating and sleeping, sexual practices, or whatever else.

Are you "sinking"? Eventually your boat, your soul, will drift away from the shipping lanes, as it were—and truly lose any forward motion in the Christian life. The numbness of heart can become hardness because you give in to thoughts of self-pity and resentment. If some major difficulty or trouble were to come into your life, it would be possible to abandon your faith and identity as a Christian altogether.

In this metaphor we see that there are some things we are responsible for, such as using the means of grace—the Bible, prayer, and church participation—in a disciplined way. There are many other things we do not have much control over—such as how well the circumstances in our lives are going as well as our emotions. If you pray, worship, and obey despite negative circumstances and feelings, you won't be drifting, and when the winds come up again, you will move ahead swiftly. On the other hand, if you do *not* apply the means of grace, you will at best be drifting, and if storms come into your life, you might be in danger of sinking.

In any case—pray no matter what. *Praying is rowing*, and sometimes it is like rowing in the dark—you won't feel that you are making any progress at all. Yet you are, and when the winds rise again, and they surely will, you will sail again before them.

The Great Feast

Those who enjoy sailing might find these nautical images helpful. However, a metaphor used more often in the Bible to describe fellowship with God is that of a feast. Isaiah looked forward to the day when God will end death, heal the world, and take his people deep into his love. He envisions this as a great feast.

> The Lord Almighty will prepare
> a feast of rich food for all peoples,
> a banquet of aged wine—
> the best of meats and the finest of wines.
> . . . he will destroy
> the shroud that enfolds all peoples,
> the sheet that covers all nations;
> he will swallow up death forever.
> The Sovereign Lord will wipe away the tears
> from all faces;
> he will remove his people's disgrace
> from all the earth.
> The Lord has spoken. (Is 25:6–8)

The word *sheet* refers to the shroud placed over dead bodies at funerals. At the end of time, we will not only receive God's forgiveness ("he will remove his people's disgrace") but also the end of "the sheet"—all suffering, death, and tears. Eating together is one of the most common metaphors for friendship and fellowship in the Bible, and so this vision is a powerful prediction of unimaginably close and intimate fellowship with the living God. It evokes the sensory joys of exquisite food in the presence of loving friends. The "wine" of full communion with God and our loved ones will be endless and infinite delight.

It is quite possible that Jesus had these prophecies of the Great Feast Day in mind when he was invited to a wedding in Cana. Jesus knew that the great banquet at the end of time was going to be a *wedding* feast (Rev 19:6–9) in which Jesus took his bride, his people, to himself (Rev 21:2–5). At Cana, when he discovered that poor planning meant the wine had run out in the middle of the days-long feast, he took water jars for purification and turned the water into wine so the joy of the occasion was not diminished but enhanced (John 2:1–11). Because Jesus himself likens his blood to wine at the Lord's Supper, we can see that Jesus' death on the cross will be the basis for that final festal joy that we will have with him forever.

Yet this spiritual wine, this fellowship with the Lord, is not wholly in the future. As we have seen, we are invited even now to "*taste* and see that the Lord is good" (Ps 34:8). We can "see" and "taste" his love, at least in part, now (2 Cor 3:18). The great eighteenth-century hymn writer William Cowper suffered from bouts of depression, but he was able to write:

Sometimes a light surprises the Christian as he sings;
it is the Lord who rises, with healing in his wings:

When comforts are declining, He grants the soul again
A season of clear shining, to cheer it after rain.

In holy contemplation we sweetly then pursue
The theme of God's salvation, and find it ever new.
Set free from present sorrow, we cheerfully can say,
Let the unknown tomorrow bring with it what it may.

It may be fitful and episodic, but fellowship with God is available now. George Herbert, remember, called prayer "the Churches banquet." Remember too Dwight Moody, who was praying one day and could say only "that God revealed himself to me, and I had such an experience of his love that I had to ask him to stay his hand."[384]

Why are we settling for water when we could have wine?

Appendix: Some Other Patterns for Daily Prayer

A Daily Office of Three Set Hours of Prayer

Morning Prayer (35 minutes)
Prayer upon Rising from Sleep (see "Daily Prayers" on next page)
Read and pray Psalm 95.
Do Robert Murray M'Cheyne Bible reading—two daily chapters.[385]
Choose favorite verses and do meditation (Martin Luther's method).
Pray your meditations to God.
Free prayer: Adoration, Confession, Supplication

Prayer upon Beginning One's Work or Study (see "Daily Prayers" on next page)

Midday Prayer (5 minutes)

Read and pray Psalm 103.
Paraphrase and pray the Lord's Prayer (Luther's method).
Self-examination: Have you been prickly and proud or gracious and

humble? Have you been cold and indifferent or warm and kind? Have you been anxious and stressed or depending on God? Have you been cowardly or truthful?

Free prayer for the challenges of the day and moment

Prayer after the Midday Meal (see "Daily Prayers" below)

Evening Prayer (20 minutes)

Read and pray two Psalms, working through the Psalter with a commentary.

Confess and repent for sins of the day.

Pray for the people with needs you met that day.

Intercessory prayer for family, friends, opponents, neighbors, people you know with cares, burdens, and afflictions, the church in general, your church in particular, the needs of your city and community, the needs of the world

Prayer before Sleep (see "Daily Prayers" below)

Daily Prayers Based on the Prayers of John Calvin[386]

Prayer upon Rising from Sleep

My God, Father, and Savior, since you have been pleased to give me the grace to come through the night to the present day, now grant that I may employ it entirely in your service, so that all my works may be to the glory of your name and the edification of my neighbors. As you have been pleased to make your sun shine upon the earth to give us bodily light, grant the light of your Spirit to illumine my understanding and my heart. And because it means nothing to begin well if one does not persevere, I ask that you would continue to increase your grace in me until you have led me into full communion with your Son, Jesus Christ our Lord, who is the true Sun of our souls, shining day and night, eternally and without end. *Hear me, merciful Father, by our Lord Jesus Christ, Amen.*

Prayer upon Beginning One's Work or Study

My good God, Father, and Savior, grant me aid by your Holy Spirit to now work fruitfully in my vocation, which is from you, all in order to love you and the people around me rather than for my own gain and glory. Give me wisdom, judgment and prudence, and freedom from my besetting sins. Bring me under the rule of true humility. Let me accept with patience whatever amount of fruitfulness or difficulty in my work that you give me this day. And in all I do, help me to rest always in my Lord Jesus Christ and in his grace alone for my salvation and life. *Hear me, merciful Father, by our Lord Jesus Christ, Amen.*

Prayer after the Midday Meal

O Lord God, I give you thanks for all the benefits and gifts you constantly shower on me. Thank you for sustaining my physical life through food and shelter; for giving me new life through the gospel; and for the certainty of the best and perfect life, which is yet to come. In light of all these blessings, I now ask that you would not allow my affections to be tangled in inordinate desires for the things of this world, but let me always set my heart on things above, where Christ, who is my life, is seated at your right hand. *Hear me, merciful Father, by our Lord Jesus Christ, Amen.*

Prayer before Sleep

O Lord God, now grant me the grace not only to rest my body this night, but to have my spiritual repose, in soul and conscience, in your grace and love, that I may let go of all earthly cares so I might be comforted and eased in all ways. And because no day passes that I do not sin in so many ways, please bury all my offenses in your mercy, that I might not lose your presence. Forgive me, merciful Father, for Christ's sake. And as I lay down in sleep to safely awake again only by your grace, keep me in a joyful, lively remembrance that whatever happens, I will someday know my final rising—the resurrection—because Jesus Christ lay down in death for me, and rose for my justification. *In his name I pray, Amen.*

Acknowledgments

No readable book is written by one person alone. Feedback from my editor, Brian Tart; my wife, Kathy; and my colleague at City to City Scott Kauffmann made this a better book than it would have been. Thanks must also go to those who make it possible for me to write during my out-of-town study leaves every year—Janice Worth, Lynn Land, Mary Courtney Brooks, and John and Carolyn Twiname. Over the years I have thanked my editor, Brian Tart, and my agent, David McCormick, for all their help. But with every passing book—and this our tenth volume done together—I have come to see the greatness of my indebtedness to them.

Selected Annotated Bibliography
on Prayer

This bibliography is confined to books that were both helpful to my thinking as I wrote and were also helpful to me personally in my own prayer life.

Theology of Prayer

Calvin, John. *Institutes of the Christian Religion.* Edited by John T. McNeill. Vol. 2. Louisville, KY: Westminster John Knox Press, 1960, Book 3, Chapter 20.

There's nothing else like Calvin's treatment of prayer. Very few systematic theologies have followed Calvin by including a major chapter on prayer. Calvin is both theological and practical, and as usual, he is very comprehensive. This is a rarity—deep theology with a spiritually elevated tone and savor that makes the reader *want* to pray.

Carson, D. A. *A Call to Spiritual Reformation: Priorities from Paul and His Prayers.* Grand Rapids, MI: Baker Academic, 1992.

This is neither a theological treatise nor a how-to volume. However, by studying Paul's actual prayers and prayer life, this book bristles with many theological and practical insights.

Carson, D. A., ed. *Teach Us to Pray: Prayer in the Bible and the World*. Eugene, OR: Wipf and Stock, 2002.

The single most comprehensive volume in this list. It explores prayer from every angle—biblically, theologically, anthropologically, historically, psychologically, and practically. Its essays also represent multiple cultural perspectives.

Clowney, Edmund P. *CM: Christian Meditation*. Nutley, NJ: Craig Press, 1979.

Long out of print but uniquely helpful. Clowney provides a trenchant critique of Transcendental Meditation, which was at its high noon of popularity in the 1970s. The basic ideas of Eastern mysticism, however, are more pervasive than ever and so this is still relevant. Clowney lays out a biblical theology not only for Christian prayer but for Christian meditation.

——— "A Biblical Theology of Prayer." In *Teach Us to Pray: Prayer in the Bible and the World*, edited by D. A. Carson. Eugene, OR: Wipf and Stock, 2002.

Not easy reading and not very practical, but this is probably the single most complete treatment of the biblical material on prayer. See also Goldsworthy's volume *Prayer*.

Davis, John Jefferson. *Meditation and Communion with God: Contemplating Scripture in an Age of Distraction*. Downers Grove, IL: InterVarsity Press, 2012.

Davis lays out a biblical theology of meditation on the Scripture. He does so by thinking out the implications of several key biblical-theological themes and doctrines. He strikes a rare balance, being positive about spiritual experience yet cautious about methods of meditation from Eastern religions as well as from Eastern Orthodoxy and Catholicism that, in his view, do not do sufficient justice to the authority of the Word and the freeness of grace.

Goldsworthy, Graeme. *Prayer and the Knowledge of God*. Downers Grove, IL: InterVarsity Press, 2003.

Goldsworthy distills the biblical data on prayer, first thematically and topically. He then re-marches through the biblical data by considering prayer in successive stages in redemptive history, from creation through the fall, Israel, and the coming of Christ. This should be read in combination with Carson's *Teach Us to Pray,* and especially Clowney's chapter, "A Biblical Theology of Prayer."

Practice of Prayer

Edwards, Jonathan. "Personal Narrative" and "A Divine and Supernatural Light." In *A Jonathan Edwards Reader*, edited by John E. Smith, Harry S. Stout, and Kenneth P. Minkema. New Haven, CT: Yale University Press, 2003.

These two pieces by Edwards are complementary. One is a personal account of spiritual experience and the other is a biblical-philosophical account of how spiritual experience works. Reading the two in combination could be life-changing, or at least should be prayer-life-changing.

Hallesby, Ole. *Prayer.* Minneapolis: Augsburg Fortress, 1975.

This little classic takes a troubleshooting approach to the subject of prayer. Rather than outlining the theology of prayer or laying out practical steps to take in praying, Hallesby takes a pastoral path, responding to a series of complaints and difficulties people have about prayer. Perhaps for this reason, the discussion sometimes feels theologically thin or speculative. Nevertheless, the overall effect of the book is to reassure strugglers that Jesus is with them and to encourage endurance.

Henry, Matthew. *A Method for Prayer: Freedom in the Face of God.* Edited by J. Ligon Duncan. Tain, Scotland: Christian Focus, 1994.

This is also a unique book. Henry mines the Scripture for hundreds of actual prayers and then organizes and classifies them as subheadings under the larger headings of praise, confession, petition, thanksgiving, intercession, and concluding our prayers. The editor, J. Ligon Duncan, outlines the whole book in an appendix. It provides scores of specific ideas on how we can go about adoring, confessing, thanking, and petitioning God. All you have to do is personalize the headings with your own issues and conditions. I have found that you can easily spend an entire day in prayer with this guide and help.

Luther, Martin. "A Simple Way to Pray" and "Personal Prayer Book." In *Luther's Works: Devotional Writings II*, edited by Gustav K. Wiencke, Vol. 43. Minneapolis: Fortress Press, 1968.

Luther's "A Simple Way to Pray" succeeds in being extremely practical and profound at the same time. I have given this little work substantial treatment earlier in my volume. It's worth reading annually.

Owen, John. "A Discourse on the Work of the Holy Spirit in Prayer." In *The Works of John Owen*, edited by William H. Goold. Carlisle, PA: Banner of Truth, 1965, 4:235–350.

——————. "On the Grace and Duty of Being Spiritually Minded." In *The Works of John Owen*, edited by William H. Goold. Carlisle, PA: Banner of Truth, 1965, 7:262–497.

_____. "Meditations and Discourses on the Glory of Christ." In *The Works of John Owen*, edited by William H. Goold. Carlisle, PA: Banner of Truth, 1965, 1:274–461.

Owen wasn't easy to read even in his own day. His writing is even harder to digest now. But his works on spiritual experience are without equal. He combines exhaustive theological reflection with the strongest calls to go beyond doctrinal subscription into full-heart knowledge of God.

Prayers and Devotion

Barbee, C. Frederick, and Paul F. M. Zahl. *The Collects of Thomas Cranmer.* Grand Rapids, MI: Eerdmans, 1999.

Presents Thomas Cranmer's collects as models for public and private prayer, with brief explanations of the theology of each prayer along with a historical note about Cranmer's development of each. They are indeed priceless models for prayer—without peer, many think, outside of the Bible itself.

Bennett, Arthur G., ed. *The Valley of Vision: A Collection of Puritan Prayers & Devotions.* Carlisle, PA: Banner of Truth, 1975.

This compendium of prayers from the Puritans is edited and put into a more contemporary idiom. The collection has stood the test of time. One reason is that the prayers are so different from those in most current devotional literature. Sin is taken much more seriously and so glory and grace shine the brighter.

Contemporary Popular Treatments

Packer, J. I., and Carolyn Nystrom. *Praying: Finding Our Way through Duty to Delight*. Downers Grove, IL: InterVarsity Press, 2009.

This book is based on a series of talks, so it is sometimes rambling and repetitious but, overall, it is the best single popular-level treatment on prayer. This covers all the bases and directly invites, exhorts, and urges us into a life of prayer.

Peterson, Eugene H. *Answering God: The Psalms as Tools for Prayer*. San Francisco: Harper & Row, 1989.

This is the best book on how to use the Psalms in prayer. It also includes along the way a very strong theology of prayer. Peterson is a champion of connecting prayer closely to the Bible both theologically and practically.

Ward, Timothy. *Words of Life: Scripture as the Living and Active Word of God*. Downers Grove, IL: InterVarsity Press, 2009.

While this is a book on the doctrine of Scripture, and hardly touches on prayer, Ward makes a case that the Bible is "the primary means God has given us for coming to encounter him." He argues for this as he expounds a very high view of the authority and inerrancy of the Bible. The implications of his definition are enormous for prayer. With this view of the Bible, prayer combined with scriptural meditation can be a true dialogue or conversation with God.

The Lord's Prayer

Packer, J. I. "Learning to Pray: The Lord's Prayer." In *Growing in Christ*. Wheaton, IL: Crossway, 2007, 153–220.

Packer's exposition of the Lord's Prayer is perhaps the most accessible and concise contemporary one available. For somewhat longer treatments, see also:

Coekin, Richard. *Our Father: Enjoying God in Prayer.* Nottingham, UK: InterVarsity Press, 2012.

Lloyd-Jones, D. Martyn. *Studies in the Sermon on the Mount.* Grand Rapids, MI: Eerdmans, 1984.

Stott, John R. W. *The Message of the Sermon on the Mount.* Downers Grove, IL: InterVarsity Press, 1985.

Wright, N. T. *The Lord and His Prayer.* Grand Rapids, MI: Eerdmans, 1997.

Contemplative Spirituality

I have given ample critique of the Christian mystical/contemplative tradition. Nevertheless, there are things to learn here for those of us who stand outside it.

Bloom, Anthony. *Beginning to Pray.* Mahwah, NJ: Paulist, 1970.
This is another well-known volume, a classic in the Eastern Orthodox tradition.

Hall, Thelma. *Too Deep for Words: Rediscovering* Lectio Divina. Mahwah, NJ: Paulist, 1988.
Hall's is perhaps the most accessible book and introduction to this tradition.

Von Balthasar, Hans Urs. *Prayer.* Ignatius, 1986.
This is perhaps the best substantial book on Roman Catholic spirituality, providing serious and thoughtful theological reflection on contemplative prayer.

Notes

INTRODUCTION—WHY WRITE A BOOK ON PRAYER?

1. Jonathan Edwards is one example. Edwards's treatments of the nature of spiritual experience are unequaled. His work *Religious Affections* and his sermon "A Divine and Supernatural Light," for example, describe in detail the "sense on the heart" that is the essence of a spiritual encounter with God. Yet Edwards speaks very little about methodology, that is, about how to meditate and pray.

2. Austin Phelps, *The Still Hour: Or Communion with God* (Carlisle, PA: Banner of Truth, 1974), 9.

3. Donald Bloesch, *The Struggle of Prayer* (Colorado Springs: Helmers and Howard, 1988). Bloesch closely follows the typology and argument of Friedrich Heiler, who wrote of "mystical" versus "prophetic" prayer. We will look at Heiler's work and this distinction in more detail in chapter 3.

4. Bloesch, *Struggle of Prayer*, 131.

5. Ibid., 154.

6. Ibid., 97–117. As a convinced Protestant, I concur with Donald Bloesch here. Protestants believe in the "sufficiency" of the Bible. That is, they believe that God's Spirit speaks to us in his Word. Timothy Ward writes of "Scripture . . . as the means by which God extends his action, and therefore himself, into the world in order to act communicatively in relation to us." Timothy Ward, *Words of Life: Scripture as the Living and Active Word of God* (Downers Grove, IL: InterVarsity Press, 2009), 113. Ward contrasts this view of the Bible's "sufficiency" with the Roman Catholic view. The Protestant Reformers such as Martin Luther and John Calvin taught that the Spirit spoke "through Scripture itself" rather than through "the increasingly authoritative ecclesiastical center in Rome" (109). A strong, Reformation view of the sufficiency of Scripture has a major shaping influence on the

practice of prayer. The Reformers denied both the Catholic teaching that the Spirit speaks through the Church (interpreting the Scripture) rather than through the Bible itself, as well as the Anabaptist claim that the Spirit gave individuals new revelations beyond the Scripture. See the Westminster Confession of Faith (1646), 1.6, for a summary of this view. Both of these alternatives ruin the idea of prayer as part of a dialogue with God through the Word. The Catholic view undermines the idea that God speaks directly to us through the Word. The Anabaptist view does as well. In the Anabaptist (later Quaker) view, we mainly hear God speaking to us in our hearts.

7. See John Piper's treatment of this theme in *Desiring God: Meditations of a Christian Hedonist* (Colorado Springs: Multnomah, 1987).

8. Bloesch notes the "persistent mystical element" in Martin Luther's teaching on prayer in *Struggle of Prayer*, 118.

9. Hans Urs von Balthasar, *Prayer* (Ignatius Press, 1986), 28, cited in Bloesch, *Struggle of Prayer*, 118–19. See a further discussion on Balthasar's views later in this volume.

CHAPTER ONE—THE NECESSITY OF PRAYER

10. Flannery O'Connor, *A Prayer Journal* (New York: Farrar, Straus, 2013), 3.

11. Ibid., 4.

12. Ibid., 20.

13. Ibid., 8.

14. Ibid., 20.

15. Ibid., 4.

16. Ibid., 23.

17. Mary Billard, "Robert Hammond: Leaving the High Life," *The New York Times*, November 27, 2013.

18. http://goindia.about.com/od/spiritualplaces/tp/Top-10-Rishikesh -Ashrams.htm.

19. David Hochman, "Mindfulness: Getting Its Share of Attention," *The New York Times*, November 1, 2013.

20. See the *Christianity Today* cover article from February 2008 by Chris Armstrong, "The Future Lies in the Past: Why Evangelicals Are Connecting with the Early Church as They Move into the 21st Century," and the sidebar "Monastic Evangelicals" by Chris Armstrong, posted February 8, 2008. Find at http://www.christianitytoday.com/ct/2008/february/22.22.html.

21. Within the Catholic Church, there has been sustained criticism of "Centering

Prayer" as being too indebted to the thought of Eastern religions rather than to Christian understandings of the divine. See the 1989 document "Aspects of Christian Meditation" as well as "Christian Reflection on the New Age." http://www.vatican.va/roman_curia/congregations/cfaith/documents/rc_con_cfaith_doc_19891015_meditazione-cristiana_en.html and http://www.vatican.va/roman_curia/pontifical_councils/interelg/documents/rc_pc_interelg_doc_20030203_new-age_en.html. For a Protestant critique of the recent evangelical interest in ancient and medieval spirituality, see D. A. Carson, "Spiritual Disciplines," in *Themelios* 36, no. 3 (November 2011). Also see Carson's older article "When Is Spirituality Spiritual?" *Journal of the Evangelical Theological Society* 37, no. 3 (September 1994).

22. See D. Martyn Lloyd-Jones, *The Sons of God: An Exposition of Chapter 8:5–17* (Romans series) (Peabody, MA: Zondervan, 1974), 275–399. Lloyd-Jones had the (frankly idiosyncratic) view that the "witness of the Spirit" described in Romans 8:15–16, the "sealing of the Spirit" described in Ephesians 1:13 (cf. Lloyd-Jones, *God's Ultimate Purpose: An Exposition of Ephesians 1:1–23* [Grand Rapids, MI: Baker, 1978], 243–48), and the "baptism of the Spirit" described in the book of Acts (cf. Lloyd-Jones, *Joy Unspeakable: Power and Renewal in the Holy Spirit* [Marietta, GA: Shaw, 2000]) were all the same experience. He saw this baptism of the Spirit as subsequent to conversion and something that only certain Christians receive as an empowering gift. Lloyd-Jones understood "revivals" as times in which this baptism of the Spirit was poured out on an unusual number of people. Like most other admirers of Lloyd-Jones, I do not accept that all these biblical terms are identical. Nor do I think they all point to a single experience. Lloyd-Jones's understanding of this biblical material was shaped by a particularly powerful experience he had when on holiday in Wales in 1949 and was struggling with exhaustion and spiritual darkness. (See "Wales and the Summer of 1949" in Iain H. Murray, *David Martyn Lloyd-Jones: The Fight of Faith 1939–1981* [Carlisle, PA: Banner of Truth, 1990], 201–21.) However, Lloyd-Jones is on more sure exegetical ground when he describes the Romans 8:16 "witness of the Spirit" as an experience of high assurance that can come to us in prayer. I believe he is right on this matter, and his exposition of it is illuminating and inspiring. Also, his description of the experience of God's love in his exposition of the prayer of Paul in Ephesians 3:13–21 is remarkable for its richness and description.

23. Thomas R. Schreiner, *Romans: Baker Exegetical Commentary on the New*

Testament (Marietta, GA: Baker, 1998), 427. Notice Schreiner's respectful disagreement with Lloyd-Jones that the witness of the Spirit is a special experience available only to some Christians (427n18).

24. William H. Goold, ed., *The Works of John Owen*, vol. 9 (Carlisle, PA: Banner of Truth, 1967), 237.

25. John Murray, *Redemption: Accomplished and Applied* (Grand Rapids, MI: Eerdmans, 1955), 169–70. Italics for emphasis are mine.

26. See Karen H. Jobes, *1 Peter: Baker Exegetical Commentary on the New Testament* (Marietta, GA: Baker Academic, 2005), 91. This biblical verse was one of Lloyd-Jones's favorite, and he gave this title to his book on the baptism of the Holy Spirit.

27. For more on how to "pray the Psalms" or use the Psalms in prayer, see the last chapter in this volume.

28. D. Martyn Lloyd-Jones, *Preaching and Preachers* (Peabody, MA: Zondervan, 1971), 169–70.

29. P. T. Forsyth, *The Soul of Prayer* (reprint of the 1916 edition; Grand Rapids, MI: Eerdmans, 2012), 9.

CHAPTER TWO—THE GREATNESS OF PRAYER

30. As we have already noted several times, the "inner life with God" here does not mean only our private, individual prayer life. Life with God is cultivated by both public and private worship and prayer. John Calvin and the other Reformers were clear that public prayer and devotion in the gathered Christian assembly was to be the formative foundation that taught us how to pray and behave toward God privately. Michael Horton, describing Calvin's understanding of the Christian life, writes: "The public ministry shapes private devotion, not vice versa." See Michael S. Horton, *Calvin on the Christian Life: Glorifying and Enjoying God Forever* (Wheaton, IL: Crossway, 2014), 154.

31. Isak Dinesen, *Out of Africa* (New York: Modern Library, 1992), 270.

32. John Owen, cited in I. D. E. Thomas, *A Puritan Golden Treasury*, (Banner of Truth, 1977), 192.

33. Phelps, *The Still Hour*, 9. The italics and emphasis are his.

34. For the prayer life of the Patriarchs, see Genesis 20:17; 25:21; 32:9; and 15:2ff. Isaac finds a wife through the prayers of Abraham's servant (Gen 24:12, 15, 45). For Moses's deployment of prayer against Pharaoh, see Exodus 8:8–9, 28–30; 9:28–29; 10:17–18.

35. Samuel was famed for his prayers and prayer life. See 1 Samuel 1:10–16; 2:1ff.

36. 1 Kings 8:22–53; 2 Chronicles 6:14–42.

37. 1 Kings 8:30, 33, 35, 38, 42, 44, 45, 49.

38. The book of Jonah is largely a record of prayers—the petition of the frightened sailors (Jonah 1), the confession of Jonah in the belly of the great fish (Jonah 2), and then the shocking complaint of Jonah against (what he felt) was the irresponsible, extravagant mercy of God (Jonah 4:2). Elijah, through prayer, called down fire from heaven before the people in the most spectacular display (1 Kings 18:36) and almost immediately, depressed and depleted, received God's tender mercy and help through prayer (1 Kings 19:4ff). Elijah's successor, Elisha, saved a boy's life and saved a city from a siege—both through prayer (2 Kings 4:33; 6:18). When King Hezekiah received a high-handed letter from the Assyrian king threatening to annihilate Jerusalem, Hezekiah took the letter and "spread it out before the Lord" and prayed. God delivered the city (2 Kings 19:14–20). Hezekiah was later delivered from illness through prayer. The book of Habakkuk is nothing but a dialogue of prayer by the prophet with God (Hab 3:1). Habakkuk waited in prayer for God's answers to his questions (Hab 2:1–3).

39. This is the view of J. Thomson in his article "Prayer" in *The New Bible Dictionary*, ed. J. D. Douglas (Grand Rapids, MI: Eerdmans, 1973), 1020. See Isaiah 6:5ff; 37:1–4; Jeremiah 11:20–23; 12:1–6.

40. Daniel's thrice-daily prayer practice is found in Daniel 6:7–12. His prayer of repentance, asking that they be released from exile, is found in Daniel 9:1–18; the response is found in vv. 21–23.

41. Nehemiah seeks the favor of the emperor to rebuild the wall of Jerusalem through prayer (Neh 1:1–11; 2:4). He used prayer also for protection until the work on the wall was done (Neh 4:9; 6:9). Later, Ezra protects people returning to Judah from exile in Babylon through prayer (Ez 8:23). Both Ezra (Ez 9:1ff) and Nehemiah repent and seek forgiveness for the sins of the people.

42. Christ taught his disciples to pray in Matthew 6:5–15; 21:22; Mark 11:24–25; Luke 11:1–13; 18:1–8. He laid hands on children to pray for them (Matt 19:13). He raised Lazarus from the dead, calling on his Father in prayer (John 11:41–42). He saved Peter from spiritual hardening, through prayer (Luke 22:32). He said the temple should be a "house of prayer" (Matt 21:13; Mark 11:17; Luke 19:46). He taught that some demons could be cast

out only through prayer (Mark 9:29). He prayed often and regularly (Matt 14:23; Mark 1:35; 6:46; Luke 5:16; 9:18), and sometimes all night (Luke 6:12). The prayer in the Garden of Gethsemane is recorded in Matthew 26:36–45; Mark 14:32–40; Luke 22:39–46. His prayer—that he would not have to suffer the cross—was denied. He died praying—crying out in agony (Mark 15:35), praying for his enemies (Luke 23:34), and giving himself to God (Luke 23:46).

43. Prayer brings the power of the Spirit in Acts 4:24, 31. Leaders are selected and appointed with prayer in Acts 6:6; 13:3; and 14:23. The apostles—the teachers and leaders of the early church—believed that they needed to give as much attention to praying as they did to teaching the Word (Acts 6:4). All Christians were expected to have a fervent prayer life (Rom 12:2; 15:30; Col 4:2), praying in all sorts of ways for all kinds of things (Eph 6:18). It was expected that spouses might even part from each other for times of sustained prayer (1 Cor 7:5). The Spirit gives us the confidence and desire to pray to God as Father (Gal 4:6; Rom 8:14–16) and enables us to pray even when we don't know what to say (Rom 8:26). All desires must be given to God in prayer—the only alternative is anxiety (Phil 4:6). All people around you should be prayed for (1 Tim 2:1), and the sick should especially be prayed for (James 5:13–16). God hears prayers and answers them (James 5:17–18). Every gift you receive should be "consecrated" through prayer—you should thank God for it lest your heart become hard through an illusion of self-sufficiency (1 Tim 4:5). Prayer should pervade your whole life—we should "pray without ceasing" (1 Thess 5:17), seeking the glory of God consciously in everything we do (1 Cor 10:31). The prayers and praise of our lips is now the most pleasing sacrifice we can offer God (Heb 13:15; cf. Rev 5:8).

44. Charles Summers, cited in Helen Wilcox, ed., *The English Poems of George Herbert* (New York: Cambridge University Press, 2007), 177.

CHAPTER THREE—WHAT IS PRAYER?

45. Philip and Carol Zaleski, *Prayer: A History* (Boston: Houghton Mifflin, 2005), 4–5. In December 2013, hundreds assembled at Bodh Gaya in India, considered the birthplace of Buddhism, to seek world peace through prayer. "Karmapa Begins Prayer for World Peace at Bodh Gaya," *The Times of India,* December 14, 2013.

46. See, for example, "Reincarnation" at the official website of the Dalai Lama, which says that people can choose their place and time of birth as well as their

future parents through the virtue of their prayers. http://www.dalailama
.com/biography/reincarnation.

47. Zaleski, *Prayer: A History*, 6–8, 23. Using songs and trances to channel energy
from the spiritual world into the physical is called shamanism. This religious
view is extremely old and seems to have been pervasive around the world. The
Kalevala, a compilation of ancient Finnish epic poetry, gives classic accounts of
shamanistic activity. Creation, healing, and combat happen through songs with
magical, powerful effects.

48. Cited in Bernard Spilka and Kevin L. Ladd, *The Psychology of Prayer: A
Scientific Approach* (New York: Guilford, 2012), 3.

49. http://www.bbc.co.uk/pressoffice/pressreleases/stories/2004/02_february
/26/world_god.shtml. This percentage of atheists and agnostics who pray
was also reported in the General Social Survey, cited by Spilka and Ladd,
Psychology of Prayer, 37.

50. "'Nones' on the Rise: One-in-Five Adults Have No Religious Affiliation,"
Pew Forum on Religion & Public Life, October 9, 2012.

51. See "Religion among the Millenials," *Pew Research Religion & Public Life Project*, February 17, 2010, accessed at http://www.pewforum.org/2010/02/17/
religion-among-the-millennials.

52. Giuseppe Giordan, "Toward a Sociology of Prayer," in *Religion, Spirituality and Everyday Practice*, ed. Giuseppe Giordan and William H. Swatos Jr.
(New York: Springer, 2011), 77. Giordan goes on to assert that prayer is a
"global experience," an effort to establish a relationship between limited,
weak human beings with something more powerful (78). Psychologists
Bernard Spilka and Kevin Ladd, authors of the most extensive scientific
psychological study of religion to date, say that likewise "prayer is . . . critical to the way most people conduct their lives." See Spilka and Ladd, *Psychology of Prayer*, 4. The most significant contemporary survey of prayer, by
Philip and Carol Zaleski, scholars who have taught at Harvard, Smith College, and Tufts University, also concludes that "wherever one finds humans, one finds humans at prayer" and that even if prayer is outlawed, "it
goes underground where it continues to wend its course into the depths of
the soul." Zaleski and Zaleski, *Prayer: A History*, 4. A classic older study,
Prayer, by the German scholar Friedrich Heiler, draws the same conclusion,
noting prayer's "astonishing multiplicity of forms" throughout the world.
Friedrich Heiler, *Prayer: A Study in the History and Psychology of Religion*
(Oxford: Oxford University Press, 1932), 353.

53. There have sometimes been claims of remote tribes who live without any religion. Daniel L. Everett, author of *Don't Sleep, There Are Snakes* (London: Profile Books, 2010), wrote of the Piraha people (a small tribe of fewer than five hundred, in the Amazonian rain forest of Brazil), who "believed the world was as it had always been, and that there was no supreme deity" and they were content to live "without God, religion, or any political authority." Despite these claims, the Piraha did believe very firmly in spirits and wore certain articles of clothing to protect themselves. See http://freethinker .co.uk/2008/11/08/how-an-amazonian-tribe-turned-a-missionary-into -an-atheist.

54. Heiler, *Prayer: A Study*, 5.

55. Quoted in Bloesch, *Struggle of Prayer*, vii.

56. Most of these kinds of prayer are described and discussed at some length in the Zaleskis' *Prayer: A History*. One empirical study in the *Journal for the Scientific Study of Religion* posited at least twenty-one types of Christian prayer alone. Kevin L. Ladd and Bernard Spilka, "Inward, Outward, and Upward: Cognitive Aspects of Prayer," *Journal for the Scientific Study of Religion* 41, 475–84; and "Inward, Outward, and Upward: Scale Reliability and Validation," *Journal for the Scientific Study of Religion* 45, 233–51. Ladd and Spilka were seeking to use objective scales and factor-analysis to verify the categories posed by Richard J. Foster in *Prayer: Finding the Heart's True Home* (San Francisco: Harper, 1992).

57. Zaleski and Zaleski, *Prayer: A History*, 27. Their treatment of the early theorists of prayer is found on pp. 24–28.

58. Ibid., 27.

59. Unlike his contemporary Sigmund Freud, Carl Jung did not see religion as a sign of repressed sexuality and psychological immaturity. Instead, he believed that religious experiences could be helpful in growing into wholeness and psychological health. Jung taught that all human beings had a personal unconscious, formed through experience, but also shared a "collective unconscious," an awareness of symbols and themes that all human beings are born with and share together, and that are not the result of personal experience. See Robert H. Hopcke, *A Guided Tour of the Collected Works of C. G. Jung*, 10th anniversary edition (Boston: Shambhala, 1999), 13–20, 68.

60. The collective unconscious is possible because Jung believed, as did Eastern thinkers, that "the world [is] a unified field in which subject and object are fundamentally one, two different manifestations of the same basic reality"

(Hopcke, *C. G. Jung*, 72). The process of growth into maturity is therefore a process of bringing one's individual consciousness into contact with the symbols of the collective unconscious so that a kind of balance is achieved. People need to be "individuated" with their own self-image, and yet they also must come to see themselves as part of the interdependent whole of reality and thereby escape egocentricity and the illusion that they are not part of the whole of reality (Hopcke, *C. G. Jung*, 14–15).

61. See Hopcke, *C. G. Jung*, 68. "[For Jung] religion was religious experience, the direct contact with the divine, that which he called the *numinosum*, a term he borrowed from Rudolf Otto, manifested in dreams, visions, and mystical experiences. Second, religion consisted of religious practice, the doctrines and dogmas as well as the rituals and enactments, which Jung saw as necessary to protect people from the awesome power of such a direct experience of the numinous. Both religious experience and religious practice were, therefore, for Jung psychological phenomena that found their source inwardly and outwardly in the collective unconscious." See also page 97, where Hopcke writes about the Jungian "archetype" within the collective unconscious of the "Self," which meant an awareness of our oneness with all reality: "Jung saw that this organizing archetype of wholeness was particularly well captured and developed through religious imagery, and he thus came to understand that the psychological manifestation of the Self was indeed the experience of God or the 'God-image' within the human soul.'" Hopcke insists that Jung was not seeking to "reduce the almighty, transcendent Divine Being to a psychological experience" but was trying to show how the "image of God exists within the psyche" (97). However, Jung's belief that one experiences God by going down into one's self and unconscious rather than by listening to words spoken by God via revelation through the prophets shows that his understanding of God was far more like the immanent, impersonal Divine being of the East than the transcendent God who speaks through revelation in the Bible. See also M. Esther Harding in "What Makes the Symbol Effective as a Healing Agent?" in *Current Trends in Analytical Psychology*, ed. Gerhard Adler (Abingdon, UK: Routledge reprint, 2001), 3. Harding explains that Jungian psychologists ascribe to the collective unconscious what religious people ascribe to God.

62. Jung wrote a foreword to D. T. Suzuki's classic *An Introduction to Zen Buddhism* (New York: Grove Press, 1964), 9–29. In this essay he argues that his view of the collective unconscious fits in with the Buddhist view that there

is "a cosmic life and a cosmic spirit, and at the same time an individual life and an individual spirit" (13). Jung also points approvingly to the similarities between the Buddhist experience of *satori* and the spiritual experience of the medieval Christian mystic Meister Eckhart. He quotes Eckhart saying, "In the breakthrough . . . then I am more than all creatures, for I am neither God nor creature: *I am what I am, and what I will remain*, now and forever. Then I receive a jerk, which raises me above all the angels. In this jerk I become so rich that God cannot suffice me, in spite of all that he is as God, in spite of all his Godly works; for in this break-through I perceive what God and I are in common. *I am then what I was*, I grow neither less nor more, for I am an immovable being who moves all things" (14).

63. See Harding, "Symbol Effective," 14. She writes that, while religious experience could help a person surrender the ego to something greater and avoid immaturity of egocentricity, particular religious doctrines were unnecessary. Though Christians, for example, might believe that their egocentricity can be countered only through "faith in the efficacy of Christ's sacrifice," psychologists knew that it "must be achieved not by faith but by understanding and conscious [psychological] work" (15).

64. See Ira Progoff, trans., *The Cloud of Unknowing* (New York: Julian Press, 1957), 24. Quoted in Zaleski and Zaleski, *Prayer: A History*, 208. Most Christian thinkers who have heavily used Jungian insights and assumptions about the unconscious have been Catholic. See T. E. Clarke, "Jungian Types and Forms of Prayer, *Review for Religious* 42, 661–76. See also Chester Michael and Marie Norrisey, *Prayer and Temperament: Different Prayer Forms for Different Personality Types* (Charlottesville, VA: Open Door, 1985). The Centering Prayer movement, led by Basil Pennington and Thomas Keating, combines Jungian thought and Catholic theology. See Spilka and Ladd, *Psychology of Prayer*, 49.

65. Heiler's distinction between mysticism and prophetic religion follows the Swedish Lutheran theologian Nathan Söderblom. While Heiler believed that the purest versions of mystical prayer are found in Eastern religions, specifically in the Upanishads and in Buddhism, he saw similar dynamics in the tradition of Christian mysticism, beginning with the writings of Pseudo-Dionysius (late fifth century), then continuing with the thirteenth-century work of Meister Eckhart, John Tauler, and *The Cloud of Unknowing*, as well as the sixteenth-century John of the Cross and Teresa of Avila (Heiler, *Prayer: A Study*, 129, 136). He granted that "Christian-God mysticism"

shows much more "personal warmth and fervor" than the "sobriety, cold-ness, and monotony of pure mysticism" in Eastern religions (Heiler, 136).

66. Mysticism is defined as "that form of intercourse with God in which the world and the self are absolutely denied, in which human personality is dissolved, disappears and is absorbed in the infinite unity of the Godhead" (Heiler, *Prayer: A Study*, 136).

67. Ibid., 284.

68. As Heiler says at one point, various types of prayer are strikingly different—not just externally but at their cores. They are different "in every way: in motive, form, and content, in the conception of God and in the relation to God implied and in the standard of prayer" (Ibid., 283).

69. Anthony Bloom, *Beginning to Pray* (Mahwah, NJ: Paulist Press, 1970), 45–56. Bloom quotes Luke 17:21 here. But Jesus is using a second person plural when he says to his disciples, "The kingdom of God is within you [all]." Most scholars believe Jesus was not saying the kingdom of God was within each individual heart but rather was within them as a community. Some translate it "The kingdom of God is among you." It is important to note that Bloom is careful to say that, while he directs people to go inward in prayer, he does not mean inward psychologically. "I don't mean that we must go inward in the way one does in psychoanalysis or psychology. It is not a journey into my *own* inwardness, it is a journey *through* my own self, in order to emerge from the deepest level of my self into the place where He is, the point at which God and I meet," 46.

70. "Belief in the personality of God is the necessary presupposition . . . wher-ever the vital conception of the divine personality grows dim, where, as in the philosophical ideal or in pantheistic mysticism it passes over into the 'One and All,' genuine prayer dissolves and becomes purely contemplative absorption and adoration" (Heiler, *Prayer: A Study*, 356).

71. Ibid., 358.

72. Ibid., 285.

73. Ibid., 30.

74. Ibid., iv. The italics are in the original.

75. Zaleski and Zaleski, *Prayer: A History*, 204–08. According to Pseudo-Dionysius, God can be known only through "the darkness of unknowing," not through the intellect. Rationality must be abandoned in an act of self-abnegation, "renouncing all the mind may conceive" in order to be "up-lifted into the divine shadow." *The Cloud of Unknowing* revises and reworks

the insights of Dionysius, insisting that what gets us beyond thought and conception is a state of perfect love. However, to achieve this requires growth in virtue and a purging of the soul from sin, a longing and passion for union with God, and finally the rigorous use of the contemplative method. The goal is to "get into the cloud of unknowing"—into the presence of God—and simply stay there, being open to God. All words and ideas are seen as distractions from awareness of him—even so-called thoughts about him. So to stay in God's presence means "rejecting all worldly thoughts," namely all "association, fantasy, and analysis." The author directs that people use repetitive prayer, urging for contemplatives "the repeated utterance of a short word, preferably of a single syllable. He proposes *God* or *love.*" This word plays a dual role: "First, it suppresses thought under the cloud of forgetting, stopping rational thought." Then, second, that frees the contemplative to "coalesce all their desire for God" around this word, "freeing the naked will to penetrate the cloud of unknowing in an act of perfect love," 206–07.

76. See the long summary of the differences between mystical and prophetic prayer in Zaleski and Zaleski, *Prayer: A History*, 283–85.

77. Donald Bloesch says, "Heiler's analysis has often been subject to severe criticism, especially by Roman Catholic and Anglican scholars who are concerned with defending the biblical foundations of Christian mysticism." Bloesch summarizes the criticisms on page 5 of his *Struggle of Prayer*. Bloesch is supportive of Heiler. In fact, his book is something of an updated, more accessible promulgation of Heiler's thesis that biblical prayer is preferable to the mysticism of Eastern religions and of some of Roman Catholicism. Bloesch rightly makes distinctions between some forms of Catholic prayer and others. (See his approval of Teresa of Avila's "prayer of quiet" on p. 5.) In his book, Bloesch contrasts mysticism with what he calls "biblical personalism." He uses this latter term to describe the view of prayer in which God is assumed to be a personal friend and father rather than simply the impersonal ground of being. Bloesch is, however, rightly concerned to not overreact to mysticism or to play down the truly experiential and mystical aspects of biblical prayer. See his chapter "Prayer and Mysticism," 97–130.

78. Zaleski and Zaleski, *Prayer: A History*, 30.

79. Even the Zaleskis cannot be fully consistent on this idea that we should embrace all kinds of human prayer. For example, they draw the line at human sacrifice, calling it "suicidal," and they point out that "the great reli-

gious traditions have come to reject it" (Ibid., 65). However, they don't say why human sacrifice is wrong, only that most people don't do it anymore.

80. Ibid., 161–71, 179–89.

81. Agehananda Bharati, *The Light at the Center: Context and Pretext of Modern Mysticism* (Santa Barbara: Ross-Erikson, 1976), 28, 43. Cited by Edmund P. Clowney in "A Biblical Theology of Prayer," in *Teach Us to Pray: Prayer in the Bible and the World*, ed. D. A. Carson (Eugene, OR: Wipf and Stock, 2002), 336n1.

82. "Belief in the personality of God is the necessary presupposition . . . wherever the vital conception of the divine personality grows dim, where, as in the philosophical ideal or in pantheistic mysticism it passes over into the 'One and All,' genuine prayer dissolves and becomes purely contemplative absorption and adoration" (Heiler, *Prayer: A Study*, 356).

83. "Personal Narrative" in *The Works of Jonathan Edwards*, vol. 16: *Letters and Personal Writings*, ed. George S. Claghorn (New Haven, CT: Yale University Press, 1998), 801.

84. Ibid., 797.

85. I do not want to give the impression that the answer is a "third way" perfectly balanced between the Zaleskis and Heiler. The reality is that the traditional Protestant understanding of prayer—and the one I will describe, unfold, and assume in the rest of this volume—is much closer to Heiler's and Bloesch's. That is not to be wondered at since, as noted, Heiler converted to Protestantism and I am a Protestant minister in the Reformed tradition. Nevertheless, the Zaleskis' brilliant and erudite survey of the practices and history of prayer forcefully reminds us that prayer is something that belongs to all human beings. It is a human instinct, not just a spiritual gift for Christian believers.

86. The first quote is from John Calvin's *Institutes of the Christian Religion*, 1.3.1. The second quote is from Calvin's commentary on John 1:5, 9. Both quotes are found in John T. McNeill, ed. *Calvin: Institutes of the Christian Religion*, vol. 1 (Louisville, KY: Westminster, 1960), 43, 43n2. Calvin quotes Cicero, who asks, "Where is there to be found a race or tribe of men which does not hold, without instruction, some preconception of the gods?" (from Cicero's *On the Nature of the Gods*, 44n4). Neither Calvin nor Cicero is saying it is impossible to sincerely and vigorously profess atheism. Cicero's statement occurs in a book where he has a dialogue with Velleius of the Epicureans, who denied the existence of the old gods. Rather, both Cicero and

Calvin are saying that, because of this inherent sense of God, prayer is a natural response unless repressed. And the instinct is difficult to eradicate. See Calvin's *Institutes*, 1.3.2: "Indeed, they seek out every subterfuge to hide themselves from the Lord's presence, and to efface it again from their minds. But in spite of themselves they are always entrapped. Although it may sometimes seem to vanish for a moment, it returns at once and rushes in with new force. . . . The impious themselves therefore exemplify the fact that some conception of God is ever alive in all men's minds" (McNeill, *Calvin: Institutes*, 45).

87. William H. Goold, ed., *The Works of John Owen*, vol. 4 (Carlisle, PA: Banner of Truth, 1967), 251–52.

88. See "The Most High a Prayer-Hearing God," in *The Works of Jonathan Edwards*, vol. 2, ed. Edward Hicks (Carlisle, PA: Banner of Truth, 1974), 117.

89. McNeill, *Calvin: Institutes*, 1.4.1., 47, "As experience shows, God has sown a seed of religion in all men. But scarcely one man in a hundred is met with who fosters it, once received, in his heart . . . all degenerate from the true knowledge of him. . . . They do not therefore apprehend God as he offers himself, but imagine him as they have fashioned him in their own presumption."

90. Another traditional Protestant theologian who acknowledges these two levels of prayer is nineteenth-century Princeton theologian Charles Hodge, who wrote: "It is principally through the efficacy of prayer that we receive the communications of the Holy Spirit. Prayer is not a mere instinct of a dependent nature, seeking help from the Author of its being; nor is it to be viewed simply as a natural expression of faith and desire, or as a mode of communion with the Father of our spirits; but it is also to be regarded as the appointed means of obtaining the Holy Ghost." Hodge shows that Christians have the "instinct of a dependent nature," but they also have prayer as a means by which the Holy Spirit communicates his gifts. He continues: "Hence we are urged to be constant and importunate in prayer, praying especially for those communications of Divine influence by which the life of God in the soul is maintained and promoted." Charles Hodge, *The Way of Life: A Guide to Christian Belief and Experience* (Carlisle, PA: Banner of Truth, 1978; reprint of an 1841 work), 231. Similarly, J. G. Vos says: "Prayer is practically universal in the human race. . . . All the non-Christian religious systems involve the practice of some kind of prayer. Non-Christian prayer, however, is not addressed to the . . . Triune God of the Scriptures . . . [and]

does not approach God through Jesus Christ as Mediator. . . . That God in his great mercy may sometimes hear and answer the prayers of non-Christians . . . we should not deny. But such prayers differ essentially from Christian prayer." Johannes G. Vos, *The Westminster Larger Catechism: A Commentary*, ed. G. I. Williamson (Phillipsburg, NJ: Presbyterian and Reformed, 2002), 512–13.

91. Eugene H. Peterson's book on prayer through the Psalms is *Answering God: The Psalms as Tools for Prayer* (San Francisco: Harper & Row, 1989). Though he uses the title "Answering God" to describe the Psalms themselves, I believe this also serves as an excellent and compressed definition for all prayer. I also draw on Clowney, who defines prayer as "personal address to a personal God" (Clowney, "Biblical Theology," 136). Much of this chapter is influenced by the outline of Ed Clowney's article. He calls prayer an address to a personal, covenant, and triune God.

92. Donald Bloesch quotes Karl Barth: "However difficult it may sound, the hearing really precedes the asking. It is the basis of it. It makes it real asking, the asking of Christian prayer" (Bloesch, *Struggle for Prayer*, 55).

93. C. S. Lewis, *That Hideous Strength* (New York: Macmillan, 1965), 318.

94. Ibid., 319.

95. We know Lewis had read Martin Buber's *I and Thou* (see C. S. Lewis, *Collected Letters*, vol. 2 [New York: HarperOne, 2004], 526, 528), which contains the phrase *Alles wirkliche Leben it Begegnung*, "All real living is meeting." See Martin Buber, *I and Thou*, trans. Ronald Gregor Smith (Edinburgh: T. & T. Clark, 1937), 20.

96. J. I. Packer, *Knowing God* (Downers Grove, IL: InterVarsity, 1993), 39–40.

97. See the longer discussion of this story in Timothy Keller, *Walking with God through Pain and Suffering* (New York: Dutton, 2013), 270–93.

98. John Knox is quoted by Bloesch, *Struggle of Prayer*, 50. The first and second quotes from John Calvin are taken from McNeill, *Calvin: Institutes*, 3.20.16, 3.20.2, 872, and 851, respectively.

CHAPTER FOUR—CONVERSING WITH GOD

99. For more on the biblical doctrine of the Trinity, see chapter 5.

100. The Father speaks to the Son and the Son to the Father: "I have brought you glory on earth by finishing the work you gave me to do. And now, Father, glorify me in your presence with the glory I had with you before the world began. I have revealed you to those whom you gave me out of the world. They

were yours; you gave them to me and they have obeyed your word. Now they know that everything you have given me comes from you. For I gave them the words you gave me and they accepted them. They knew with certainty that I came from you, and they believed that you sent me" (John 17:4–8). The Father and the Son speak to the Spirit: "But when he, the Spirit of truth, comes, he will guide you into all the truth. He will not speak on his own; he will speak only what he hears, and he will tell you what is yet to come. He will glorify me because it is from me that he will receive what he will make known to you. All that belongs to the Father is mine. That is why I said the Spirit will receive from me what he will make known to you" (John 16:13–15).

101. See Vern S. Poythress, *God-Centered Biblical Interpretation* (Phillipsburg, NJ: Presbyterian and Reformed, 1999), 16–25, from which many of the ideas in this part of the chapter are taken.

102. Nicholas Wolterstorff quotes Sandra M. Schneiders for an example of this view. She writes: "Divine discourse cannot be taken literally. . . . Words . . . are the intelligible physical sounds emitted by the vocal apparatus (or some substitute for that apparatus). . . . Language . . . is a human phenomenon rooted in our corporeality as well as in our discursive mode of intellection and as such cannot be literally predicated of pure spirit." Put another way, words are physical sounds (or physical marks on a page) that exist only for physical creatures. To talk about God, a pure spirit, speaking is wrong. Taken from Sandra M. Schneiders, *The Revelatory Text* (San Francisco: Harper, 1991), 27–29. Quoted in Nicholas Wolterstorff, *Divine Discourse: Philosophical Reflections on the Claim That God Speaks* (Cambridge: Cambridge University Press, 1995), 11.

103. Clowney, "Biblical Theology," 136.

104. Ward, *Words of Life*. This is one of the main burdens of Ward's entire volume.

105. Ibid., 22.

106. Ibid., 25.

107. Ibid., 27. The italics are in the original, not added.

108. Ibid., 31–32.

109. Eugene H. Peterson, *Working the Angles: The Shape of Pastoral Integrity* (Grand Rapids, MI: Eerdmans, 1987), 49.

110. Ibid., 48.

111. Peterson, *Answering God*, 14.

112. Bloesch, *Prayer: A Study*, 101.

113. Thomas Merton, *The Ascent to Truth* (New York: Harcourt, Brace, 1951), 83. Quoted in ibid.

114. Quoted in Bloesch, *Prayer: A Study*, 101.

115. John Jefferson Davis, *Meditation and Communion with God: Contemplating Scripture in an Age of Distraction* (Downers Grove, IL: InterVarsity Press, 2012), 16. Davis quotes Diana Eck in stating that the crossing over of Eastern meditation practices into Christianity is "one of the most important spiritual movements of today" and that Buddhist meditation "is becoming an important strand of Christian spirituality." Quotes from Diana L. Eck, *Encountering God: A Spiritual Journey from Bozeman to Banaras* (Boston: Beacon Press, 1993), 153. Davis cites Eck's research that shows how explicitly many Roman Catholic teachers have brought Buddhist and Hindu practices into their own practices of prayer and meditation (Davis, *Meditation and Communion*, 16n22).

116. See Thomas Keating, "The Origins of Centering Prayer," in *Intimacy with God* (New York: Crossroad, 1994), 11–22; and *Open Mind, Open Heart: The Contemplative Dimension of the Gospel* (New York: Continuum, 1992).

117. In *Prayer: A History*, 204–08, the Zaleskis provide an excellent summary of the teaching of the anonymous work *The Cloud of Unknowing* and its roots in the Neoplatonic text *The Mystical Theology* of Pseudo-Dionysius the Areopagite, from the sixth century. But they are critical—almost dismissive—of the way the Centering Prayer movement of Thomas Keating, William Menninger, and Basil Pennington has domesticated and perhaps commodified the wild, difficult path to contemplation marked out by medieval writers such as the author of *The Cloud*. The three basic steps of Centering Prayer:

    Rule 1: At the beginning of the Prayer we take a minute or two to quiet down and then move in faith to God dwelling in our depths; and at the end of the Prayer we take several minutes to come out, mentally praying the "Our Father" or some other prayer.

    Rule 2: After resting for a bit in the center of faith-full love, we take up a single, simple word [such as *God* or *love*] that expresses this response and begin to let it repeat itself within.

    Rule 3: Whenever in the course of the Prayer we become *aware* of anything else, gently return to the Presence by the use of the prayer word (M. Basil Pennington, O.C.S.O, *Centering Prayer: Renewing an Ancient Christian Prayer Form* [Garden City, NY: Image, 1982], 65).

    The Zaleskis comment (in *Prayer: A History*, 208): "It's easy to discern in

Notes

this program the bare bones of the teaching of *The Cloud*, especially the effort to suppress awareness of created things and the use of a single prayer word. But one misses the boldness of the original, here replaced with painfully polite expressions. . . . For the author of *The Cloud*, contemplative prayer is an arduous trial with an uncertain end; the centering prayer movement . . . has turned it into a comfortable exercise with a foregone conclusion." They end by observing that today's Centering Prayer has "little in common with *The Cloud*'s hard-eyed realism and seems rather to partake of the Zeitgeist of the late twentieth century, with its spiritual eclecticism and optimism."

118. John Jefferson Davis's telling critiques of Centering Prayer and the Jesus Prayer are found on pages 134–42 of his *Meditation and Communion*. Davis rightly criticizes Centering Prayer not only as not comporting with the biblical teaching on God's speech and personality, but also as not fitting with Christian beliefs about the goodness (versus the illusory nature) of the creation and the fact of Jesus' permanent incarnation. Eastern mysticism and the Neoplatonism that *The Cloud of Unknowing* represents see the physical world and personality/rationality as illusions or at least merely epiphenomenal and temporary. But that's not the biblical view. Davis writes: "The fact of the incarnation means that even now in heaven, and into eternity, the historical Jesus will still have a definite, though glorified, bodily form. . . . For all eternity the glorified Jesus will still have a human nature and consequently a human experience of the knowledge of God—a knowledge of God that of course transcends our knowledge, but is not *utterly dissimilar* to it. By leaving words and images behind, an exclusively apophatic style of meditation tends to erase the boundaries between Eastern (Buddhist, Hindu) and Christian forms of meditation."

119. Davis, *Meditation and Communion*, 141.

120. Zaleski and Zaleski, *Prayer: A History*, 143. The Zaleskis treat the Jesus Prayer very sympathetically, but they admit that the prayer often functions as a "magical operation" (143–44).

121. Ibid., 138.

122. Ibid. The question poses itself: If we accept all the warnings and cautions about mysticism, how are we to interpret the experience of the medieval Christian mystics? Were they connecting to the true God or not? I believe we have to answer that on a case-by-case basis. Many of the mystics seem to be praying to a very personal, triune God of holiness and love, both transcendent and immanent. Though their manner of prayer does not ground

their prayer in the Word as much as a Protestant would want, it appears that their heart and imagination were shaped enough by the Bible that the God they meet is the biblical God. Other mystical Christian writers, however, appear to have had the kinds of alterations in psychological consciousness that can be brought on by many forms of meditation and physical deprivation. I can't be as confident those experiences are the same as that described by the biblical writers. It is also possible that some mystical authors have had both kinds of experiences, and it is difficult, at least for me, to distinguish which were genuine encounters with God and which were not.

123. J. I. Packer and Carolyn Nystrom, *Praying: Finding Our Way through Duty to Delight* (Downers Grove, IL: InterVarsity Press, 2009) 65.

124. Ibid.

125. Anne Lamott, *Help, Thanks, Wow: The Three Essential Prayers* (New York: Penguin, 2012), 2–3.

126. Lamott (*Help*, 67) briefly alludes to confession once in passing. "So I prayed: 'Help me not be such an ass.'" Then Lamott adds in parentheses: "This is actually the fourth great prayer, which perhaps we will address another time." Nevertheless, while she calls it the "fourth great prayer," it is neither named nor treated elsewhere in the book.

127. See Augustine's Letter 130 (AD 412) to Proba found in Philip Schaff, ed., *Nicene and Post-Nicene Fathers*, First Series, vol. 1, 1887 (Christian Classics Ethereal Library), 997–1015; Martin Luther, "A Simple Way to Pray" in *Luther's Works: Devotional Writings II*, ed. Gustav K. Wiencke, vol. 43 (Philadelphia: Muhlenberg Press, 1968), 187–211.

128. However, I think it is fair to say that Lamott does not really follow her own principle consistently. For example, she writes: "Most good honest prayers remind me that I am not in charge, that I cannot fix anything, and that I open myself to being helped by something, some force, some friends, some something. . . . I am clueless, but something else isn't" (Help, 35). This is an assertion about God's sovereignty and power and our dependence on him. Such theological statements are unavoidable, really, because we can't pray to God without some conception in our mind of his nature. But since Lamott has not chosen to ground her book on prayer in biblical narratives, we aren't told why we should believe that God "isn't clueless" or where that knowledge comes from.

129. Clowney, "A Biblical Theology," 136. Compare the words of Arthur W. Pink: "In the great majority of books written, and in the sermons preached upon prayer, the human element fills the scene almost entirely. It is the

conditions which we must meet, the promises we must claim, the things we must do, in order to get our requests granted; and God's claim . . . rights . . . [of] glory are often disregarded." From Arthur W. Pink, *The Sovereignty of God* (Carlisle, PA: Banner of Truth, 1961), 109.

130. Christian Smith's *Soul Searching: The Religious and Spiritual Lives of American Teenagers* (New York: Oxford University Press, 2005) explores the faith and spiritual lives of young American adults, who he describes as being characterized by "moralistic, therapeutic deism." This is belief in a God who exists but who is not particularly involved in day-to-day affairs, where human free will and choices determine things. In this view, God's main desire for us is that we live good lives, being kind and fair to others. If we live that way, he then provides "therapeutic benefits"—self-esteem and happiness (pp. 163–64). This view of God has a profound effect on prayer. Smith found that American teens personally prayed frequently; 40 percent prayed daily or more, and only 15 percent said they never prayed. However, their motivation for prayer was pervasively that of meeting psychological and emotional needs. "If I ever have a problem I go pray." "It helps me deal with problems, 'cause I have a temper, so it calms me down for the most part." "When I have a problem, I can just go bear it and he'll always be supportive." "Praying just makes me feel more secure, like there's something there helping me out." "I would say prayer is an essential part of my success" (pp. 151–53). Smith points out that from young Americans' prayers there were at least two things missing. First, repentance is virtually absent. "This is not a religion of repentance from sin," Smith writes. Second, prayer to this God is almost devoid of adoration and praise, because he is a "distant God" who is "not demanding. He actually can't be, because his job is to solve problems and make people feel good. There is nothing here to evoke wonder and admiration" (p. 165).

In Smith's subsequent study of the faith of "emerging adults" (ages 18–29), *Souls in Transition: The Religious and Spiritual Lives of Emerging Adults* (New York: Oxford University Press, 2009), he observes "an increase in the selfish and instrumental use of personal prayer" (102). In summary, instead of adoration and repentance—two forms of prayer that put the one praying into perspective as small, limited, weak, and dependent— younger adults pray almost exclusively for help with their problems or to feel better and happier. Studies of younger adults in Europe have shown a similar shift in the use of prayer from seeking God to becoming "a path of discovery of the 'true self.' . . . God, according to these interviewees, can be found only inside the 'true self.'" See Giordan and Swatos, *Religion, Spirituality*, 87. See also Giuseppe Giordan and Enzo Pace, eds., *Mapping Religion and Spirituality in a Postsecular World* (Leiden, Netherlands: Brill, 2012). A thin or vague view of God does not simply reduce prayer's content but also reverses its motive. In the prayer of younger Americans, God is a means to the end of a happy life for themselves. Glorifying God is not in view—and indeed, would be an opaque and confusing concept. Instead, prayer is used on a cost-benefit (to the self) basis.

131. Peterson, *Answering God*, 5–6.

132. This story is recounted in John Pollock, *George Whitefield and the Great Awakening* (Oxford: Lion Publishing, 1972), 205–08; and Arnold A. Dallimore, *George Whitefield: The Life and Times of the Great Evangelist of the Eighteenth-Century Revival*, vol. 2 (Carlisle, PA: Banner of Truth, 1979), 168–69. See also Harry S. Stout, *The Divine Dramatist: George Whitefield and the Rise of Modern Evangelicalism* (Grand Rapids, MI: Eerdmans, 1991), 170. Pollock points out that a carriage near-accident that was averted when his wife was pregnant helped convince him that his son's life was being preserved because God had great things in store for him. Dallimore adds that Whitefield's assumption that God spoke to him directly through his impressions was a habit of mind Jonathan Edwards had warned him against earlier, and seemingly, it was advice Whitefield had not appreciated. Stout contributes the fact that Whitefield blamed himself for John's death, fearing he had made an "idol" of his son. While Stout thinks Whitefield was wrong to interpret such misfortunes as punishment for his sins, Whitefield was certainly right that he had turned his infant son into an idolatrous focus of his own longing for usefulness and influence. If the child had grown to maturity, he would have been extraordinarily burdened with his father's expectations and hopes.

Chapter Five—Encountering God

133. Ward, *Words of Life*, 48. The italics are in the original, not added. Ward goes on to show also that the Bible is a covenant document. When God enters into a relationship with us human beings, it is not merely personal but also covenantal. It means we are bound to God and he to us by promises to be faithful to one another—and now we have right of access to him. It is analogous to the covenant of marriage. Both the Bible *and* prayer, then, are covenantal privileges. God speaks to his people (through the Bi-

ble) and listens to his people (through prayer), who are bound to him in the covenantal relationship. See Ward, 22–23.

134. Many object that since the word *Trinity* does not appear in the Bible and since the doctrine was not formulated until the third and fourth centuries after Christ, the doctrine is an imposition of later theology on the biblical text. Nothing could be further from the truth. There are three things the New Testament says repeatedly about God: (1) there is only one God, (2) the Father, the Son, and the Holy Spirit are all equally God, indeed "*all* of the fullness of the deity" dwells in each (cf. Col 2:9), not just one-third of the divinity, and (3) the three persons know and love one another and work together in distinctive ways for our salvation. Only the doctrine of the Trinity accounts for all three biblical propositions. J. I. Packer uses the illustration of something being "in solution." Sugar dissolved in tea is not visible—it is "in solution," but a chemist could crystallize it if necessary. Packer rightly insists that the Trinity was "in solution" in the Bible, and all the early church did was crystallize it. Packer and Nystrom, *Praying: Finding Our Way*, 23–24.

135. When God said he would "make his name dwell" in the tabernacle (Deut 12:5, 11; cf. 1 Kings 8:16, 29), he meant he was going to live there himself. When the psalmist says God's "name is near," he means God himself is near (Psalm 75:1). And every time a human being in the Bible went through a deep transformation of character or nature, the name was changed, from Abram to Abraham, Simon to Peter, Saul to Paul. In the Bible, your name is your nature. So when Jesus says that the Father, Son, and Holy Spirit have a single name, the divine name, it tells us that, though three persons, they are one being and share one nature.

136. R. T. France, *The Gospel of Matthew: New International Commentary on the New Testament* (Grand Rapids, MI: Eerdmans, 2007). He adds, "The fact that the three divine persons are spoken of as having a single 'name' is a significant pointer toward the Trinitarian doctrine of the three persons in one God" (1118).

137. See the Westminster Larger Catechism, Q. 9 and 10. "*Q. 9. How many persons are there in the Godhead?* A. There be three persons in the Godhead, the Father, the Son, and the Holy Ghost; and these three are one true, eternal God, the same in substance, equal in power and glory; although distinguished by their personal properties. *Q. 10. What are the personal properties of the three persons in the Godhead?* A. It is proper to the Father to beget the Son, and to the Son to be begotten of the Father, and to the

Holy Ghost to proceed from the Father and the Son from all eternity." This summarizes the doctrine of the Trinity. (1) There is one God existing in three persons, and (2) these persons are equal in power, divinity, and glory. These three are not merely different modes for the same person, nor are the persons interchangeable. They know and love one another and work together for the creation and redemption of the world—in which the Father sends the Son, and the Father and the Son send the Spirit.

This is one place where all branches of Christianity—Orthodox, Catholic, and Protestant—agree. If you don't believe in the Trinity, you do not merely misunderstand prayer, but you twist Christianity completely out of shape so it is not itself. If you deny (1) one way, saying there is only one God with one person, that is Unitarianism. If you deny (1) the other way, saying there are three Gods in three persons, that is polytheism. If you deny (2), saying God the Father is the real God and the other two are derivatives, that is subordinationism. If you deny (3), saying there is one God but he inhabits different forms or shapes at different times, that is modalism. None of those are Trinitarianism. There is one God in three equally divine persons, who know and love one another and work together as a team to create and redeem the world. The entire Christian church throughout all the centuries has always said this is true. Without this, your understanding of everything else goes wrong.

It is worth noting that while various analogies can be used to illustrate certain aspects of the Trinity, any single analogy taken exclusively skews too much toward one aspect (oneness or threeness, equality or diversity). Common analogies include a cube with its height, width, and depth; the sun with its source, heat, and light; social analogies—in which God is a family or community; or psychological analogies, such as the lover, the self one loves, and the love with which the lover loves the self. See Augustine's efforts to find images of the Trinity in the human mind in Book 9 of *De Trinitate*. As intriguing and as often illuminating as they are, any analogy adopted exclusively leads the thinking in the direction of one of the heresies mentioned above.

138. Paul Ramsey, ed., *Ethical Writings: The Works of Jonathan Edwards*, vol. 8 (New Haven, CT: Yale University Press, 1989), 403–536.

139. William G. T. Shedd, "Introductory Essay" to Augustine's *On the Trinity*, in *A Select Library of the Nicene and Post-Nicene Fathers of the Christian Church*, ed. Philip Schaff, vol. 3 (Grand Rapids, MI: Eerdmans, 1979), 14. "Here is society within the Essence, and wholly independent of the universe; and communion and blessedness resulting therefrom. But this is impossible to an

essence without personal distinctions. Not the singular Unit of the deist, but the plural Unity of the Trinitarian, explains this. A subject without an object could not know. What is there to be known? Could not love. What is there to be loved? Could not rejoice. What is there to rejoice over? And the object cannot be the universe. The infinite and eternal object of God's infinite and eternal knowledge, love, and joy, cannot be his creation: because this is neither eternal, nor infinite. There was a time when the universe was not; and if God's self-consciousness and blessedness depends upon the universe, there was a time when God was neither self-conscious nor blessed" (14–15).

140. This fact—that the metaphor of adoption combines the forensic legal aspects of salvation (such as pardon and justification) with the relational (such as regeneration and sanctification)—means that the biblical doctrine of adoption is getting a lot of attention in current theological scholarship. See J. Todd Billings, "Salvation as Adoption in Christ: An Antidote to Today's Distant yet Convenient Deity," in *Union with Christ: Reframing Theology and Ministry for the Church* (Grand Rapids, MI: Baker Academic, 2011), 15–34. Billings sees the doctrine of adoption as an especially potent antidote to the "Moralistic Therapeutic Deism" (as Christian Smith calls it) of younger American adults. This term means belief in a God who is there but only for emergencies and who otherwise makes no demands. See also Michael S. Horton, "Adoption: Forensic and Relational, Judicial and Transformative," in *Covenant and Salvation: Union with Christ* (Louisville, KY: Westminster John Knox Press, 2007), 244–47. As Horton's subtitle suggests, the doctrine of adoption in Christ gives Protestants an answer to the charge that their belief in full legal acceptance—justification by faith alone apart from any inward change or personal merit—encourages Christians to make no changes or effort to live holy and righteous lives. Adoption unites the forensic/legal and the relational/transformative. An adopted child has a changed legal status *and* radically changed life patterns and lived relationships all at once. The two go intrinsically together. Anyone who is truly justified by faith in Christ apart from good works *will* necessarily produce good works. The conception of adoption prevents us from pitting aspects of our salvation in Christ against one another.

141. The quote is from a radio talk by J. Gresham Machen, "The Active Obedience of Christ," from early in the twentieth century. The fuller quote: "[The] covenant of works was a probation. If Adam had kept the law of God for a certain period, he was to have eternal life. If he disobeyed, he was

to have death. Well, he disobeyed, and the penalty of death was inflicted upon him and his posterity. Then Christ by his death on the cross paid that penalty . . . but if that is all Christ did for us, do you not see that we should be back in just the situation in which Adam was before he sinned? The penalty of his sinning would have been removed from us because it had all been paid by Christ. But for the future the attainment of eternal life would have been dependent upon our perfect obedience to the law of God. We should simply have been back in the probation again. As a matter of fact, [Christ] has not merely paid the penalty of Adam's first sin (and the penalty of the sins which we individually have committed), but also he has positively merited for us eternal life. He was, in other words, our representative both in the *penalty paying* and in *probation keeping.* He paid the penalty [of failed probation] for us, and he stood the probation for us. . . . [Christ not only took the punishment by his death] but merited for them the reward by his perfect obedience to God's law. . . . Those are the two things he has done for us." This can be found in J. Gresham Machen, *God Transcendent* (Carlisle, PA: Banner of Truth, 1982), 187–88.

142. See Edwards's sermon "Justification by Faith Alone," in *The Works of Jonathan Edwards,* vol. 19, *Sermons and Discourses, 1734–1738,* ed. M. X. Lesser (New Haven: Yale University Press, 2001), 204.

143. C. E. B. Cranfield, *A Critical and Exegetical Commentary on the Epistle to the Romans,* vol. 1 (Edinburgh: T. & T. Clark, 1975), 400. In the well-known article "*Abba* isn't 'Daddy,'" *The Journal of Theological Studies* 39 (1988), 28–47, James Barr tries to correct the emphasis of Joachim Jeremias and others who stressed that *Abba* meant "Daddy" and was a term of supreme familiarity. Barr determines that the word *Abba* was not used only by small children but also by Jewish children when they were fully grown. There was another Greek word—*pappas*—that was used only by children and discarded later and so would be the equivalent of "Dada" or "Daddy." Barr's point was that it wasn't appropriate to address the Almighty God in prayer as Daddy. Nevertheless, Barr's point can also be overdone. In most cultures, children—especially males—do tend to discard the baby terms (e.g., from "Daddy" to "Dad"). Nevertheless, when an adult continues to call a parent Mama or Papa, it mixes respect with the old intimacy, delight, and access they had as little children.

144. Cranfield, *Critical and Exegetical Commentary,* 400.

145. Martin Luther, "Personal Prayer Book," in *Luther's Works: Devotional*

Writings II, ed. Gustav K. Wiencke, vol. 43 (Minneapolis: Fortress Press, 1968), 29.

146. Some commentators argue that the groans here are only the groans of the Spirit, not ours. We are, therefore, entirely unaware of them. They arise to God beside our petitions. The Spirit's intercession, therefore, arises constantly and happens essentially apart from us and our prayers. (Commentators on Romans 8:26–27 who take that view include Douglas J. Moo and Joseph A. Fitzmyer.) Others believe that while it is strictly true grammatically that the groans are the Spirit's—the point of the promise is that we feel weak and don't know how to pray and the Spirit helps us in that. After all, God is a "searcher of hearts" (Rom 8:27), and this means God is looking into believer's hearts. So the groanings of the Spirit are believers' groanings and longings after conformity to God's will originating from the Holy Spirit. Commentators such as John Murray, Peter O'Brien, John Stott, and Thomas Schreiner take this latter view. See Schreiner, *Romans: Baker Exegetical*, 445–47.

147. "Accordingly, we know not what to pray for as we ought in tribulations" Augustine Letter 130, in Schaff, *Nicene and Post-Nicene Fathers*, 1011.

148. Clowney, "Biblical Theology," 170.

149. Graeme Goldsworthy, *Prayer and the Knowledge of God* (Downers Grove, IL: InterVarsity, 2003), 169–70.

150. John Murray, *The Epistle to the Romans* (Grand Rapids, MI: Eerdmans, 1968), 330.

151. See *Nicomachean Ethics*, Book VIII.7, trans. W. D. Ross, Digireads, 2005.

152. This is D. A. Carson's explanation in *The Gospel According to John*, Pillar New Testament Commentary series (Grand Rapids, MI: Eerdmans, 1991), 496–97.

153. McNeill, *Calvin: Institutes*, 3.2.36., 585–84.

154. McNeill, *Calvin: Institutes*, 1.2.1., 41.

155. McNeill, *Calvin: Institutes*, 1.2.2., 43.

156. Of course, many things we do now, including prayer and praise, can be called a "pleasing sacrifice" to God (Heb 13:15–16), but they are no longer an *appeasing* sacrifice. In Hebrews 13, Christian prayer is depicted as a thank offering for a salvation already secured by Christ. Prayer is not, on New Testament terms, an atoning or appeasing sacrifice that turns aside God's wrath and procures and merits God's attention and favor.

157. My own translation. For a literal version of this, see the New American

Standard Bible—"For my father and mother have forsaken me, but the Lord will take me up."

158. McNeill, *Calvin: Institutes*, 3.20., 850.

CHAPTER SIX—LETTERS ON PRAYER

159. Calvin's *Institutes* are something like what we would today call a systematic theology. It is striking and somewhat puzzling, then, that even writers of systematic theology in Calvin's Reformed tradition do not usually have a chapter on prayer. One exception was Charles Hodge, the nineteenth-century Princeton theologian, whose systematic theology contains a substantial section on prayer, and particularly on the implications of the Christian doctrine of God for Christian prayer. See Charles Hodge, *Systematic Theology*, vol. 3 (Grand Rapids, MI: Eerdmans, 1965), 692–700.

160. Schaff, *Nicene and Post-Nicene Fathers*, 997–1015.

161. Ibid.

162. See chapter 8 for more on Augustine's exposition of the Lord's Prayer.

163. Quoted in Mark Rogers, "'Deliver Us from the Evil One': Martin Luther on Prayer," *Themelios* 34, no. 3 (November 2009).

164. Luther, "A Simple Way to Pray," 193. It is worth noticing that Luther says that this twice-daily prayer regimen could be in private in your room or in a church with an assembled congregation. He writes: "When I feel that I have become cool and joyless in prayer . . . I hurry to my room, or, if it be the day and hour for it, to the church where a congregation is assembled" (193). This is testimony to the importance of corporate worship in Luther's theology. We do not conquer a hard, cold, prayerless heart only on our own, through personal exercises. The public house of worship of the people of God was a place where you could hear the Word of God through the preached Word—not just through the read Word as in private—and where the response of prayer and praise was corporate, not just individual.

165. Martin Luther, *Luther's Large Catechism*, trans. F. Samuel Janzow (St. Louis: Concordia, 1978), 79.

166. Calvin too believed it was crucial to engage the heart and mind in prayer, and like Luther, he counsels to do it with disciplined meditation on the meaning of the Word and what is being said. He writes: "A fault that seems less serious but is also not tolerable is that of others who, having been imbued with this one principle—that God must be appeased by devotions—mumble prayers without meditation. Now the godly must particularly

beware of presenting themselves before God to request anything unless they yearn for it with sincere affection of heart, and at the same time desire to obtain it from him. Indeed, even though in those things which we seek only to God's glory we do not seem at first glance to be providing for our own need, yet it is fitting that they be sought with no less ardor and eagerness. When, for example, we pray that 'his name be sanctified' [Matt 6:9; Luke 11:2], we should, so to speak, eagerly hunger and thirst after that sanctification" (McNeill, *Calvin: Institutes*, 3.20.6., 857).

167. Luther, "A Simple Way to Pray," 194.

168. The only subject Luther proposes for this meditation that is not strictly Scripture is the Apostles' Creed, perhaps because Luther was so thoroughly convinced that it was nothing but a distillation of biblical truth. Luther gives examples of how to meditate on the Creed in "A Simple Way to Pray," 209–11.

169. Ibid., 200.

170. Ibid., 200–01.

171. Ibid., 196–97.

172. Ibid., 198.

173. Luther's advice on how to meditate and then how to paraphrase and personalize the Lord's Prayer can be applied to any part of Scripture. Praying the Psalms and other parts of the Bible back to God is a very ancient and time-tested Christian practice. But seldom has it been outlined and presented in a more accessible way than Luther does here. We also have in Luther's "A Simple Way to Pray" an implicit approval of praying prayers written for you by others. While some, like John Bunyan, were completely against using scripted prayers, Luther's *Small Catechism* offers some written prayers to be prayed in families before going to work and school in the morning and going to bed at night. Calvin provided the same thing. Luther had no problem with the use of scripted prayers, as long as we internally personalized the prayer as we pray—otherwise it would be but "idle chatter and prattle." See "Daily Prayers" in *Luther's Small Catechism with Explanation* (St. Louis: Concordia, 1986), 30–32.

174. Luther, "A Simple Way to Pray," 198.

175. Ibid., 201–02.

Chapter Seven—Rules for Prayer

176. McNeill, *Calvin: Institutes*, 3.20.5., 854.
177. Kenneth Grahame, *The Wind in the Willows*, chapter 7, "The Piper at the Gates of Dawn."
178. McNeill, *Calvin: Institutes*, 856. This is the chapter heading for 3.20.6. It is marked with an asterisk, meaning that the editor supplied it—it was not original to Calvin. Nevertheless, it is a good summary of this second rule of Calvin's for prayer.
179. Ibid., 857.
180. Francis Spufford, *Unapologetic: Why, Despite Everything, Christianity Can Still Make Surprising Emotional Sense* (New York: HarperOne, 2013), 27.
181. McNeill, *Calvin: Institutes*, 3.20.7., 858.
182. McNeill, *Calvin: Institutes*, 3.20.8., 859.
183. McNeill, *Calvin: Institutes*, 3.20.11., 862.
184. McNeill, *Calvin: Institutes*, 3.20.13., 867.
185. McNeill, *Calvin: Institutes*, 3.20.15., 872.
186. McNeill, *Calvin: Institutes*, 3.20.16., 872.
187. McNeill, *Calvin: Institutes*, 3.20.17., 874–75.
188. McNeill, *Calvin: Institutes*, 3.20.15., 870.
189. Goldsworthy, *Prayer and the Knowledge of God*, 48.
190. Ibid.
191. R. A. Torrey, *The Power of Prayer and the Prayer of Power* (Grand Rapids, MI: Fleming H. Revell, 1924), 106–07.

Chapter Eight—The Prayer of Prayers

192. For Luther, see not only "A Simple Way to Pray" but his "Personal Prayer Book" in *Luther's Works* and both his *Large Catechism* and *Small Catechism* as well as *Luther's Works: The Sermon on the Mount and the Magnificat*, vol. 21 (St. Louis: Concordia, 1968). For Calvin, besides his *Institutes*, see David and Thomas Torrance, eds., *A Harmony of the Gospels: Matthew, Mark, and Luke*, vol. 1 (Grand Rapids, MI: Eerdmans, 1994). For Augustine, see especially Paul A. Boer, ed., *St. Augustine of Hippo: Our Lord's Sermon on the Mount according to Matthew & the Harmony of the Gospels* (CreateSpace, 2012), taken from Philip Schaff, *Nicene and Post-Nicene Fathers*, vol. 6 (Christian Literature, 1886).
193. McNeill, *Calvin: Institutes*, 3.20.36., 899.

194. Luther, "Personal Prayer Book," 29.

195. McNeill, *Calvin: Institutes*, 3.20.36., 901.

196. *Luther's Large Catechism*, 84.

197. Augustine, Letter 130, in Schaff, *Nicene and Post-Nicene Fathers*, chapter 12.

198. McNeill, *Calvin: Institutes*, 3.20.41., 903–04.

199. Augustine, "Our Lord's Sermon on the Mount," trans. S. D. F. Salmond, in *Nicene and Post-Nicene Fathers*, ed. Philip Schaff, vol. 6, 1886 (Electronic edition, Veritatis Splendor, 2012), 156.

200. McNeill, *Calvin: Institutes*, 3.20.42., 905.

201. Luther, "Personal Prayer Book," 32.

202. Ibid., 33.

203. Augustine, "Our Lord's Sermon on the Mount," 158–59.

204. Luther, "Personal Prayer Book," 34.

205. McNeill, *Calvin: Institutes*, 3.20.43., 907.

206. George Herbert, "Discipline," in *The English Poems of George Herbert*, ed. Helen Wilcox (New York: Cambridge University Press, 2010), 620.

207. Augustine, Letter 130, in Schaff, *Nicene and Post-Nicene Fathers*, chapter 12.

208. McNeill, *Calvin: Institutes*, 3.20.44., 907–08.

209. *Luther's Large Catechism*, 92.

210. *Luther's Large Catechism*, 93.

211. McNeill, *Calvin: Institutes*, 3.20.45., 912.

212. Augustine, "Our Lord's Sermon on the Mount," 167.

213. McNeill, *Calvin: Institutes*, 3.20.46., 913.

214. Ibid.

215. *Luther's Large Catechism*, 96–97.

216. Augustine, Letter 130, in Schaff, *Nicene and Post-Nicene Fathers*, chapter 12. See also his "Our Lord's Sermon on the Mount," 171.

217. McNeill, *Calvin: Institutes*, 3.20.47., 915–16.

218. McNeill, *Calvin: Institutes*, 3.20.49., 917.

219. McNeill, *Calvin: Institutes*, 3.20.47., 915.

220. Horton, *Calvin on the Christian Life*, 154.

221. C. S. Lewis, *The Four Loves* (New York: Harcourt, 1960), 61.

222. Ibid., 62.

CHAPTER NINE—THE TOUCHSTONES OF PRAYER

223. Forsyth, *Soul of Prayer*, 9–10.

224. Ibid., 62.

225. Phelps, *The Still Hour*, 61–62.

226. Ole Hallesby, *Prayer* (Minneapolis: Augsburg, 1975), 89–90.

227. See the important and extensive discussion of the conflict between the Puritans and the Quakers in Peter Adam, *Hearing God's Words: Exploring Biblical Spirituality* (Downers Grove, IL: InterVarsity Press, 2004), 175–201. Adam sides with the Puritans, who charged that the Quakers separated Word and Spirit, but he adds it is possible to overidentify the Spirit with the Word so that there is no way that the Spirit can influence us at all apart from our reading the Bible. That is an opposite mistake. "Too close an identification of Spirit and Word falls down when we reflect that the Spirit indwells believers even when they are not thinking the words of Scripture. Too radical a separation between Spirit and Word diminishes two of the means God has provided and chosen to use: Bible and Bible teacher" (199).

228. J. I. Packer, "Some Lessons in Prayer," in *Knowing Christianity* (Wheaton, IL: Harold Shaw, 1995), 129–30.

229. See the evidence for this conclusion in Wayne R. Spear, *The Theology of Prayer: A Systematic Study of the Biblical Teaching on Prayer* (Grand Rapids, MI: Baker, 1979), 28–30; and Graeme Goldsworthy, *Prayer and the Knowledge of God*, 82–83.

230. Packer, *Knowing Christianity*, 127.

231. Westminster Larger Catechism, Q. 189.

232. Phelps, *The Still Hour*, 55.

233. Hallesby, *Prayer*, 16.

234. Packer, *Knowing Christianity*, 128.

235. Forsyth, *Soul of Prayer*, 10.

236. The moment we believe in Christ, we are said to be "in Christ"—united with him. Sinclair Ferguson discerns several aspects of our union with Christ—we are united with him legally, by faith, spiritually, and vitally (S. Ferguson, *The Christian Life*, [Carlisle, PA: Banner of Truth, 1981], 107–10).

237. Clowney, "A Biblical Theology of Prayer."

238. Westminster Larger Catechism, Q. 182.

239. John Newton, "Letter II to Mr. B****," in *The Works of John Newton*, vol. 1 (Carlisle, PA: Banner of Truth, 1985), 622.

240. Westminster Larger Catechism, Q. 174.

241. William Guthrie, *The Christian's Great Interest* (Glasgow: W. Collins, 1828), 156.

242. Forsyth, *Soul of Prayer*, 18–19.

243. Westminster Larger Catechism, Q. 105. Here, explaining the first commandment—not to have any other gods before the true God—the catechism tells us that we are to root out "self-love, self-seeking, and all other inordinate and immoderate setting of our mind, will, or affections upon other things, and taking them off from him in whole or in part . . . and ascribing the praise of any good we either are, have, or can do, to fortune, idols, ourselves, or any other creature."

244. McNeill, *Calvin: Institutes*, 1.1.1.

245. Clowney, "A Biblical Theology of Prayer," 142.

246. Hodge, *Systematic Theology*, 703.

247. Hallesby, *Prayer*, 61–118.

248. Cited in Bloesch, *Struggle of Prayer*, ix.

249. Hallesby, *Prayer*, 76.

250. Packer and Nystrom, *Praying: Finding Our Way*, 40.

251. Ibid.

252. A paraphrase of Romans 7:19–20, 22–23.

253. McNeill, *Calvin: Institutes*, 3.20.1., 850.

CHAPTER TEN—AS CONVERSATION: MEDITATING ON HIS WORD

254. Peterson, *Answering God*, 23–24.

255. Edmund P. Clowney, *CM: Christian Meditation* (Nutley, NJ: Craig Press, 1979), 11.

256. Modern people might think that the term "law of the Lord" meant only the Ten Commandments or the books of the Bible that were explicitly filled with divine legislation. But the broad usage of the term "law of the Lord" in the Bible shows that the term can and does often refer to all of the Scripture. The Scripture is all "law" in the sense that it is all normative, all binding on the believer as an expression of God's will, whether taking the form of actual legal precepts or of a story with a lesson.

257. Derek Kidner, *Psalms 1–72, Tyndale Old Testament Commentaries*, vol. 15 (Downers Grove, IL: InterVarsity Press, 1973), 48.

258. New Testament words that are associated with the work of meditation include the word *logizdomai*, a favorite of Paul's, which means to "calculate, to assess the value, to count up" (1 Cor 13:5; 2 Cor 2:6) or "to evaluate,

estimate, consider" (Rom 2:26; 9:8) or "to think about, ponder, let one's mind dwell on" (Phil 4:8; 2 Cor 10:11). See P. T. O'Brien, *The Epistle to the Philippians: A Commentary on the Greek Text* (Grand Rapids, MI: Eerdmans, 1991), 436. Similar terms in Paul are seen in Ephesians 3:18, where he prays for "the power to grasp how wide and long and high and deep is the love of Christ"—the term meaning to comprehend or take in, referring to both the intellect and the affections.

259. Luther, "A Simple Way to Pray," 200.

260. Lindsay Gellman, "Meditation Has Limited Benefits, Study Finds," *The Wall Street Journal*, January 7, 2014. The study found no benefits for mantra meditation and a few limited ones for "mindfulness" meditation or "present focused awareness."

261. Clowney, *CM*, 7.

262. Douglas J. Moo, *The Letters to the Colossians and to Philemon, Pillar New Testament Commentary* (Grand Rapids, MI: Eerdmans, 2008), 286. Moo rightly points out that since the "you" in Colossians 3:16 is plural, he is talking not merely of individual meditation on the Scripture but corporate study and contemplation of the Word.

263. Two classic Protestant treatments of meditation from the seventeenth century were written by Richard Baxter, in *The Saints' Everlasting Rest*, and John Owen, in *The Grace and Duty of Being Spiritually Minded*. Baxter wrote of two basic movements within meditation. First, there was "consideration"—meaning long, thoughtful reflection—and second was "soliloquy" meaning preaching to oneself, self-communing, and exhortation. See Richard Baxter, *The Saints Everlasting Rest*, abridged by Benjamin Fawcett (The American Tract Society, 1759). See Peter Adam's summary of Baxter's teaching on meditation in Adam, *Hearing God's Words*, 202–10. John Owen's main work on meditation is *The Grace and Duty of Being Spiritually Minded*, in *The Works of John Owen*, ed. William H. Goold, vol. 7 (Carlisle, PA: Banner of Truth, 1965), 262–497. Owen's steps of meditation—to "fix the mind" on truth and then to "incline the heart" toward it—are parallel to Baxter's. See also Owen's "Meditations and Discourses on the Glory of Christ," in *Works of John Owen*, ed. William H. Goold, vol. 1 (Carlisle, PA: Banner of Truth, 1965), 274–461. Here we have an extended example of an actual meditation by Owen on various aspects of the glory of Jesus Christ.

264. Owen, *The Grace and Duty of Being Spiritually Minded*, 384. See also p. 270, where he lists the three stages or parts of meditation. "Three things

may be distinguished in the great duty of being spiritually minded . . . [1—Fixing the mind] The actual exercise of the mind, in its thoughts, meditations, and desires, about things spiritual and heavenly. . . . They mind them by fixing their thoughts and meditations upon them. [2–Inclining the heart] The inclination, disposition, and frame of the mind, in all its affections, whereby it adheres and cleaves unto spiritual things . . . from the love and delight . . . in them and engagement unto them. [3–Enjoying the Lord] A complacency of mind, from that gust, relish, and savor, which it finds in spiritual things, from their suitableness unto its constitution, inclinations, and desires. There is a salt in spiritual things, whereby they are condited and made savory unto a renewed mind; though to others they are as the white of an egg, that hath no taste or savor in it. In this gust and relish lies the sweetness and satisfaction of spiritual life. Speculative notions about spiritual things, when they are alone, are dry, sapless, and barren. In this gust we taste by experience that God is gracious, and that the love of Christ is better than wine, or whatever else hath the most grateful relish unto a sensual appetite. This is the proper foundation of that 'joy which is unspeakable and full of glory,'" 270–71.

265. Ibid.

266. Cited in Adam, *Hearing God's Words*, 209.

267. This is taken from John Owen, *Meditations and Discourses on the Glory of Christ*, 400–01.

268. Ibid., 400.

269. Ibid., 401.

270. Owen, *Works*, vol. 7, 270–71.

271. Ibid., 393.

272. Ibid.

273. Ibid., 394.

274. It is interesting to compare Owen's three steps of meditation to those of the traditional Catholic and Benedictine practice of *lectio divina*, or "divine reading," as described by Thelma Hall in *Too Deep for Words: Rediscovering* Lectio Divina (Mahwah, NJ: Paulist Press, 1988). The four steps of *lectio divina* are reading, meditating, prayer, and contemplation. (1) *Reading the Scripture* in *lectio divina* means slow, meditative perusal of a Biblical passage. In *lectio* it is not recommended that you try to theologically analyze the text for doctrinal meanings. Instead you should wait on the Holy Spirit to show you something within the text especially for you. Wait for something to draw your interest and grab your attention and note it. You are

looking for something that seems very relevant for "me, now" in my current situation (pp. 36–38). Once you have done this, move on to (2) *Meditation*. Hall suggests two kinds of meditation. One is using the imagination, putting yourself into the biblical scene (if it is a narrative) and thinking of what it would have been like to see the actions and hear the words yourself. If Jesus is in the passage, imagine him looking into your eyes and saying the words to you (p. 40). The second approach is to take the actual words and repeat them to yourself, pondering the meaning of each word or phrase. Hall says that meditation in any form is basically a cognitive and intellectual activity. But the goal of meditation, regardless of the method is to start to feel God's love (pp. 40–41). Once you begin to feel your heart warmed with this love, you should move into (3) *Prayer*. A metaphor of fire is used at this point, taken from Teresa of Avila. When meditation leads to a small fire of feeling and love, don't keep meditating—that is like throwing more wood on the fire, and too much fuel can smother the fire. Instead, now we should begin to just pray, just talking to God the way you would talk to a loved one. Nurture the love-fire with small pieces of "fuel"—a glance at a Scripture now and then—and just begin to pray, by longing for union with the one we love. This leads, finally, to (4) *Contemplation*. This Hall defines as "interior silence." Any kind of thinking of thoughts, analysis, and reasoning, is basically being "in charge" and not surrendering to God. She recommends books about "centering prayer" to help us achieve, not thinking any thoughts "about" him, but experiencing direct, wordless, adoring awareness of him and his presence (pp. 45–55).

The similarities and differences between Owen/Luther's approach and this description of *lectio divina* are easy to see. The Protestant thinkers agree that the Bible must be meditated on in order to engage the affections as a means to respond and pray to God with the whole person. They too want us to deliberately work the biblical truth into the heart until it "catches fire" and they believe the Holy Spirit can directly apply the inscripturated Word to our lives. But Owen and Luther do not advise that we ignore the theology of the text and look for a "personal word." Luther actually proposes regular meditation on the Apostles' Creed. Owen and Luther want us to think out the implications and applications of our doctrine and theology until the Holy Spirit makes the truths real in our affections. Second, Luther and Owen would not expect or advise that we only or mainly aim to know God's love. Of course the knowledge of his love and grace in Christ must constantly be present, otherwise we would have no confidence that we could approach him at all. We pray only "in Jesus' name." But his power, holiness, majesty, sovereignty, or his wisdom could be the dominant theme of the biblical text rather than his love and therefore what we encounter that day. Finally, Owen and Luther would not say we are trying to get beyond thinking or thoughts into pure awareness. They assumed that the Scripture *is* the way God is actively present in the world and our lives (see the beginning of chapter 4, "Conversing with God") and would not, again, pit thinking and feeling against each other as the contemplative tradition seems to do.

Having registered all these criticisms, it is worth noting that the essential order of things Hall lays out—reading the Scripture (fixing the mind), meditating (inclining the heart), and prayer (enjoying God's presence)—are roughly similar to both Owen and Luther's directions.

275. Richard F. Lovelace, *Dynamics of Spiritual Life: An Evangelical Theology of Renewal*, (Eugene, OR: Wipf and Stock, 2012), 213.

CHAPTER ELEVEN—AS ENCOUNTER: SEEKING HIS FACE

276. Westminster Larger Catechism, Q. 182.

277. McNeill, *Calvin: Institutes*, 3.1.1., 537.

278. McNeill, *Calvin: Institutes*, 3.2.36.

279. See D. M. Lloyd-Jones for a searching sermonic exposition of this prayer, to whom I am indebted for many of the insights in this chapter. D. Martyn Lloyd-Jones, *The Unsearchable Riches of Christ: An Exposition of Ephesians 3:1 to 21* (Grand Rapids, MI: Baker, 1979), 106–315.

280. This is Lloyd-Jones's understanding of what Paul means here. See also P. T. O'Brien, *The Letter to the Ephesians* (Grand Rapids, MI: Eerdmans, 1999). "At first sight it seems strange for Paul to pray that Christ may dwell in the hearts of believers. Did he not already live within them? In answer, it is noted that the focus of this request is not on the initial indwelling of Christ but on his continual presence . . . to establish believers on a firm foundation of love" (pp. 258–59).

281. See chapter 5, "The Night of Fire," in Marvin Richard O'Connell, *Blaise Pascal: Reasons of the Heart* (Grand Rapids, MI: Eerdmans, 1997), 90.

282. William R. Moody, *The Life of Dwight L. Moody* (Albany, OR: Book for the Ages, Ages Software, 1997), 127.

283. See O'Brien, *Letter to the Ephesians*, 258.

284. "O Jesus, King Most Wonderful" by unknown author, twelfth century, trans. Edward Caswall, 1814–78.

285. O'Brien, *Letter to the Ephesians*, 255.
286. Suzanne McDonald, "Beholding the Glory of God in the Fact of Jesus Christ: John Owen and the 'Reforming' of the Beatific Vision" in *The Ashgate Research Companion to John Owen's Theology*, ed. Kelly M. Kapic and Mark Jones (Surrey: Ashgate, 2012), 142.
287. Owen, *Works*, vol. 1, 288. Cited also McDonald, "Beholding the Glory," 143.
288. Ibid., 307–08.
289. Many will recognize in Owen's discussion of the beatific vision many of the basic ideas on spiritual experience later developed by Jonathan Edwards. Edwards believed that the difference between a Christian regenerated by the Holy Spirit and a merely religious and moral person is that the Christian experiences "a change made in the views of his mind, and the relish of his heart whereby he apprehends a beauty, glory, and supreme good in God's nature as it is in itself" (*The Works of Jonathan Edwards*, vol. 2, *Religious Affections*, ed. John E. Smith, [New Haven: Yale, 1959], 241). Elsewhere he describes the change like this: " 'Tis the soul's relish of the supreme excellency of the divine nature, inclining the heart to God as the chief good" (*The Works of Jonathan Edwards*, vol. 21, *Writings on the Trinity, Grace, and Faith*, ed. Sang Hyun Lee, [New Haven: Yale, 2002], 173). The two things Edwards discerns in genuine spiritual experience are: (1) a whole-person change (both views of the mind and the "relish" of the heart) (2) in which God becomes no longer a means to an end to other goods, but now becomes the supreme good. Edwards puts this in other ways—previously God was useful to us but now he is beautiful to us, satisfying for who he is in himself. God's glory and happiness now *become* your glory and happiness. Behind both Owen and Edwards, of course, stands Augustine, with his teaching that sin is disordered love, and only if the heart's greatest joy is changed, and God is loved supremely, will other virtues begin to develop and the character be renewed.
290. Owen, *Works*, vol. 1, 307. See also McDonald, "Beholding the Glory," 143.
291. In her important article, Suzanne McDonald points out that John Owen's emphasis on the beatific vision put him somewhat at odds with other Protestants in his day. Most of his colleagues saw the vision as too otherworldly and too "Catholic." Only Francis Turretin, Reformed Protestant theologian in Geneva and Owen's contemporary, gave it attention. Thomas Aquinas and Turretin, however, both thought of the vision as basically one of intellectual apprehension of God in general, with Jesus as a kind of conduit for it (see

McDonald, "Beholding the Glory," 151–54). Owen accepted the idea of the beatific vision but then "reformed" it along what he considered less speculative and more biblical lines, putting it into a Protestant and Reformed theological framework. Rather than understand it as some generic apprehension of the infinity of God, he understood it as centering on the person and work of Christ. Christ was not a mere vehicle for the vision; he was its central object. Indeed, Owen argued, even in the future it would be in Christ's glorified human nature that we would continually see God. Instead of a completely future, intellectual experience, then, Owen described the beatific vision as something that could happen in part by faith now, and would affect the whole person through its impact on the heart. Owen made the apparently esoteric concept of the beatific vision into a practical basis for prayer and experience right now. Because we can be shaped by the foretaste of the beatific vision, it can profoundly shape how we actually live day by day in the world.

Owen looked at the 2 Corinthians texts and noticed the unusual nature of the verb "behold as in a mirror." In 1 John 3:2, we are told that the vision of Christ is future, but in 2 Corinthians 3:18, we are told that we can see and contemplate the glory of Christ now. The Greek verb *katoptrizdomenoi* is a compound word, meaning "to gaze at an image reflected in a mirror." This makes sense of the two texts. When we look in a mirror, we are not seeing the object itself; we are seeing a two-dimensional reflection of a three-dimensional object. We can "see" Christ now, though only by faith.

What does it mean to behold Jesus by faith? "For Owen, the mirror through which we behold Christ's glory is the gospel. We do not have unmediated access to Christ's person in his ascended glory; we behold the glory of Christ, in his divinity and humanity, through the mirror of the Scriptures" (Ibid., 149. Owen also makes this case in *Works*, vol. 1, p. 305. "We have 'the light of the knowledge of the glory of God in his face alone.' . . . This is the principal fundamental mystery and truth of the Gospel." Cf. chapter 2 in *Meditations and Discourses on the Glory of Christ*, 293–309. Owen also makes the same point throughout his work *The Grace and Duty of Being Spiritually Minded*). So it is when the gospel of Christ's salvation is preached and explained that the glory of Jesus' person and work is unveiled. It is as we meditate especially on gospel truths as they are set forth in the Bible that, with the Spirit's help, the truth begins to shine, the love of God becomes palpable, and the glory of Christ dazzles, moves, melts, and transforms us.

This reading of the 2 Corinthians passages has good support by commentators today (see Paul Barnett, *The Second Epistle to the Corinthians* [Grand Rapids, MI: Eerdmans, 1997], 206). "What will be Paul's torch to shine the glory of that light into the hearts of others? It is 'the gospel,' the word of God," by which the "knowledge of God" lights up the hearts of Paul's hearers (2 Cor 4:4, 6; cf. Gal 1:16). Paradoxically, therefore, Paul's readers *see* the glory of Christ as they *hear* the gospel, which in turn gives the knowledge of God" (206). See Murray J. Harris, *The Second Epistle to the Corinthians: A Commentary on the Greek Text* (Grand Rapids, MI: Eerdmans, 2005). "'The glory of the Lord' is God's glory as it is revealed in his image, Christ. If we must identify the 'mirror' in which God's glory is seen, it is more likely to be Christ as present in the gospel, the essence of which is Christ, or the gospel along with the Christian life as lived in the Spirit, than gospel ministers or Christians in general" (315).

So, Owen concludes, our "sight" of Christ is only by faith through the gospel, and partial. In the future, we will see him face-to-face (1 Cor 13:12).

292. Owen, *Works*, vol. 7, 348.

293. Owen, *Works*, vol. 4, 329–30.

294. Owen, *Works*, vol. 1, 401.

295. All these items are taken from Owen's chapter on the "Mental Prayer" of Rome. Ibid., 328–38.

296. Owen, *Works*, vol. 1, 401.

297. Owen, *Works*, vol. 7, 345–46.

298. Von Balthasar, *Prayer*, 28.

299. Ibid., 28–29. Von Balthasar says that Protestant pietism and revivalism has tried to recapture the missing element of the reality of the indwelling Spirit, but the attempts have not succeeded because "of the lack of an objective and official ecclesial act of worship with its surrounding liturgy," 29. It is obviously a very sweeping statement to say Protestant efforts to promote spiritual experience have basically failed.

300. I stand with others in making a distinction between the modern movement of Centering Prayer and the older medieval mystics—this despite the fact that Centering Prayer proponents go to great lengths to argue that their approach is just a modernization of the medieval tradition. Among the more surprising critics of Centering Prayer are the Zaleskis. Despite their (overly) broad sympathies for nearly all kinds of human prayer, they see Centering Prayer as a consumeristic "dumbing down" of the older mystical tradition of *The Cloud*

of Unknowing. "It's easy to discern in this program the bare bones of the teaching of *The Cloud*, especially the effort to suppress awareness of created things and the use of a single prayer word. But one misses the boldness of the original, here replaced with painfully polite expressions. . . . For the author of *The Cloud*, contemplative prayer is an arduous trial with an uncertain end; the centering prayer movement . . . has turned it into a comfortable exercise with a foregone conclusion. . . ." Centering Prayer has "little in common with *The Cloud*'s hard-eyed realism and seem rather to partake of the Zeitgeist of the late twentieth century, with its spiritual eclecticism and optimism" (Zaleskis, *Prayer*, 208). For an appreciative but sharp Protestant critique of both the older traditions and practices such as the Jesus Prayer, see John Jefferson Davis, *Meditation and Communion*. See also Edmund P. Clowney, *CM: Christian Meditation*; and Peter Adam, *Hearing God's Words*.

301. Carl Trueman, "Why Should Thoughtful Evangelicals Read the Medieval Mystics?" *Themelios* 33, no. 1 (May 2008).

CHAPTER TWELVE—AWE: PRAISING HIS GLORY

302. C. S. Lewis, *Reflections on the Psalms* (New York: Harcourt, Brace, 1958), 90–98.
303. Ibid., 90–91.
304. Ibid., 92.
305. Ibid., 95.
306. Ibid., 94.
307. James K. A. Smith, *Desiring the Kingdom: Worship, Worldview, and Cultural Formation* (Grand Rapids, MI: Baker, 2009), 46–47.
308. Quoted in David K. Naugle, *Reordered Love, Reordered Lives: Learning the Deep Meaning of Happiness* (Grand Rapids, MI: Eerdmans, 2008), xi.
309. "Now he is a man of just and holy life who forms an unprejudiced estimate of things, and keeps his affections also under strict control, so that he neither loves what he ought not to love, nor fails to love what he ought to love, nor loves that equally which ought to be loved either less or more, nor loves less or more which ought to be loved equally. No sinner is to be loved as a sinner; and every man is to be loved as a man for God's sake; but God is to be loved for His own sake. And if God is to be loved more than any man, each man ought to love God more than himself" (Augustine, *On Christian Doctrine*, vol. 1, 27, 28). Quoted in David K. Naugle's 1993 paper "St. Augustine's Concept of Disordered Love and Its Contemporary Application," available online at http://www3.dbu.edu/naugle/pdf/disordered_love.pdf.

310. Ibid.

311. Smith, *Desiring the Kingdom*, 51.

312. C. S. Lewis, *Letters to Malcolm: Chiefly on Prayer* (New York: Harcourt, Brace, 1963), 90.

313. Ibid., 91. Another figure who used the pleasures of the natural world for adoration is Jonathan Edwards. See his "Images of Divine Things," in *Typological Writings: The Works of Jonathan Edwards*, ed. Wallace E. Anderson, vol. 11 (New Haven, CT: Yale University Press, 1993).

314. See C. Frederick Barbee and Paul F. M. Zahl, *The Collects of Thomas Cranmer* (Grand Rapids, MI: Eerdmans, 1999), ix–xii.

315. See both Matthew Henry, *Method for Prayer: Freedom in the Face of God*, ed. J. Ligon Duncan (Christian Heritage, 1994), *A Way to Pray*, ed. and rev. O. Palmer Robertson (Carlisle, PA: Banner of Truth, 2010).

316. Peterson, *Answering God*, 128.

317. Ibid., 96–97.

CHAPTER THIRTEEN—INTIMACY: FINDING HIS GRACE

318. For the Scripture references and the theology of this paragraph and the next, I am indebted to D. A. Carson, *Love in Hard Places* (Wheaton, IL: Crossway, 2002), 74–77.

319. Disputation of Doctor Martin Luther on the Power and Efficacy of Indulgences, 1517, Thesis 1.

320. John R. W. Stott, *Confess Your Sins: The Way of Reconciliation* (Word Books, 1974), 19.

321. The premier and unparalleled guide to what Stott calls "forsaking" sin, and older theologians called the mortification of sin, is John Owen's "On the Mortification of Sin" in *Works*, ed. William Goold, vol. 6 (Carlisle, PA: Banner of Truth, 1965). Owen's work is in archaic English and is difficult to read, but it is a unique work of Reformed Protestant spirituality.

322. Stott, *Confess Your Sins*, 20. In his book, Stott distinguishes "confessing sin" (which he considers the same as admitting sin) from "forsaking sin" (which he sees as working a deeper attitude of contrition in the heart). I agree that "confession proper" is a more mental process in which you end blame shifting and take responsibility for sin as sin. What Stott calls "forsaking" sin is then the heart work that John Owen and the Puritans call "mortification." I would rather refer to both the mental admission and the heart contrition as two parts of confession or repentance.

323. Stott, *Confess Your Sins*, 21.

324. See Owen, "On the Mortification of Sin." "In a time of some judgment, calamity, or pressing affliction; the heart is then taken up with thoughts and contrivances of flying from the present troubles, fears, and dangers. This, as a convinced person concludes, is to be done only by relinquishment of sin, which gains peace with God. It is the anger of God in every affliction that galls a convinced person. To be quit of this, men resolve at such times against their sins. Sin shall never more have any place in them; they will never again give up themselves to the service of it. Accordingly, sin is quiet, stirs not, seems to be mortified; not, indeed, that it hath received any one wound, but merely because the soul hath possessed its faculties, whereby it should exert itself, with thoughts inconsistent with the motions thereof; which, when they are laid aside, sin returns again to its former life and vigour" (pp. 26–27). "The true and acceptable principles of mortification shall be . . . insisted on . . . [namely] hatred of sin as sin, not only as galling or disquieting. . . . Now, it is certain that that which I speak of proceeds from self-love. Thou settest thyself with all diligence and earnestness to mortify such a lust or sin; what is the reason of it? It disquiets thee, it hath taken away thy peace, it fills thy heart with sorrow, and trouble, and fear; thou hast no rest because of it" (p. 41).

325. "To load it daily with all the things which shall after be mentioned, that are grievous, killing, and destructive to it, is the height of this contest." Ibid., 32.

326. See Ibid., 54–118.

327. Ibid., 58.

328. Owen, "A Discourse Concerning the Holy Spirit," in *Works*, vol. 3, 547.

329. This is not to say that Christians who understand gospel truths can't go to the law of God for help in weakening sin. In many places he tells Christians to "bring their sin" to the law *and* to the gospel ("Mortification of Sin," *Works*, vol. 6, 57–58). Nevertheless, such counsel comes with warnings to remember that Christians cannot come back under legal condemnation for their sin, and that too much emphasis on the danger of sin and the law can lead to the legalistic spirit that can only stop sinful acts temporarily and not change the heart.

330. Alexander B. Grosart, ed. *Works of Richard Sibbes* (Carlisle, PA: Banner of Truth, 1973), 47.

331. George Whitefield, quoted in Arnold Dallimore, *George Whitefield: The Life and Times*, vol. 1, 140.

Chapter Fourteen—Struggle: Asking His Help

332. Quoted in Horton, *Calvin on the Christian Life*, 159.

333. For much more on this topic, see Keller, *Walking with God through Pain and Suffering*, especially chapter 6, "The Sovereignty of God," pp. 130–46.

334. Phelps, *The Still Hour*, 27–28.

335. Packer and Nystrom, *Praying: Finding Our Way*, 157.

336. Ibid., 158.

337. Ibid., 157.

338. Packer and Nystrom, *Praying: Finding Our Way*, 55.

339. McNeill, *Calvin: Institutes*, 3.20.52., 919.

340. Ibid., 178.

341. Ibid., 179.

342. This is my paraphrase of Edwards's headings. The sermon is "Christian Happiness" and can be found in Wilson H. Kimnach, ed., *The Works of Jonathan Edwards*, vol. 10, *Sermons and Discourses 1720–1723* (New Haven: Yale, 1992), 296–307. Edwards's thesis is that the Christian can be happy whatever the outward circumstances.

343. I address this kind of prayer at greater length in chapter 12—"Weeping," in *Walking with God through Pain and Suffering*, 240–54.

344. Packer and Nystrom, *Praying: Finding Our Way*, 181.

345. Ibid.

346. The descriptive terms for categories of complaint prayer in this paragraph come from Packer and Nystrom, *Praying: Finding Our Way*, 194–99.

347. See Keller, *Walking with God through Pain and Suffering*, 240–42.

348. Smith, *Soul Searching*.

349. Packer and Nystrom, *Praying: Finding Our Way*, 192–93. For more on processing our complaints and suffering in prayer, see my *Walking with God through Pain and Suffering*, especially chapters 12–16, 240–322.

Chapter Fifteen—Practice: Daily Prayer

350. Alan Jacobs, *The "Book of Common Prayer": A Biography* (Princeton: Princeton University Press, 2013), 24. Jacobs relies on Eamon Duffy, *The Stripping of the Altars: Traditional Religion in England c. 1400–c.1580* (New Haven, CT: Yale University Press, 1992).

351. Edgar C. S. Gloucester, ed. *The First and Second Prayer Books of Edward VI* (Wildside Press, reprint of 1910 edition), 3.

352. Ibid., 8.

353. Jacobs, *The "Book of Common Prayer,"* 24–27.

354. English translations can be found in Elsie Anne McKee, *John Calvin: Writings on Pastoral Piety* (Mahwah, NJ: Paulist Press, 2001), 210–17.

355. McNeill, *Calvin: Institutes*, 3.20.50., 917–18. Calvin adds, however, that stated hours of daily prayer should not become a "superstitious observance . . . as if paying a debt to God."

356. There are many versions of the calendar online. See http://www.mcheyne .info/calendar.pdf.

357. See Matthew M. Boulton, *Life in God: John Calvin, Practical Formation, and the Future of Protestant Theology* (Grand Rapids, MI: Eerdmans, 2011) for an extensive argument that Calvin's Christian formative practices represented a kind of "lay monasticism." This is especially interesting in light of what is today called the New Monasticism or Lay Monasticism. The original monastic ideal was for a way of daily work and life completely framed by Christian practices of prayer, Bible reading and instruction, Psalm singing and recitation, and corporate worship. This ordinarily meant interrupting daily work with fixed-hour observances of both private prayer and community worship. Monastics also submitted to close accountability for their lives with others as well as modest living standards and a commitment to serving others. The New Monasticism has grown largely through evangelicals dissatisfied with current church life and practice. It seeks to create a lay monasticism, not requiring members to leave secular work or live literally under the same roof, but nonetheless calling them to live in close geographic proximity, to accountability, concern for the marginalized, and practices from the contemplative tradition including common daily liturgical fixed-hours prayer. One main rationale given for the movement is the death of Christendom. As our culture becomes more post-Christian, believers need to be more immersed in communal Christian practices lest they be too assimilated to the values of the surrounding culture. See Jonathan Wilson-Hartgrove, *New Monasticism: What It Has to Say to Today's Church* (Brazos, 2008); and Rob Moll, "The New Monasticism," *Christianity Today*, April 24, 2008. Those who promote the new, lay monasticism almost always look to either Catholic or Anabaptist historical resources, and this is to some degree because Anabaptist Protestants have functioned as somewhat embattled minorities for centuries, and the original monastic ideal has been inherited from Catholicism. But it is arguable that Calvin proposed

the first serious effort to do lay monasticism. His program was far more extensive than Luther's. As Boulton explains, Calvin was concerned to re-form an entire city, in the midst of medieval Catholic Europe, along the lines of what he considered biblical Christian faith. Calvin, therefore, provides many resources for those looking to develop spiritually formative Christian community today in the postmodern West. See also Scott Manetsch, *Calvin's Company of Pastors* (New York: Oxford University Press, 2012).

358. *Quiet Time: An InterVarsity Guidebook for Daily Devotions* (Downers Grove, IL: InterVarsity Press, 1945). Although the authors are given as InterVarsity Staff, the book was compiled out of the writings of many longtime evangelical missionaries, including Bishop Frank Houghton, W. Graham Scroggie, Paget Wilkes, and Mrs. Harry Strachan. C. Stacey Woods, Australian-Canadian founder of InterVarsity in the United States, took the British book, edited out its "Anglicanisms," and published it in the United States. See A. Donald MacLeod, *C. Stacey Woods and the Evangelical Rediscovery of the University* (Downers Grove, IL: InterVarsity, 2007), 107.

359. Cf.: One of the best was *Appointment with God: A Practical Approach to Developing a Personal Relationship with God* (The Navigators, 1973).

360. *Quiet Time*, revised edition 1976 (InterVarsity Press), 21.

361. Ibid., 15–16. Later in the booklet a different outline for prayer is offered—thanksgiving, worship, and adoration using the names of God, confession, intercession for others, and committal of the new day to God (p. 21). This reflects the fact that despite being quite short, the book is a compilation of reflections on daily devotions by seven different authors.

362. *Appointment with God*, 16.

363. Phyllis Tickle, *The Divine Hours, Prayers for Springtime: A Manual for Prayer* (Image, 2006); *The Divine Hours, Prayers for Summertime: A Manual for Prayer* (Image, 2006); *The Divine Hours, Prayers for Autumn and Wintertime: A Manual for Prayer* (Image, 2006).

364. See John Bunyan, *Prayer* (Carlisle, PA: Banner of Truth, 1965).

365. Owen, *Works*, vol. 4, 348.

366. See Owen's entire chapter "Prescribed Forms of Prayer Examined," in *Works*, vol. 4, 338–51.

367. Horton, *Calvin on the Christian Life*, 154.

368. Luther, "A Simple Way to Pray," 193.

369. Arthur G. Bennett, *The Valley of Vision: A Collection of Puritan Prayers and Devotions* (Carlisle, PA: Banner of Truth, 1975).

370. David Hanes, ed., *My Path of Prayer* (Wales: Crossway UK Books, 1991).

371. Ibid., 57–65.

372. Packer and Nystrom, *Praying: Finding Our Way*, 286.

373. See Barbee and Zahl, *Collects of Thomas Cranmer*. This volume not only provides one year (fifty-two weeks) of Cranmer prayers but a short explanation and meditation for each one. This makes this book extremely useful for the initial "evocation/invocation" moment of daily prayer.

374. D. A. Carson et al., eds., *New Bible Commentary*, 21st Century Edition (Downers Grove, IL: InterVarsity Press, 1994).

357. Henry, *A Method for Prayer*. See also a shorter edition, Henry, *A Way to Pray*. The editor of the first edition, Ligon Duncan, outlines the whole book in an appendix. The appendix alone provides scores of specific ideas on how to adore, confess, thank, petition, and intercede with God. To use the book in prayer you need only to personalize the headings and pray in your own words and with your specific needs.

376. This is from Luther's "A Simple Way to Pray," which is quoted in Packer and Nystrom, *Praying: Finding Our Way*, 288. Packer here is quoting from a translation by Walter Trobisch, in his classic booklet, *Martin Luther's Quiet Time*.

377. Quoted in Gordon Wenham, *The Psalter Reclaimed: Praying and Praising with the Psalms* (Crossway, 2013), 39.

378. The following are taken from T. M. Moore, *God's Prayer Program: Passionately Using the Psalms in Prayer* (Christian Focus, 2005).

379. Ibid., 83.

380. Ibid., 88.

381. Ibid., 95.

382. Many people seeking to pray the Psalms find themselves confused and put off by the "imprecatory" Psalms in which the psalmist prays down God's wrath and punishment on his enemies, often in violent terms. One such prayer comes at the end of Psalm 137, where the psalmist hopes that someone will do to the Babylonians what they did when they sacked Jerusalem. He hopes warriors will seize their infants by the feet and kill them by dashing their heads upon the rocks (vv. 8–9). Old Testament scholar Derek Kidner wisely points out that Christians must not pray in the same way now, in light of the cross, but we still must be able to understand such prayers. He writes about Psalm 137: "Our response to such a scripture should, we suggest, be threefold. First, to distil the essence of it, as God

himself did with the cries of Job and Jeremiah. Secondly, to receive the impact of it. This raw wound, thrust before us, forbids us to give smooth answers to the fact of cruelty. To cut this witness out of the Old Testament would be to impair its value as revelation, both of what is in man and of what the cross was required to achieve for our salvation. Thirdly, our response should be to recognize that our calling, since the cross, is to pray down reconciliation, not judgment. . . . So this psalm takes its place in Scripture as an impassioned protest, beyond all ignoring or toning down, not only against a particular act of cruelty but against all comfortable views of human wickedness, either with regard to the judgment it deserves or to the legacy it leaves; and not least, in relation to the cost, to God and man, of laying its enmity and bitterness to rest" (Derek Kidner, *Psalms 73–150: An Introduction and Commentary* [Downers Grove, IL: InterVarsity Press, 1975], 497).

383. For much more on this subject, read Eugene Peterson, *Answering God*; Tremper Longman, *How to Read the Psalms* (Downers Grove, IL: InterVarsity Press, 1988); and Derek Kidner, *Psalms: An Introduction and Commentary* in 2 volumes (Downers Grove, IL: InterVarsity Press, 1973).

384. Moody, *Life of Dwight L. Moody*, 127.

APPENDIX—SOME OTHER PATTERNS FOR DAILY PRAYER

385. By reading two chapters a day from the M'Cheyne Bible Reading Calendar—one in the morning and one in the evening—you will read through the Old Testament once and the New Testament twice in two years. See http://www.mcheyne.info/calendar.pdf.

386. These are very freely adapted from prayers composed by John Calvin and placed in the 1545 Geneva Catechism to provide guidance for the occasions of private prayer Calvin wanted individuals and families to observe. Original English translations are found in Elsie A. McKee, ed. and trans., *John Calvin: Writings on Pastoral Piety*, 210–17.

REDEEMER

The Redeemer imprint is dedicated to books that address pressing spiritual and social issues of the day in a way that speaks to both the core Christian audience and to seekers and skeptics alike. The mission for the Redeemer imprint is to bring the power of the Christian gospel to every part of life. The name comes from Redeemer Presbyterian Church in New York City, which Tim Keller started in 1989 with his wife, Kathy, and their three sons. Redeemer has begun a movement of contextualized urban ministry, thoughtful preaching, and church planting across America and throughout major world cities.

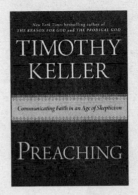
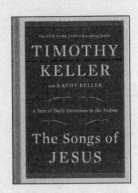

ALSO AVAILABLE AS EBOOKS

The Father and Son

The First Christian

The Great Enemy

The Grieving Sisters

The Insider and the Outcast

The Mother of God

The Obedient Master

The Skeptical Student

The Two Advocates

The Wedding Party

VIKING

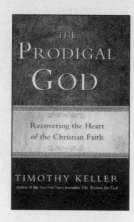